SIGNS

of

HOPE

In praise

of

ordinary

heroes

SIGNS

of

HOPE

In praise

of

ordinary

heroes

SELECTIONS
FROM
HOPE MAGAZINE

Edited by
Jon Wilson
and
Kimberly Ridley

PUSHCART PRESS • WAINSCOTT, NEW YORK

This collection is gratefully dedicated to

the writers on these pages who have summoned

the courage to reveal their truths and their hearts

in so evocative and compelling a manner,

thus illuminating a way to heart and

truth for the rest of us.

....

For further information contact:
Pushcart Press, P.O. Box 380, Wainscott, NY 11975

For further information on *Hope* magazine write to:
P.O. Box 160, Brooklin, ME 04616
www.hopemag.com

Distributed by W.W. Norton & Co.
500 Fifth Avenue, New York, NY 10110

Library of Congress Catalog Card Number 00-130320
ISBN 1-888889-20-9

Design by Sherry Streeter

Acknowledgements

This work would not have been possible without the considerable effort and commitment of many individuals over time, and acknowledgement here hardly suffices to express our gratitude. To begin with, there are the many who have put their shoulder to the wheel on behalf of *Hope* magazine over the years. When the magazine was barely an idea, the staff of WoodenBoat Publications, Inc. were always supportive and ready to help out in numerous ways. As the idea for *Hope* became increasingly real, Kimberly Ridley came on board to help give it substance, bringing not only great heart, but a solid journalistic orientation. Sherry Streeter took on the challenge of trying to design our too-many words-and-pictures pieces into an attractive and compelling magazine, and shared her many valuable editorial ideas and insights with us, as well. Though she no longer designs the magazine, we're fortunate to have her design in this book. Valerie Chiasson broke the trail in *Hope*'s initial advertising sales and marketing efforts, making call after call, struggling to get strangers to pay attention to this altogether new idea. Kathleen Brandes rigorously proofread our earliest issues. Behind all this was Jim Miller, working to make sure we could finance this venture, even though it would clearly lose money. These are the ones who were there at the creation, and who have continued to believe that *Hope* might yet prevail.

Since then, we have benefited from the hard work of many others: Susan Snyder, who was a devoted volunteer until she became so indispensable that we had to hire her; Kathleen Caldwell, who continues to be an invaluable resource to us; Deborah Brewster, Jane Crosen, and Pat Lown, our indefatigable team of proofreaders. Frances Lefkowitz was part of the magazine's early editorial team, and Amy Rawe and Lane Fisher are critical members of the current team. Adrienne Ricci has helped us keep track of the details. Eric Jacobssen, Jessica Francis, and Wendy Sewall have worked to keep the advertising sales and marketing side running smoothly and energetically, and James Bartick, Sally Bowen, and Blythe Heepe, of *WoodenBoat*'s art department, have rescued us on many occasions.

The same holds for this book. Though many have played greater and lesser roles at various stages, we have especially to thank Scot Bell, Pat Lown, and James Bartick, who made the scanning and translation of articles from back issues less problematic than it might otherwise have been. And of course, Sherry Streeter, that rare designer for whom content means as much as design, and who approaches every design project as if it really matters to the world—because it really does. To the founder and Publisher of Pushcart Press, the brilliant and crazy Bill Henderson, we owe much gratitude. His gift for seeing the profound in small things is renowned. That he saw it in the issues of *Hope* is most gratifying.

Finally, of course, to the many writers who replied with an unhesitating yes when we asked if we could include their pieces in this collection, we are deeply grateful. We had the difficult task of choosing from more than 250 published pieces, and there are many that we would like to have included, but we could not fit them in. Any one of them would have been worthy in its own right. Our hope is that this selection is only the beginning.

Contents

Introduction

Our search for meaning takes us on strange expeditions. We seek inside ourselves, outside ourselves, alone, with others, and from others alone. We seek it in our work, in our diversions, in physical relationships, spiritual relationships, and beyond relationships. Everything we do is linked to our yearning for meaning and connection; to our need to be more human in a world becoming overwhelmingly technological. The deep urge for connection and contact, for empathy and identification—the need to reach out to others—takes myriad fascinating forms, including not so lovely ones. Some forms, like working with the desperate and disenfranchised to bring them hope, take a commitment many of us wish we had but suspect we don't, and we make heroes of those so clearly courageous. But we may fail to realize that we can also be heroes; that our own stories might also inspire courage and action in others; that the intentions and accomplishments—even small kindnesses—of *all* of us can have unseen effects. This is the reason we have gathered these stories together; these are the yearnings given voice on these pages.

It's easy to feel overwhelmed by the challenges and questions facing ourselves and our society: crime, punishment, education, poverty, health, community, politics, family, self, environment, greed. There is so much pain in the world; so much need. Trying to answer these needs, to make a difference for good, feels like shoveling sand against the surf. How are we supposed to think about saving the world? Do we even *want* to, when certain friends are just realizing, to their relief, that they *don't* have to save the world? In fact, that they *cannot* save the world? Yes. Because don't they just mean save it *alone*? That's the impossible dream. No one can do it alone. But just because we cannot do it alone doesn't mean that we should do nothing. Is there not some glowing ember in each of us that really *wants* to save the world—or at least some small part of it? Yet where do we start? What do we do? What *could* we do? I am only sure of what we *shouldn't* do: hide from the need.

Most of us suffer from a sense that we are very different from others: That no one else fears what we fear, longs for what what we long for, needs what we need deep down in our tender, vulnerable hearts. So we try to be strong, to take care of ourselves, to be among Darwin's finest. But when we assume that our place and purpose on the planet are simply about survival and acquisition, we anchor our isolation from one another in ways that deny our deep and common humanity. We only see the world through the refractions of our own lenses. This is the challenge that *Hope* magazine was founded to explore and illuminate by inviting honest, courageous, and evocative writing from men and women who have thought hard about *what can actually be done* to make the world a better place, and ourselves better people.

Our current headlong rush to the future is leaving too many behind in too many ways, and the social, educational, and economic disparities in our culture are growing more jagged-edged than ever. It feels wrong, somehow—as if we cannot possibly continue this without innumerable negative consequences. The fact is, we *can* get away with it for a while. We can continue to look out only for ourselves and our loved ones, and life will go on. It will even get better for some. But it will get a lot worse for a lot more, and it is then that we will wonder what we have wrought in our society. Because by then we will have homes that are not havens but fortresses from which we try to ignore the realities outside—but we cannot lock out the world. And when we leave others behind in our onward rush, we leave something of ourselves, as well. This just cannot be who we truly are—that we merely take care of our own needs, throwing occasional charity dollars at causes that touch us only skin deep.

Somehow, our inherent capacity to express and embody human love has become severely impaired, and we're wreaking havoc on the spirit and substance of humanity as a result. We're losing touch with society's most integrating elements, especially *connection* with one another. The essence of real human love, as uncommon and irrelevant as it might seem in our high-tech world, is exactly what this book is about.

What is wonderful and powerful about these writings is that they bring us to a sense of recognition and connection with ourselves and one another. They help us remember that we are not alone, that we share common strengths and common flaws, that we are in this together, and that, together, we could create a world in which love and justice and caring and community are absolute realities, not merely dreams. There are unimaginable cycles of pain ripping through homes and families in neighborhoods and nations right now—for reasons that are both perfectly clear and perfectly unthinkable. We cannot go into these homes and stop these cycles, though legions of social workers, police, and aid workers have tried. But we can inform ourselves more thoroughly, and understand the problems on a more human, individual scale. If we're really going to change the world, it will require the efforts of every single one of us. But it will require first that we *understand* one another better; that we feel our *place* in relation to one another. These writings bring us insights, aspirations, and disclosures from eloquent kindred souls—our ordinary heroes. If we could share this kind of honesty, authenticity, and intention in more of our everyday encounters in the world, the effects might be incandescent. In fact, we *could* change the world. Together.

Jon Wilson
Kimberly Ridley

Fences and Fields

by Andre Dubus III

It was a dry summer, and so hot it was a mistake to go barefoot on the sidewalk. When a rare breeze blew off the ocean, one or two miles east, we could hear the rattle of leaves in the tree branches, and smell the soft rubber and hot metal of cars in the street and driveway. Every Saturday I would drive to my father's house to cut his grass, but last summer I could wait three weeks or more before the yellowed lawn needed a trim. Joggers exercised only after dark. Dogs slept all day in the shade of maples and beech, or under parked cars I'd worry would drive over them the way I drove over my own dog, Dodo, when I was nineteen. At night we kept all our windows open and I put two fans in my son's room, one to suck hot air out the screen, the other directed at his crib, where he slept in only a diaper, his curly hair matted in wet ringlets to his temples and neck. In the other bedroom I lay alongside my wife, and waited for sleep with my hand on her swollen belly, the olive skin there stretched tight. Our second child's due date had come and gone two weeks earlier; my wife's mother and aunt had stayed with us then, but no contractions came, and my mother-in-law had to go back to work. So now we waited.

Those days I was doing carpentry work just two blocks from our house, building a gate and fence in a treeless yard. Between post holes, I had to dig a trench a foot deep, and by mid-morning I'd be wearing only shorts and boots, headband and bug spray, my torso slick with sweat, my hair as wet as if I'd just gotten cool. Every time I heard the ring of a phone coming from someone's house I would pause in my work and look up, and whenever a car drove slowly by, I'd wait for it to stop, expecting to see my lovely pregnant wife, her belly a full curved promise, come to tell me it was time.

One morning, as I was setting in my second post, holding my level to it, poised to kick more dirt into the hole once I'd found plumb, I heard breathing that wasn't my own and turned to see a little girl squinting up at me in the sunlight. She was thin, her pale arms and legs poking out of clothes that didn't match: a sleeveless green and yellow flowered shirt, faded pink shorts with white ruffles on the hem, red sneakers with no socks, and white ankles coated with dust from the street and dry back yards. Her hair was dusty too, and so straight and fine that her normal ears stuck out. I think I blurted out a startled hello but she just pointed to the four-foot level I was still holding to the post: "So what are you doing with that?"

"Trying to make the post straight up and down."

"I'll help you," she said, and kicked in some dirt before I was ready. It was after coffee break, the morning shade from the house gone now, and the cool dark soil I'd shoveled earlier was already dry and cracked and flaking under my boots. My headband was saturated, the sweat beginning to burn my eyes, and this trench was taking longer than I'd estimated; I was beginning to fear I'd given too low a price for the work. At home there was a whole new cycle of bills coming in and I still didn't have another job lined up after this one and I felt sure our new baby would come any minute. I wanted to get this fence done as soon as I could; I wanted this little girl to go play somewhere else.

I asked her not to kick in any dirt until I said to. She stood quickly, looked over the job site, then picked up the spade shovel, its handle twice as long as she was.

"Now?"

I found myself nodding and she squatted and scraped a small mound of dirt into the hole, the shovel knocking against the post. I pushed in more and tamped it with my boot. She dropped the shovel and began to stomp around the base of the four-by-four, her thin leg fitting all the way into the hole, her red sneaker leaving nothing more than light prints in the soil. But we got into a rhythm. We set that post, then another, and I knew the job wasn't going any faster with her, but not slower, either, and as we worked I asked her name and told her mine. I asked if she lived in one of the houses nearby, and did her parents know where she was.

"My mom thinks I'm at my friend's. I don't have a father, just a stepfather. Well, he's not really my stepfather, just my mother's boyfriend. They're gonna get married when they save enough money."

A jug of spring water sat near my tool bag and she walked over, uncapped it, and drank. The jug was half empty but she had to hold it with two hands and she spilled some water onto her flowered shirt. She put the cap back on, then left it leaning against the tools and hurried back to the new post hole. "I was thirsty."

I was holding the level to the four-by-four. I considered telling her it's polite to ask someone for a sip of their water before drinking it, but I was glad I'd had the water when she needed it, so let it go. "Do you ever see your father?"

"He died when I was little." She looked up at me and made a sad face, as if she were no longer sad but felt she still should be, that it wouldn't be right to say her father was dead without showing me her downturned lips.

"Do you remember him?"

Now she did look sad, her gray-blue eyes looking off into the dry brush at the yard's edge. "Know what I wish?"

"What?"

"That he was here and my mom was with him and she didn't even know her boyfriend."

Something fell away inside me. I began to get an image I didn't want of this tiny girl lost under some man. I said her name and she looked at me, her eyes not quite seeing me.

"Does your mother's boyfriend treat you okay? Is he good to you?"

She shrugged her shoulders. "Nah, he doesn't even look at us." She began to kick more dirt into the post hole and I let out a breath.

"He doesn't?"

"He hardly remembers our names."

A breeze picked up. It blew a feathering of sawdust into the trench. It cooled my back and legs. The girl's fine hair blew sideways in her face and as she worked she reached up with her finger and stuck a loose strand behind one ear. I guessed her to be eight or nine years old, but at that moment, pulling the hair from her face so she could keep working and not stop, her eyes on what she was doing, but not really, she looked for a moment like every hard-time girl and woman I'd ever worked with in halfway houses and group homes and pre-parole. They were either lean and scrappy or else obese and resilient; they moved with intent or didn't move much at all, but smoked cigarette after cigarette, drank too much coffee or Diet Coke, talked too loud or kept silent—

all of them, it seemed, doing essentially this: stomping dirt into a hole with a tiny red shoe, trying to cover and bury and hide their solitary hearts.

I called her name.

"What?" She pulled her leg out of the hole, picked up the too-long shovel, and began to push in more soil.

"Your dad will always be with you, you know."

She straightened and looked at me, the shovel hanging in her hands; her mouth hung partly open and in her eyes was a tentative light. I'd seen that look on my two-and-a-half-year-old son whenever I would try to explain away something common that frightened him, like a balloon or a clown's face; when each word I spoke was a step on the high wire over the valley of his normal fears and terrors. She blinked and looked at me harder, and for a second I was afraid my choice of words would be wrong, that I'd stumble and drop her into a worse place than she'd been before. But this doubt faded quickly; I began to imagine being dead, with my young child still on earth, and I felt sure I was telling her the absolute truth.

"Your father loves you too much to leave you alone. He'll watch over you your whole life."

"He will?" Now her eyes were bright and alert.

"Of course he will. He's probably watching over you right now."

"Can I see him?"

"Probably not."

She looked down at the shovel in her hands.

"But you might be able to feel him, sometimes." The breeze picked up again. It blew through the brush and high grass at the yard's edge. It began to dry the sweat on my neck and upper back. "Feel this wind? That could be him trying to cool you off."

She cocked her head at me, skeptical, standing as still as if her very body was in danger of plummeting into deep disappointment. I began to wish I'd kept quiet, once again in my life wrestling with the question of what true helping really was.

We continued working, the sun directly over us. The breeze died down, then blew in one last time. I felt a chill and knew it was sunburn. My post was leaning out of plumb and I put the level to it, then tamped the dirt at the base. She dropped the shovel for me to pick up and use, I thought, but as I reached for it I glanced at her and saw her standing there in the hot breeze, her eyes closed, her chin raised slightly, a solitary hair quivering against her cheek, her small dirty hands held up close to her chest.

We worked together until almost lunchtime. She abandoned the shovel and began to pull the dirt into the hole with her hands. The air was heavy and so hot my lungs felt tender. The girl's mother called her from the front stoop three doors down and out of sight. Her voice was shrill and coarse. From too much daily yelling, I imagined, too much alcohol and cigarette smoke, too much of some things and not enough of another, and I wanted to protect my young helper from it. She jerked at the sound, dropped the shovel, and without a word cut through the back yard the way she'd come, wiping her hands off on her pink shorts, leaving light footprints in the sawdust and dirt.

Soon after, I covered my tools with a tarp and walked home for lunch, and I think I knew then our second child would be a girl, that I would be the father of a son and a daughter. I think I made yet another silent prayer for our baby to be born safely, for my wife to come through it well, and if the baby was a boy to please not be hurt that I'd had the premonition of a girl. But as I walked down the shaded street, I began to sense deeply we would have a girl, and that loving a daughter would be different from loving a son, the way loving rivers is not the same as loving mountains, loving a half moon through the trees is different from loving the sun on your back.

And then she was born; early on an August afternoon when it was almost a hundred degrees and there was a full moon we couldn't see in the cloudless sky, she came. After twenty hours of labor there was the blinding light of the operating room, my exhausted wife's bright blood, our daughter coming head-first out of the incision, her hazel eyes wide open and a nurse almost jumping back from the table. I held my tiny daughter and she cried and I cried and her valiant mother cried, lying on the table, the surgeons still working on her behind a raised blue sheet.

Later, as my wife began to recover in her room and our son played with his grandmother and aunts and our baby girl slept in the hospital nursery, a pink name tag attached to her clear plastic basinette, I went outside into the heat with my brother and father. We drove to a package store, then to the river, two blocks from the hospital, its banks thick with trees. We sat in the shade at the edge of a jogging path, my father in his wheelchair, my brother and I sitting on a railroad tie. It was late afternoon and we were sweating under our clothes. A hundred yards away on the other side of the jogging path was a softball field, and people were playing, men and women, I think, though it could have been teenagers, their voices high with a winded purpose that sometimes sounded cruel to me. Already I wanted to keep that sound from ever entering my tiny daughter's ears, and her older brother's, too. We could see the bright sunlight on the water through the trees, and we drank beer and smoked our cigars. I began to speak, though I could not do it without crying, for the word daughter was ringing through my blood, her name already deep in my heart with her brother's, as if both had been there since my own delivery nearly thirty-six years earlier. With my son's birth, a love had opened up in me that forever left my small heart behind the way a flood scatters sandbags. And now the walls of my heart seemed to fall away completely and become a green field inside me. Through tears I told my father and brother how much I felt, and that even that faithless corner of my heart that worried about money, worried that once this fence job was through nothing would follow—even that part of me was assuaged. Because how can there be green fields inside us and no food on our tables?

My brother had a disposable camera and he was taking pictures of me, but I was seeing a picture of him, twenty-three years old, holding his blue-eyed baby boy, whispering to him, a mischievous and delighted smile on his son's face, playing imaginary games on the floor with him, eating cheese and crackers at the table, painting pictures, laughing, all before he had to drive him back home to his mother. I told my brother I loved him and grieved for his truncated fatherhood. I told him I knew his son would be in his life more fully one day, a presumptuous thing to say, and again I found myself on the verbal high wire over the depths of another's pain. But I was certain what I said was true, and as my brother, father, and I wept, I knew I would feel none of this certainty without my baby daughter and lovely son, without the horizonless love and attendant faith and hope that opens up in us when we are given the gift of children.

A woman jogged by, my age or older. Her T-shirt was wet with sweat, the wires of her bra were easy to see, and her hips wide beneath jogging shorts. I think she glanced in our direction as she passed, her flushed face a mask she'd chosen to give us—three men drinking and smoking in the mottled heat. It said: I can take care of myself and I can outrun you and I will if I have to. And I felt so keenly then that my new child was a female and not a male and I wanted to shield my daughter from all the forces that had ever put that look on that woman's face. I wanted to stand and say: "It's okay, we're fathers. We're fathers!" But I of course knew better; she could not see the green fields inside us—and how many fathers had torched their own fields and burned their children, leaving their own hearts nothing but ashen caves they continued to poke around in as if they were still living?

My beer can was empty. The sting of sweat was in my eyes, and I squinted out at the sun on the river through the tree trunks. I remembered last winter at a restaurant in Boston, a friend in his forties saying over a Thai dinner that he would never bring children into such a violent and ugly world. My wife was sitting pregnant beside me and he apologized, and his girlfriend, who is the mother of a twenty-year-old daughter, turned to him and said, "But you can't have a child without having hope, too. It comes with the birth."

I glanced over at my father. I am his second child of six, and he looked broad and handsome in the wheelchair that will be his legs the rest of his life. His forehead was beaded with sweat, his eyes ringed and moist. I saw pride and love in his eyes, pride and love for his two weeping sons. I believe he still grieves the three broken marriages behind him and knows the pain it caused us, his children, and he knows all too well the challenges facing our own young marriages. But sitting there then, his beard gray and white, I saw only hope in his eyes, hope for all of us.

But hope is one-dimensional without resolve, and in the last few moments I'd been picturing my baby girl still alone in the hospital nursery, swaddled in her clear plastic basinette, her mother recovering from surgery while her father smoked and drank down by the river. Yet, I knew I was doing far more than that; I was communing with my father and only brother; I was sinking back into the arms of all the manhood I would need and more; I was celebrating the historic and ephemeral moment of my daughter's birth that was already fading away and becoming something else, the first hours of her infancy. I stood, and as we drove the two blocks back to the hospital, our windows open, the hot August air blowing in our faces, I thought of that fatherless girl who started coming daily to the job site to work with me, her dirty ankles thin and bony, her fine hair clinging to her skull, her small face already beginning to take on the same mask as the woman jogger. And I imagined her father's spirit fighting deep sky and rains and wind to be her breeze in the heat of a small dirty yard; to hold her upturned face in his airy hands, to gently thumb a strand of hair from her eye, her face—in that moment, as open and vulnerable as a newborn's; and I could hardly sit still. I wanted to be in the hospital nursery cradling my baby daughter in my arms, her entire body fitting from my elbow to palm; I wanted to smell her new skin and hair;

I wanted to kiss her sleeping eyes and rock her and hold her to my chest, her tiny ear and cheek pressed to where she could feel the beating of her father's heart—my grateful, hopeful heart.

Andre Dubus III is the author of the novels Bluesman, *and* House of Sand and Fog, *as well as a collection of short fiction entitled* The Cage Keeper and Other Stories. *A carpenter and an actor, he also teaches writing at Emerson College and Tufts University.*

The Street Where We Live
by Mark Harris

In June, my oldest daughter, Sylvie, finished kindergarten at the elementary school around the corner from where we live in Bethlehem, Pennsylvania. And if my wife Theresa and I have our way, Sylvie will graduate from this same school in another five years. Our modest goal for our daughter isn't just about academic accomplishment—it's also about community. I'm eyeing Sylvie's distant graduation because I want this little schoolhouse to be her only elementary school—and this town of Bethlehem to be her hometown.

Both goals—one grade school, and a hometown—are ones that have eluded me. My father was an officer with the Army Corps of Engineers, and by the time I headed into middle school—started in Miami, ended outside the D.C. Beltway—I had a full roster of elementary schools on my transcript. Our transient lifestyle offered a rare and grand upbringing, but it also came at a cost. Of all those people I befriended on the run, for instance, I've maintained contact with exactly one. And there's not one of those exotic and prosaic locales where we set up housekeeping that I'd claim as a hometown. When fixing my roots, about the best I can offer is this: I'm generally from everywhere and exactly from nowhere.

I have something different in mind for Sylvie and her two-year-old sister, Linnea. I want them to have that hometown I missed. It would be a place they know intimately, care about, return to with a thrill. Neighbors would know their names, their personalities, would accept them as members of the community and watch them grow up in it. Maybe a few would help them along. My goal for my kids? I want them to be native to a place.

So when Theresa took a teaching post at a small college in Bethlehem, we figured: This is where we stay put. That was five years ago, and the transition from transience to permanence was rough going. The dying steel town that was Bethlehem when we first arrived here couldn't help but pale next to Chicago, where we'd moved from, or to the cool ecotopias where we had envisioned ourselves living. The comparisons were grossly unfair, we knew, but that didn't stop us from decrying the paucity of indie movie houses, used book stores, decent coffee shops, good public transportation, and great ethnic food.

We found instead a string of faceless strip malls, cornfields yielding to suburban subdivisions, and everywhere the automobile. Conventional attitudes prevailed. The funkier south end of town was better, but it had been hit hard by urban blight, evidenced by decaying steel mills, mom-and-pops struggling behind grungy storefronts, and rising crime rates. It was hard to imagine blossoming in such a place.

But at some point in that first year here, I'm not sure why, exactly— maybe we got tired of being the incessant whiners—we made a shift. I guess we figured if we were serious about our intent to go local and, not coincidentally, be happy, we'd better start accepting our locus on its own terms. If there is an art to settling in, it has to start with acceptance. So we began to seek out the good things in Bethlehem, of which, we discovered, there are many. In short order, we turned up the cozy breakfast spot where alternative souls congregate; the children's corner of the public library; the folk music club that draws top acts to a venue no bigger than our living room; the welter of parks.

Where we found good places, we invariably found good people. Slowly their numbers increased. Soon, we discovered we had knit together a circle of dear friends. We began to see a life for ourselves here stretching into the distance. My girls formed their little friendships, too. Sylvie has a close friend she's known since before she could talk. I like to think of those friendships continuing into adulthood, with their slumber parties in grade school or the kibitzing they'll do about their high school boyfriends (the ones my girls will be dating after I'm dead, of course).

As our friendships strengthened, so too did an unspoken belief that we'd be here for each other over the long haul. We'd watch each other's children grow up, offer them a hand where we could, follow and support each other though the career changes, the joys and trials of parenthood, and the permanent hair loss. When my neighbors helped me refurbish my decrepit front porch last summer, I'm sure we all figured we'd share many a late evening on it—as indeed, we have.

We literally cemented our commitment to our friends and to Bethlehem when we bought a house a block from my wife's college three years ago. It's a Craftsman-style townhouse that, barring a visit from the Prize Patrol, will certainly require a lifetime to renovate. And it may be located on the most communal block on the eastern seaboard. On most days life here is a picture of grandma's old neighborhood—children running amok, parents assembling on porches after work. There's a yearly block party, joint tag sale, and more potluck dinners than I can tally. One neighbor commemorates the end of summer by inviting everyone over for homemade funnel cakes, another ushers in the beginning of the school year with homemade pies. We've celebrated both of Linnea's birthdays with a bash on our front lawn. I knew we had found that rare community when thirty of our friends and neighbors—from tyke to senior—serenaded my daughter with Happy Birthday.

On Saturday mornings many of us converge downtown at the bagel shop, and from there head to the park. The shopkeepers know us—Andy at the bagel shop, Francoise in the deli, Louise at the bookstore. They greet me and my children by name, hand out a goodie. To the old-timers here, all this— the friendly hello, the Friday beers on the porch, block parties, the simple life of community—might be unremarkable. But to the vagabond, this acceptance is heart-warming, nourishing, and ultimately sustaining.

Our good community hasn't come free. We've worked to support and improve it—we volunteer at Sylvie's school; I sit on the city's planning commission; Theresa and I select movies that are shown at the college's foreign film series; we shop at businesses on Main Street.

So, are we here for good? The college's tenure review committee has a big say in that. But if we have our way, we say yes. That's not to say my itinerant heritage doesn't tug sometimes. I think I'll always feel the draw of greener pastures, brighter lights, the hipper place down the road. I feel that acutely whenever I visit progressive enclaves like Northampton, Massachusetts. Bethlehem, for all its progress since we've moved here, may never match the charms of such a place. So why resist its pull? Because I think it's a mistake to take for granted the good community we've fashioned here, or to assume we'd luck into one somewhere else.

In the end, good and lasting community arises from a commitment to it, be it Bethlehem or Northampton. And there's no more basic requirement of commitment than being present, and staying put. After five years in this town, we're part of a real community in a real place; we're connected to people we care about and who, I believe, care about us. My daughters are growing up with this nurturing community around them, every day of their lives, and, as this transient sees it, that's just all the more reason to settle down.

Mark Harris is a work-at-home father, a freelance magazine writer, and a frequent contributor to Hope.

Imagining Family
by Nell Bernstein

In 1988 I spent a year in a house with six modern-day orphans—group home girls who had been taken from their families because of abuse or neglect. They had a loneliness I couldn't touch, and if I tried, my supervisor warned me about "boundary issues."

At the twice-weekly, quasi-therapeutic ritual of "group" they were sullen and restless, disinclined to participate in the "working through their feelings" that was required of them. But late at night, when they were supposed to be in bed, they'd creep down, one at a time, to talk to me. Tiny Tracy, wanting a sandwich—she'd refused to eat the lasagna I'd cooked for dinner because it was made from government cheese. Or bossy Lorena, looking childlike without her heavy makeup, wanting to know why the boys only liked the stupid girls, the ones who held their tongues.

I could never be a parent to these girls. I was practically their age, and when they asked me, "Who the fuck are you to tell me what to do?" it seemed to me a good question. But curled up on the floor of the office for those late-night talks—my clipboard laid down, the requirement that I constantly assess and regulate them set aside for the moment—we were sometimes able to muster up a feeling that approached the sisterly.

I quickly learned not to mention these private conversations to my supervisor. Stepping out of roles, speaking to the girls as equals, was dangerous. It could generate feelings of intimacy; intimacy felt too much like family; and family was what had screwed them up to begin with. When I left the group home, I was warned not to contact even the girls I had been closest to. When

I'd been a stranger to these girls I was expected to replace their parents; now that I knew them, I was to treat them as strangers.

Once or twice a year I run into one of them—Crystal on the bus, looking stoned; Maria in the grocery store with a couple of babies in the front of the cart. It always takes us a moment to recognize each other, and they rarely want to talk to me for long—they have little nostalgia for the era of their lives that I was part of. They are vague about what they are doing when I ask them; if I spot them from a distance they seem to be wandering rather than heading somewhere: unmoored, drifting off the map. I can only imagine their present lives.

If I look at the small amount of research that's been done on young people after they "age out" of foster care, this is what I might presume: A third of the girls will have been homeless; a third arrested; a third will have serious, untreated health problems. Though a number of them will have babies, few will have managed to form lasting relationships with other adults, including the fathers of their children. They'll have high levels of substance abuse and depression, too many car accidents, a lot of dental problems. Looking back at the period when I shared responsibility for their care, I can't remember signing them up for driver training, or reminding them to floss. Maybe it happened on someone else's shift.

In the years following the "family values" fiasco of the 1992 Republican Convention, a surprisingly broad consensus has emerged that "the family" is falling apart, and children are falling through the cracks. Thirty percent of children are born to unmarried mothers; forty percent live without their fathers; fifty percent of marriages end in divorce. There are 1.5 million runaways and "throwaways" on the street right now; half a million children entering foster care each year, twice as many as ten years ago; and more than 1.5 million children coming home each afternoon to empty houses.

No matter how you measure it, a generation of children is growing up alone. But few analysts have gotten any further than the implicit or explicit suggestion that the only answer is to undo history to reweave what we perceive as unraveling. We hold rallies in sports stadiums where we call on men to take up the old mantle—to commit to supporting their families—ignoring the decline in real wages that has made that impossible for many. We take seriously proposals to "restigmatize" single motherhood and divorce, as if the only thing binding us to each other is shame. There are no more utopian visions of "reinventing family"—the best we can do is recover what's been lost. We pretend we can go back because we lack the imagination to go forward.

The "family breakdown" frenzy indicates that we are beginning to suspect the blood bond can't be trusted. That a mother's love knows no limit was one of our favorite fantasies. Then we met Susan Smith. At the same time, technology and law are testing the limits of the relationship between parenthood and biology. We're willing to ponder the possibility that a child raised with our seed in another's womb is "ours," and we're outraged by court cases in which "mere biology" is privileged over the care adoptive parents have given a child. But the increasing number of children growing up outside of their families is pushing us even further. We grudgingly give them our tax dollars. Do we owe them anything else? What could make us take responsibility for children other than those we conceive? Why should we? What is a family, anyway?

I've spent a good part of the last decade working with the young people whose fates are now being so publicly bemoaned: group home girls doing their best to get pregnant; eight-year-old boys turned predatory already by the violence in their homes; teenagers who have been raising themselves in institutions or empty houses as long as they can remember. It is these young people, the ones who are most alone, who offer the only maps I've seen—however vaguely sketched—of the twenty-first-century family.

The last thing these kids who have "fallen through the cracks" want is to crawl back up through them. They've no use for our nostalgia, and no choice but to look forward. There's an American romance to the idea of the young person alone in the city, leaving Mom back home in the suburbs saying, "Why don't you ever call?" But these young people are alone in the least romantic way—they've left no one behind at all.

David, who is now twenty-two, was abandoned by his mother when he was twelve. ("Do you mind if I go to Europe?" she asked one morning, packing.) After six months on his own, followed by fourteen foster homes in three years, David moved in with his best friend Ray and Ray's mother Suzanne. He spent his teen years in a basement apartment in Berkeley, California, with his "brothers" Ray and Keith—a runaway from the South whom the two older boys conspired to shelter when they learned of the abuse he had suffered from his father. (David took the Greyhound South with Keith to check things out, got beat up by Dad himself, and put Keith back on the bus to California.) Keith's younger brother followed him west and moved into Suzanne's basement, too. One time he went back home, then returned to Berkeley and got chewed out by Suzanne. "This is family" she told him, "and once you're in a family you work everything out here."

David is desperate for roots, but roots to him are something you grow, not something you trace. And "family" is people who choose each other (unlike blood), and who don't change their minds (unlike blood). In social work lingo a kid who gets kicked out of somewhere has "failed the placement," never the other way around. "You have to go in and sell yourself," David says of the foster home experience. "If I got into trouble at school I'd be afraid to go home, 'cause I was thinking they'd send me back." A child learns from the system exactly what he learned from the family that abandoned him first: You get to stay as long as it "works," as long as everyone is pleased with you, but screw up and you're out of here. When a child breaks a window or swallows bleach (two common methods of failing a placement), he is saying: I want a place where I can stay no matter how bad I am, a home even for my worst self.

David refers to the woman who gave birth to him as "my real mother," but he says the word "real" like it means "fake." Suzanne, who lives upstairs, is "Moms." If you get confused and ask David to whom he's referring when he says "my brother," he looks at you with a hint of pity like you don't know what love is. The chance intersection of lives, David's experience insists, can be transmogrified into family.

Ida Locket also grew up in the system. Now the founder of a foster-youth advocacy group, the twenty-six-year-old Locket says you can throw the kid out of the system, but you can't throw the system out of the kid: "All you know is [how] to hustle the system. You get pregnant to get welfare if you're a girl; boys normally go from the system of care to the system of the military or the system of prison." While Locket believes foster youth must become family to each other, she also thinks the government must start fulfilling the responsibility it has assumed. "The state is supposed to be your parent," she points out. "Normally parents don't leave you completely alone at eighteen."

Meanwhile, Locket makes her one-bedroom apartment in Sacramento available to a constantly shifting array of recently "emancipated" young people. One of them is Michelle, a feather-voiced twenty-one-year-old who grew up in "the system" from the age of twelve. Michelle has a six-month-old daughter and some short-term plans. Having worn out her welcome on various friends' couches in Sacramento, she's leaving in a few days for Cleveland, where she worked in a sandwich shop and lived for six months with a half-brother until she became pregnant and he threw her out. In Cleveland she plans to get her "tax money" so she can put down a deposit on an apartment back in Sacramento, where she grew up. I try to explain to Michelle that she can get her tax refund by mail, she doesn't have to buy a plane ticket, but someone else has told her otherwise. "I really put my trust in older people," she says vaguely, stroking her baby's hair. "I just believe what they tell me."

"Wound up" is Michelle's favorite phrase—"I wound up moving out of that place;" "I wound up in Ohio;" "I wound up getting pregnant." She guesses she's lived in about ten different places in the last three years, and hasn't spoken once to a counselor or social worker, but she has kept in touch with the girls she grew up with. "I was the last one to have a baby," says Michelle. "We stay in contact, trying to survive the best we can. That's the only way you're really gonna be able to make it. You don't have any family, no blood family or anything like that, and they just open the door and push you out."

The kids I know who've been raised outside of their natural families may not have all the answers, but they do offer one clear mandate: Commitment to care can be based on blood, court order, career choice, or simple affection; but once you make it, keep it. Blood is one good reason for a family to stay together: The abandoned children I know all swear up and down they'd never leave their own kids. But blood is not the only reason: They also say they wouldn't walk by a stray child on the street.

At the news service where I now work, grown professionals mix with system kids all the time, and, blessedly, nobody talks about "boundary issues." Sometimes we succeed in shaking each other hard enough to achieve a new synthesis; other times we revert to oil and water. At a book party at a dim sum house in San Francisco last spring, eighteen-year-old Cash showed up at the buffet table with a ten-day-old Rottweiler up his sleeve. A tiny, slit-eyed thing that sucked madly at whatever it could get its gums on, the dog drew admiring attention from everyone it met. But over and over a concerned party guest would pat the dog's head and then take me aside and inform me that it was far too young to be on its own—without mother's milk it would miss crucial antibodies; weaned too early, it would inevitably grow up mean.

I tried telling them what Cash had told me: The dog was abandoned when he found it; nobody knew where its mother was. They glanced at Cash across the room and repeated their diagnosis: That dog is too young to be away from its mother. Cash, meanwhile, snuck away from their scrutiny and fed the dog puppy formula from a baby bottle he kept in his pocket. Every expert in the room knew how things ought to be. The kid with the baby bottle in his pocket was concerned with how things were.

One way to define "growing up" is learning to see the big picture, becoming "realistic." As a society we've been doing a lot of growing up lately. We've been taking a hard look at welfare, for example, weighing a child's hunger against the incentive it might provide his mother to get a job and get off the dole, or at least stop reproducing. We tell ourselves we are making the hard choices.

Meanwhile, study after study—not to mention elementary common sense—shows that the one thing capable of redeeming the most troubled child is a solid, lasting, intimate connection with at least one adult. And yet, over and over, when caring for children was my job, that was exactly what I was forbidden to provide. Everyone I ever worked for warned me about "boundary issues," and instructed me not to take the work home with me. At the group home, there was a strict rule against any form of physical contact ("p.c.") between residents and staff. If we needed to offer tangible encouragement, we could resort to an "air hug"—a bizarre, bloodless encircling less intimate even than an auntie's perfumed smooch an inch from the cheek. If the girls then turned to boys for physical comfort—the kind that had an unfortunate tendency to lead to pregnancy—we were expected to profess disappointment and surprise.

The explicit rationale for the "no p.c." rule was that many of the girls had been sexually abused and might misinterpret a touch, thereby opening us up to legal liability or trouble with the state. The subtext was that these girls were tainted, literally untouchable—fit not for messy human love but only for clinical affection doled out by the book.

Denied the touch of the only parents the state that claimed them has provided them, how do these girls learn to hold a baby, or a lover, or a friend? One young woman I know, who grew up in group homes and psychiatric wards, recalls retreating to the bathroom, and hugging herself when nobody else would. Now she dreams of a real home, with curtains and linens and matched sets of furniture. In this dream home, she's the sole inhabitant.

But here is Ida Locket's dream: "If they took some of the abandoned apartment complexes, the crack apartments, and tore them down, and rebuilt them, they could have emancipated foster kids live there all together. That would be family."

Young people like these hold the key to what binds and divides us after

the blood bond breaks. But, even as we squabble over the costs and consequences of their care, we continue to turn away from the real questions that
their lives raise. Deprived of the family ties that are weakening for so many
of us, do these children belong to a generation in which the capacity for intimate relationships has been irrevocably stifled? Are they fated to live out their
lives alone, hugging themselves on the bathroom floor? Or are they—in their
efforts to be family to each other, in their struggle to create themselves from
whole cloth—offering us new ways of measuring our responsibility to each
other in a post-nuclear family era?

Having missed out on the central lesson of American morality (You are
responsible for your family) they are blissfully ignorant of its corollary (You
are responsible *only* for your family). That they are not responsible for each
other doesn't cross these kids' minds. "My homeys are my family," they'll tell
you—so frequently, in fact, that it's become the cliche of choice among experts
on the appeal of the gang. "That's my play sister," is something else you'll
hear, or "That's my cousin," when technically, it's not.

Unlike the children of the Sixties, the babies we have since thrown out
with the bath water haven't let "family" become a bad word; they've just rede-
fined it. Their terminology reminds me that family—even the strictly bio-
logical kind—is an act of the imagination. The wedding ritual works by
magically forging family beyond blood—a transformation enacted over the
centuries through the exchange of precious talismans and the utterance of
an archaic spell. And then there's the matter of paternity: Accepting that this
sex act is responsible for that child certainly involves a little faith. So, to imagine that family might also include biologically-unrelated others who wander
into one's circle of care doesn't take a revolution in thinking—just a little bit
of a stretch.

The children we've left behind are already, out of necessity, several steps
ahead of us. With a little courage and a little imagination, we might hope to
follow them.

*Nell Bernstein is an editor at Pacific News Service in San Francisco. She writes
frequently about young people.*

If Lightning Hits, We'll Die Together
by Janisse Ray

Every day, my eight-year-old son Silas and I play his favorite game, one we invented together. He pretends to be a baby animal, maybe a king snake or a pterodactyl, and crawls inside a sheet or a towel.

"I'm in the egg now, Mama," he says. Today he's an eaglet, and I know what to do. I touch the egg and say how much I long for my baby to hatch, how I can't wait to see my baby bald eagle. He starts making noises that mimic the egg cracking, then out he pops from the sheet, wide-eyed, mouth puckered like a fish's, awed. He gurgles. He snuggles. I croon.

He will repeat this over and over, for a solid hour, because he loves to hear my exclamations of surprise and joy at his arrival. He wants to hear me say, "baby bald eagle, welcome to the world. I'm so glad you're here. Thank you so much for coming to live with me." For experiment's sake I tried to inject a father into the game one midnight while we drove home from a contra dance. "Papa Crocodile," I said to an absent third party, "I hope our baby comes soon." Silas immediately lifted the jacket and spoke in his real voice, "Papa is out of the game."

I think this game sprang from some unspeakable wisdom, and that it is less child's play than self-preservation—my obedience school for love. When I first discovered that I was pregnant with Silas, it seemed as if my life was about to shut me out, like a yellow jacket who flies home to find a cement block checking her underground passage. It has taken me years to want Silas fully.

I got pregnant during a passionate romance with a man eleven years older than I; a handsome, restless musician. Funny thing is, he kept pressuring me to have a baby, and I never wanted to. We hadn't been able to make any kind of commitment to each other. A baby would change that.

It didn't. Our problems increased, although we did manage to build a house together in rural north Florida, and to plant a garden, and set out thirty or so fruit trees. I remember nailing tongue-and-groove siding on the bedroom wall, crying: I knew I'd never live in that house.

Silas: "Do octopuses have eyebrows?"

When Silas was a few months old, his father and I were officially married in the courthouse in downtown Quincy, Florida, and less than a year later we divorced there. During that time two separations had occurred. Within another year we had moved thousands of miles from each other, across an ocean.

Silas's father is not entirely absent in his son's life. As the years have passed, he has grown to accept and love him. He sends a $300 check monthly, without fail, and Silas has spent part of the last three summers with him.

I'm the parent, however, who drops Silas off at school on weekdays, and watches his skinny legs pump across the playground into the big brick building. I'm the one who reads bedtime stories. I'm the parent who wrestles him and practices punting and cajoles him to finish homework. I'm the one he depends upon.

Silas, looking out the window of the car: "Can you catch the wind?"

A few weeks ago I stood at the counter in Office Depot, computer ribbon in hand, waiting for the cashier to notice me. She was talking to a stocker, telling him about her new maybe-boyfriend. She had met this man who seemed to like her. He'd called the night before from Camp Something (he was in the Army Reserves), and she'd only known him a couple of weeks. "He sent me a dozen roses the day after we met," she said. She was probably twenty-four, big-boned, with long blonde hair puffed up on top. Even after I wrote the check she kept talking. "I haven't been out in over two years, and I'd given up on finding anybody," she said. "This guy just seems too good to be true. But he called last night, all the way from Kentucky."

"I have a little boy," she said to me, "and that makes it harder."

"I know what you mean," I replied. Her child was two years old; his father abandoned both of them when the cashier got pregnant. Both her parents were dead, and she was rearing him alone.

Then there's Gayle. When I arrived recently in Missoula, Montana, to begin graduate school, the first person I met was Gayle, a dark-eyed Native American woman just turned fifty. Gayle is a single parent with three children, the youngest ten years old. She works in home health care, and supports her family of four on less money than I make as a teaching assistant at the university, which is a pittance. We have become good friends. Her husband had asked for a divorce during his midlife crisis, she told me. "I wish I'd demanded more child support," she said. "He couldn't have afforded it. Then he would've worked out his midlife crisis with us around."

My best friend back in Tallahassee, a red-headed schoolteacher, is raising her two children after the dissolution of a seventeen-year marriage. Another friend, a lawyer, is raising her eight-year-old alone, and has for years. The child is epileptic, with learning disabilities. So far, both of the babysitters I've called from the university's reference have been single parents, one of a toddler daughter, the other of four children. At one small birthday party recently I met three more single parents. The list goes on and on. They're everywhere.

Riding home after school in a vigorous thunderstorm, we watch fat raindrops dance on the warm pavement. "Look!" Silas exclaims, "It's like little people jumping on a trampoline."

In the Spring 1995 issue of *Marriage and Family Review*, Suzanne Bianchi reported that the number of single-parent families has increased so significantly in the past three decades that now approximately four of every ten children will be part of a single-parent family in their lifetimes. Small wonder that single parents had been turning up everywhere.

I hear how single-parenting contributes to the rise in crime, the decline in interest in the outdoors, the failure of public education, the welfare crisis. I hear the implications that single mothers are licentious, lustful, reprehensibly irresponsible. Ours are the "broken" homes, and we don't constitute families. Our children lag behind. When I hear these stories, I think about all the single parents I know. I think how hard-working, dedicated, unselfish, ambitious, and loving they are. I think about the long, lonely task of single-parenting, and how often it comes by default rather than choice, and how few resources are available, and how, despite all this, they manage to rear great children.

Silas: "Have you ever seen a house eating a stop sign?"

If I had the time, I would become a national advocate for single parents—lobby for child-support enforcement, get parenting resources into communities across the country, help single parents create their own support groups and childcare exchanges. I would promote clear thinking about societal trends in child-rearing, and I would call the Missoula Adult Education and tell them that if they really want attendees in their "Single Parenting— Is Sanity Possible?" class, they'd better not offer it on Monday evenings from 7:00 to 9:00, exactly bedtime, if they cannot provide childcare.

I'd speak as a single mother from the ranks of American working women. I'd speak in memory of my grandmother Clyo, a stout and determined woman who found herself raising eight young children alone when her husband vanished during the Great Depression. She ran the Greasy Spoon Cafe in Baxley, Georgia, and bootlegged whiskey on the side, just to put cornbread on her kitchen table. My father remembers hiding jars of whiskey in the baby's cradle when the deputies drove into the yard. He remembers going hungry. Single parenting is not the problem, I would say. It's lack of resources. It's absentee parents.

On a trip: "Mom, will you tell me things I don't know while I'm sleeping?" (pause) "I'm asleep now."

Before I went back to school, this was my life: Dawn came and someone flipped a big hourglass. All day as the sun arced across the gray Lego landscape laid out like a child's dream, dun-colored sand drained through. Before I could even reach for the day it lay in a pile at my feet.

Before dawn I was up. In the hour before we left the house I showered, dressed, made breakfast and two lunches, and maybe folded the two loads of laundry that had been unstrung from the clothesline for three days, so one never knew if the hamper was full of clean clothes or of dirty ones.

I let Silas sleep as late as possible, because he played hard all day and because I moved faster without him. Then I got him up, dressed him, fed him (no, he *couldn't* have frozen yogurt), coaxed him to put on his shoes and tie them himself, and raced him downstairs and out the door. I kissed him good-bye at school, flew to work and never got there on time. If I skipped lunch I could leave at four so Silas wasn't the last kid to be picked up from after-school care.

The evening was a hungry elephant. If I was lucky I got to run in the park, Silas biking alongside. Back home there was a fast supper, a long, hot bath for Silas, an argument over whether he would brush his teeth or I would have to do it, two or three stories read aloud—Andersen or White—speeding toward bedtime by 8:00, 8:15, 8:30.

"Will you leave the door open a little bit more?" He asked this same question every night.

"Honey I don't want the light to keep you awake. I'm right here in the kitchen, doing the dishes. Now go to sleep."

All got quiet and I washed dishes like a machine, thinking I might get a minute to myself.

"Mom," Silas called, "Is dirt alive?"

Why is he thinking? He should be sleeping.

"No, but things in it are. Go to sleep."

"Nan at school says that dirt is alive."

"Some people think that. Now go to sleep. It's way past your bedtime." I didn't have the time or energy to explain anything. It was always like that. Sometimes I swept and picked up around the house, did a load of laundry, made phone calls, paid bills. When I got to my journal or the revision of a poem, it was late. I thought, if I weren't so tired, I could laugh at the absurdity of my life.

"Mama, I wish I had three hands." "What would you do with the extra hand, Silas?" "I'd play with this hand and this hand." He holds them up, then touches near his shoulder, "and this hand."

I've spent a lot of time thinking almost scientifically about single-parenting, trying to pinpoint the worst of it. If I can make any discoveries, I may be able to ease someone's burden. Or my own.

The worst is the constancy, I decide; that the responsibility never lifts, not for long. No, it's loneliness—isolation, decisions made alone, the knowledge of the fallibility of independent thinking, the necessity for decisiveness despite uncertainty. That's the worst. Then I'll remember loss, the want of family, of father, of husband. But the night Silas lost his first tooth I knew definitively the worst of it.

That afternoon I had pinned myself to the extra chair in Dr. Brooks's office. A milk tooth Silas damaged as a toddler was infected and had to be extracted. I watched the needle, thick with painkiller, enter the tiny cliff of his pink gum. This little mammal who for five years had clung to me, suckled from me, was now captive in the huge chair of pain. With one quick snap the brown tooth was out and in his hand.

Back home I called my friend Sharon, divorced mother of two orange-haired children. "How much money do I leave under his pillow?" I asked her. When I was little, the Tooth Fairy left a quarter or fifty cents, but that was twenty-five years ago. Was a dollar enough? Shouldn't it be much more?

"It all depends," Sharon told me. "Usually a dollar or two. Once I left twenty dollars."

"Wow," I said, "Why?"

"I wanted to," she said.

That night I slipped a dollar under Silas's pillow and confiscated the ugly gauze-wrapped sprout of a tooth. Then it hit me that I'd become the Tooth Fairy, too.

Tooth Fairy. Mother. Nurse. Counselor. Teacher. Father. Firm Hand. Nurturer. Easter Bunny, Santa Claus. Bread-winner. Decision-maker. Role model. Fan. School Volunteer. The worst of single parenting is that one person has to be everything for his or her child.

Silas wakes up: "Mama, there was a wolf chasing me, up the steps," he says accusingly. "I was yelling for you. You should've come with a knife and killed it."

I cannot remember a specific scene that will illustrate how frustrated and furious I can get with Silas. I decided against corporal punishment before he was born, and I've spanked him only four or five times, and those left me aghast. I have been careful to keep his spirit separate from his behavior, and conscientious even of semantics in parenting.

Not to say "I have to change you," but, "I have to change your clothes." I'm proud of that. But there were times I'd be exhausted, worried about money, lonely and depressed, and I know I was not a kind parent then. I remember one fight Silas and I had over popsicles. I said that Silas had to eat certain vegetables on his plate before he got dessert, and he refused. He was stubborn and I was determined. Before long we were both screaming; me about needing him to stay healthy and have good teeth and be strong and eat food besides sweets, and him about how mean I was and how he wanted a popsicle and I was always screaming at him and he wanted his daddy. Before long I was physically dragging him away from the refrigerator, holding him so he wouldn't kick or hit me. It seems as if that fight lasted a long time, and it ended with me throwing the popsicles out the back door, off the balcony (our kitchen was upstairs), and ordering him to his room, or maybe locking myself in my own room.

Perhaps it's good that the fights are fuzzy in my memory. As Silas has gotten older, I have matured. I've learned parenting tricks and how to play more. Everybody told me it gets better and better, and it does. Now, there's seldom an argument.

Silas: "I remember when you were a giant."

Around the time of the popsicle incident I attended an evening parenting workshop. I had to call five babysitters before I found one available. The meeting would run past his bedtime, which would put him off schedule, which would probably mean he'd be cranky the next day and so would I. I sat grimly, watching people arrive, hoping the program would be worth the effort of coming. I watched a man come in, then another, and as I looked around I noticed that a great portion of the participants were male. The sight of men at a parenting workshop completely unnerved me—what were they doing here?

As we went around the room introducing ourselves (most of the people had partners), I learned the men were parents who wanted to be great parents; one man wasn't a parent, but wanted to learn parenting skills in order to strengthen his relationships with young people.

I realized how isolated I had become in my world of mothering. Because Silas's father wasn't present, I had forgotten that any men were. As I sat there, my rage and grief grew until finally we got a chance to pair up and listen to each other for ten minutes. I turned to a woman near me and started to sob. "I had no idea that men would be here," I said. What hurt was that Silas's father, not as a man but as a person, wasn't in that room. What I realized then was that we make individual decisions to be responsible to our children.

To prove a woman can teach her son outdoor skills, I take Silas fishing for white bass the winter he is five. "How long will we be there?" he asks. "About three hours," I say. "Catching fish?" he asks incredulously. "Why?"

After Silas and I moved to Missoula, I began trying to fashion a support system for myself, and at Lewis and Clark Elementary's Open House I heard that a local nonprofit support group, called "Families First," was beginning. Child care would be provided, so I went. Only three of us showed up, and I couldn't help but wonder about the hundreds of single parents in Missoula who weren't there.

One woman, not yet twenty, the mother of a toddler daughter, was so overwhelmed that it was obvious she was almost insane. She said as much. She'd stopped being able to function; she was a university student, but she hadn't been able, psychologically, to attend classes. If she dropped out, she wouldn't get the grant money she needed to live on. What she wanted was a break from the constant care her daughter demanded. Her parents wouldn't help. The child's father wouldn't agree that the girl was his, and the woman couldn't afford genetic testing to prove it. She didn't know where to turn.

The other woman parented two older boys, pre-teens. She was outgoing and jovial, a graduate student in social work who lived on Aid to Families with Dependent Children. Her boys, the little I saw of them before they went downstairs to play, seemed well-adjusted and loving. She came, she said, because she craved adult contact.

The support group leader was a happily re-married psychologist whose one slim claim to credibility was that he had co-parented his child for a few years after his divorce. He readily admitted that co-parenting is different from single-parenting, and that single-parent men seem to have more resources than single-parent women, not just in salary but in personal offers of assistance. It seems that people are more willing to pity single-parent men.

I can say that I didn't find support at that meeting. What I realized, however, is that there are single parents whose situations are exponentially worse than mine. I wanted to do something for the crazy woman, but I never did. Sometimes I think we single parents should band together and depend on each other, but more often I think that others (volunteer non-parents, parents of grown children, family advocate organizations) could do the helping.

In the middle of the night, crying with stomach virus pains: "Mama, I want a new stomach."

"When are you going to die?" Silas asks me one day. He has to worry about me dying, and about what will happen to him if I vanish from the earth. I explain that I have no idea when I'll die, but I don't think it'll be soon, that maybe we can feel when it's time. I don't feel ready yet, and maybe he'll be grown before I die. A few days later he asks, "Is today the day it's getting soon to die?" Coming in late on another day, unlocking the door as a thunderstorm rages, Silas presses his small body into mine. His head almost reaches my navel. "If lightning hits, we'll die together," he says.

Silas: "I pulled something out of my nose and it was a space ship."

This story of tragic joy is one that's happening in every neighborhood, among people you know, a story so complicated that we can only scratch the surface of its implications. It's my story, and even as I tell it I rob hours from my son, time in which he will not get my attention nor my care. Yet the story has to be told, so we can begin to rethink familial structures and figure out how to make them work.

I worry how being reared with one parent, my interests further divided by my own desires, will affect Silas. I spend long, sleepless spells running choices through my head: Should I try to bring his father back? Should I move in with my parents, so they can help? Should I remarry? Should I try co-housing with another single parent?

For now; this is where I am—alone, descending the steep mountain of every day, my baby bald eagle in his nest asleep, his father out of the game. For now I search for doorways leading down lucky passages and I wait, living on the hope that one day Silas will understand enough to forgive me for the hard times, and for all the ways I could not be everything.

All summer, Silas has been trying to summon the nerve to jump off the low dive at Wakulla Springs. Without a word, one afternoon, he does it. "I just looked at it really hard and jumped," he said.

On the last day I spend with Silas before he leaves for two months with his dad, we go to our land in Sycamore and pick a bushel of apples and enough blackberries for a cobbler. But first we hike to the creek, sliding our way down the ravine, wary of snakes.

The creek is a silver glint beneath magnolias. Recent heavy rains have swept the dross of the creek high up its banks, so that the creek seems lined with aeries. When we get to our bathing spot two red-shouldered hawks begin to call, nearby, alarmed. They're nesting. Silas and I climb the bank and track the nest, tracing through cinnamon fern, dog hobble and star anise to stand beneath a strong-limbed magnolia. The nest is fifty feet up, and the parents are wild with worry.

"Let's leave them alone," I whisper.

Where we creep back out onto the stream bank, we find a cougar track, and that's exciting. Another one marks the junction of the stream from the lake. Silas and I gather stones to skim, to pore over for fossils, and to take home. We rub clay on our faces, and balance on a log high across the creek, ribbed with two colors of shelf lichens.

I watch every movement he makes, trying to memorize the way his little belly sticks out, the skinniness of his legs, the set to his face as he inches out across the log—preparing myself. We build a sand fort and float magnolia leaf boats downstream.

We leave via the deer trail that is lined with white, purple, orange, yellow, and red mushrooms. It reminds me that Wendell Berry defined a path as "little more than a habit that comes with knowledge of a place." I think of it in the context of my life, which so often seems well-traveled and worn. So habitual, and hard. But the path itself is not a bad thing. Off in the woods something thuds; it sounds like a rotted tree limb.

In the afternoon we buy red wigglers at Triple-D Store and go to Mill Creek below Greensboro. Silas catches a five-inch bream right away on his cane pole. That night, when I'm putting him to bed, he says simply, "Mom, today was a great day."

That's the best I can do.

Janisse Ray's book, Ecology of a Cracker Childhood, *is about growing up on a junkyard in the longleaf pine ecosystem of southern Georgia.*

Why Schools Don't Educate

by John Taylor Gatto

When John Taylor Gatto was named New York City's Teacher of the Year (for the second year in a row) in 1990, his acceptance speech was not a quiet thank-you, but a loud-and-clear challenge to the conventional wisdom about education, family, and society today. Not just about New York City schools and children, his remarks address concerns that educators and parents feel, more or less deeply, no matter where they reside. The challenges we face in the education and engagement of our children are serious and complex, and they are not simply the responsibility of our schools. Yet schools can provide much of the context necessary for making our society and our world the kind of place in which we all want to live. So we take pleasure in publishing the impassioned remarks of one of the most vocal and articulate champions of education reform. —JW

"I accept this award on behalf of all the fine teachers I've known over the years who've struggled to make their transactions with children honorable ones: men and women who are never complacent, always questioning, always wrestling to define and redefine endlessly what the word "education" should mean. A "Teacher of the Year" is not the best teacher around—those people are too quiet to be easily uncovered—but a standard-bearer, symbolic of these private people who spend their lives gladly in the service of children. This is their award as well as mine.

We live in a time of great social crisis. Our children rank at the bottom of nineteen industrial nations in reading, writing, and arithmetic. The world's narcotic economy is based upon our own consumption of this commodity. If we didn't buy so many powdered dreams the business would collapse—and schools are an important sales outlet. Our teenage suicide rate is the highest in the world—and suicidal kids are rich kids, for the most part, not the poor. In Manhattan seventy percent of all new marriages last less than five years.

Our school crisis is a reflection of this greater social crisis. We seem to have lost our identity: Children and old people are penned up and locked away from the business of the world without precedent; nobody talks to them anymore. Without children and old people mixing in daily life, a community has no future and no past; only a continuous present. In fact, the name "community" hardly applies to the way we interact with each other. We live in networks, not communities, and everyone I know is lonely because of that. In some strange way, a school is a major actor in this tragedy; just as it is a major actor in the widening gulf among social classes. Using school as a sorting mechanism, we appear to be on the way to creating a caste system, complete with untouchables who wander through subway trains begging, and sleep on the streets. I've noticed a fascinating phenomenon in my twenty-five years of teaching—that schools and schooling are increasingly irrelevant to the great enterprises of the planet. No one believes anymore that scientists are trained in science classes, or politicians in civics classes, or poets in English classes. The truth is that schools don't really teach anything except how to obey orders. This is a great mystery to me because thousands of humane, caring people work in schools as teachers and aides and administrators, but the abstract logic of the institution overwhelms their individual contributions. Although teachers do care and do work very, very hard, the institution is psychopathic; it has no conscience. It rings a bell, and the young man in the middle of writing a poem must close his notebook and move to a different cell, where he learns that man and monkeys derive from a common ancestor.

Our form of compulsory schooling is an invention of the State of Massachusetts around 1850. It was resisted—sometimes with guns—by an estimated eighty percent of the Massachusetts population, the last outpost in Barnstable on Cape Cod not surrendering its children until the 1880s, when the area was seized by militia and children marched to school under guard. Now here is a curious idea to ponder: Senator Ted Kennedy's office released a paper not too long ago claiming that, prior to compulsory education, the state literacy rate was ninety-eight percent, and after it, the figure never again reached above ninety-one percent, where it stands in 1990. I hope that interests you.

Here is another curiosity to think about: The home-schooling movement has quietly grown to a size where one and a half million young people are being educated entirely by their own parents. Last month the education press reported the amazing news that children schooled at home seem to be five or even ten years ahead of their formally trained peers in their ability to think.

I don't think we'll get rid of the schools anytime soon, certainly not in my lifetime, but if we're going to change what's rapidly becoming a disaster of ignorance, we need to realize that the school institution "schools" very well, but it does not "educate." That's inherent in the design of the thing. It's not the fault of bad teachers or too little money spent. It's just impossible for education and schooling ever to be the same thing.

Schools were designed by Horace Mann, Barnas Sears, W. R. Harper of the University of Chicago, Thorndyke of Columbia Teachers College, and others, to be instruments of the scientific management of a mass population. Schools are intended to produce, through the application of formulae, formulaic human beings whose behavior can be predicted and controlled.

To a very great extent schools succeed in doing this. But our society is disintegrating, and in such a society the only successful people are self-reliant, confident, and individualistic—because the community life which protects the dependent and the weak is dead. The products of schooling are, as I've said, irrelevant. Well-schooled people are irrelevant. They can sell film and razor blades, push paper, and talk on telephones, or sit mindlessly before a flickering computer terminal, but as human beings they are useless—useless to others and useless to themselves.

The daily misery around us is, I think, in large measure caused by the fact that—as Paul Goodman put it thirty years ago—we force children to "grow up absurd." Any reform in schooling has to deal with its absurdities.

It is absurd and anti-life to be part of a system that compels you to sit in confinement with people of exactly the same age and social class. That system effectively cuts you off from the immense diversity of life and the synergy of variety. It cuts you off from your own past and future, sealing you in a continuous present much the same way television does.

It is absurd and anti-life to be part of a system that compels you to listen to a stranger reading poetry when you want to learn to construct buildings, or to sit with a stranger discussing the construction of buildings when you want to read poetry.

It is absurd and anti-life to move from cell to cell at the sound of a gong for every day of your youth in an institution that allows you no privacy and even follows you into the sanctuary of your home demanding that you do its "homework."

"How will they learn to read?!" you say, and my answer is "Remember the lessons of Massachusetts." When children are given whole lives instead of age-graded ones in cellblocks they learn to read, write, and do arithmetic with ease if those things make sense in the life that unfolds around them.

But keep in mind that in the United States almost nobody who reads, writes, or does arithmetic gets much respect. We are a land of talkers; we pay talkers the most and admire talkers the most and so our children talk constantly, following the public models of television and schoolteachers. It is very difficult to teach the "basics" anymore because they really aren't basic to the society we've made.

Two institutions at present control our children's lives—television and schooling, in that order. Both of these reduce the real world of wisdom, fortitude, temperance, and justice to a never-ending, non-stop abstraction. In centuries past, the time of a child and adolescent would be occupied in real work, real charity, real adventures, and the real search for mentors who might teach what one really wanted to learn. A great deal of time was spent in community pursuits, practicing affection, meeting and studying every level of the community, learning how to make a home, and dozens of other tasks necessary to becoming a whole man or woman.

But here is the calculus of time the children I teach must deal with:

Out of the 168 hours in each week, my children must sleep fifty-six. That leaves them 112 hours hours a week out of which to fashion a self.

My children watch fifty-five hours of television a week, according to recent reports. That leaves them fifty-seven hours a week in which to grow up.

My children attend school thirty hours a week, use about eight hours getting ready, going and coming home, and spend an average of seven hours a week in homework—a total of forty-five hours. During that time they are under constant surveillance, have no private time or private space, and are disciplined if they try to assert individuality in the use of time or space. That leaves twelve hours a week out of which to create a unique consciousness. Of course my kids eat, too, and that takes some time—not much, because we've lost the tradition of family dining. If we allot three hours a week to evening meals we arrive at a net amount of private time for each child of nine hours.

It's not enough, is it? The richer the kid, of course, the less television he watches, but the rich kid's time is just as narrowly proscribed, by a broader catalogue of commercial entertainments and inevitable assignments to a series of private lessons—in areas seldom of his choice.

And these things are, oddly enough, just a more cosmetic way to create dependent human beings, unable to fill their own hours, unable to initiate lines of meaning to give substance and pleasure to their existence. It's a national disease, this dependency and aimlessness, and I think schooling and television and lessons—the entire Chatauqua idea—have a lot to do with it.

Think of the things that are killing us as a nation: drugs, brainless competition, recreational sex, the pornography of violence, gambling, alcohol, and the worst pornography of all—lives devoted to buying things—accumulation as a philosophy. All are addictions of dependent personalities and that is what our brand of schooling must inevitably produce.

I want to tell you what the effect is on children of taking all their time— time they need to grow up—and forcing them to spend it on abstractions. No reform that doesn't attack these specific pathologies will be anything more than a facade.

1. The children I teach are indifferent to the adult world. This defies the experience of thousands of years. A close study of what big people were up to was always the most exciting occupation of youth, but nobody wants to grow up these days, and who can blame them. Toys are us.

2. The children I teach have almost no curiosity, and what little they do have is transitory; they cannot concentrate for very long, even on things they choose to do. Can you see a connection between the bells ringing again and again to change classes, and this phenomenon of evanescent attention?

3. The children I teach have a poor sense of the future, of how tomorrow is inextricably linked to today. They live in a continuous present; the exact moment they are in is the boundary of their consciousness.

4. The children I teach are ahistorical; they have no sense of how the past has predestined their own present, limiting their choices, shaping their values and lives.

5. The children I teach are cruel to each other; they lack compassion for misfortune, they laugh at weakness, they have contempt for people whose need for help shows too plainly.

6. The children I teach are uneasy with intimacy or candor. They cannot deal with genuine intimacy because of a lifelong habit of preserving a

secret self inside an outer personality made up of artificial bits and pieces of behavior borrowed from television, or acquired to manipulate teachers. Because they are not who they represent themselves to be, the disguise wears thin in the presence of intimacy, so intimate relationships have to be avoided.

7. The children I teach are materialistic, following the lead of school-teachers who materialistically "grade" everything—and television mentors who offer everything in the world for sale.

8. The children I teach are dependent, passive, and timid in the presence of new challenges. This timidity is frequently masked by surface bravado, or by anger or aggressiveness, but underneath is a vacuum without fortitude.

I could name a few other conditions that school reform will have to tackle if our national decline is to be arrested, but by now you will have grasped my thesis, whether you agree with it or not. Either schools, television, or both have caused these pathologies. It's a simple matter of arithmetic. Between schooling and television, all the time children have is eaten up. That's what has destroyed the American family; it no longer is a factor in the education of its own children.

What can be done? First, we need a ferocious national debate that does not quit, day after day, year after year; the kind of continuous emphasis that journalism finds boring. We need to scream and argue about this school thing until it is fixed or broken beyond repair, one or the other. If we can fix it, fine; if we cannot, then the success of home schooling shows a different road that has great promise. Pouring the money back into family education might kill two birds with one stone, repairing families as it repairs children.

Genuine reform is possible but it shouldn't cost anything. We need to rethink the fundamental premises of schooling and decide what it is we want all children to learn and why. For 140 years this nation has tried to impose objectives from a lofty command center made up of "experts," a central elite of social engineers. It hasn't worked. It won't work. It is a gross betrayal of the democratic promise that once made this nation a noble experiment. The Russian attempt to control Eastern Europe has exploded before our eyes. Our own attempt to impose the same sort of social orthodoxy, using the schools as an instrument, is also coming apart at the seams, albeit more slowly and painfully. It doesn't work because its fundamental premises are mechanical, anti-human, and hostile to family life. Lives can be controlled by machine education, but they will always fight back with weapons of social pathology—drugs, violence, self-destruction, indifference, and the symptoms I see in the children I teach.

It's high time we looked backward to regain an educational philosophy that works. One I like particularly well has been a favorite of the ruling classes of Europe for thousands of years. I think it works just as well for poor children as for rich ones. I use as much of it as I can manage in my own teaching; as much, that is, as I can get away with, given the present institution of compulsory schooling.

At the core of this elite system of education is the belief that self-knowledge is the only basis of true knowledge. Everywhere in this system, at every age, you will find arrangements that place the child alone in an unguided setting with a problem to solve. Sometimes the problem is fraught with great risks, such as the problem of galloping a horse or making it jump, but that, of course, is a problem successfully solved by thousands of elite children before the age of ten. Can you imagine anyone who had mastered such a challenge ever lacking confidence in his ability to do anything? Sometimes the problem is that of mastering solitude, as Thoreau did at Walden Pond, or Einstein did in the Swiss customs house.

One of my former students, Roland Legiardi-Laura, though both his parents were dead and he had no inheritance, took a bicycle across the United States alone when he was hardly out of boyhood. Is it any wonder that in manhood he made a film about Nicaragua, although he had no money and no prior experience with film-making, and that it was an international award-winner—even though his regular work was as a carpenter?

Right now we are taking from our children the time they need to develop self-knowledge. That has to stop. We have to invent school experiences that give a lot of that time back. We need to trust children from a very early age with independent study perhaps arranged in school, but which takes place away from the institutional setting. We need to invent a curriculum where each kid has a chance to develop uniqueness and self-reliance.

A short time ago, I took seventy dollars and sent a twelve-year-old girl with her non-English speaking mother on a bus down the New Jersey coast. She took the police chief of Sea Bright to lunch and apologized for polluting his beach with a discarded Gatorade bottle. In exchange for this public apology, I had arranged for the girl to have a one-day apprenticeship in small-town police procedures. A few days later, two more of my twelve-year-old kids traveled alone from Harlem to West 31st Street, where they began an apprenticeship with a newspaper editor. Next week, three of my kids will find themselves in the middle of the Jersey swamps at six in the morning studying the mind of a trucking company president as he dispatches eighteen-wheelers to Dallas, Chicago, and Los Angeles.

Are these "special" children in a "special" program? They're just nice kids from Central Harlem, bright and alert but so badly schooled when they came to me that most of them couldn't add or subtract with any fluency. And not a single one knew the population of New York City, or how far it is from New York to California.

Does that worry me? Of course. But I am confident that as they gain self-knowledge they'll also become self-teachers, and only self-teaching has any lasting value.

We've got to give the kids independent time right away because that is the key to self-knowledge, and we must reinvolve them with the real world as fast as possible so that the independent time can be spent on something other than more abstractions. This is an emergency. It requires drastic action to correct. Our children are dying like flies in our schools. Good schooling or bad schooling, it's all the same—irrelevant.

What else does a restructured school system need? It needs to stop being a parasite on the working community. I think we need to make community service a required part of schooling. It is the quickest way to give young children real responsibility.

For five years I ran a guerrilla school program where I had every kid, rich and poor, smart and dipsy, give 320 hours a year of hard community service. Dozens of those kids came back to me years later, and told me that this one experience changed their lives, taught them to see in new ways, to rethink goals and values. They were thirteen, and in my Lab School program—made possible only because my rich school district was then in chaos. When "stability" returned, the Lab closed. It was too successful, at too small a cost, to be allowed to continue. We made the expensive, elite programs look bad.

There is no shortage of real problems in this city. Kids can be asked to help solve them in exchange for the respect and attention of the adult world. Good for kids, good for the rest of us.

Independent study, community service, adventures in experience, large doses of privacy and solitude, a thousand different apprenticeships—these are all powerful, cheap, and effective ways to start a real reform of schooling. But no large-scale reform is ever going to repair our damaged children and our damaged society until we force the idea of "school" open—to include family as the main engine of education. The Swedes realized this in 1976, when they effectively abandoned the (national system) of adopting unwanted children and instead spent national time and treasure on reinforcing the original family so that children born to Swedes were wanted. They reduced the number of unwanted Swedish children from 6,000 in 1976 to fifteen in 1986. So it can be done. The Swedes just got tired of paying for the social wreckage caused, and they did something about it. We can, too.

Family is the main engine of education. If we use schooling to break children away from parents—and make no mistake, that has been the central function of schools since John Cotton announced it as the purpose of the Bay Colony schools in 1650, and Horace Mann announced it as the purpose of Massachusetts schools in 1850—we're going to continue to have the horror show we have right now.

The curriculum of family is at the heart of any good life. We've gotten away from that curriculum—it's time to return to it. The way to sanity in education is for our schools to take the lead in releasing the stranglehold of institutions on family life: to promote during school time confluences of parent and child that will strengthen family bonds. That was my purpose in sending the girl and her mother down the Jersey coast to meet the police chief.

I have many ideas to make a family curriculum, and my guess is that a lot of you will have many ideas, too, once you begin to think about it. Our greatest problem in getting the kind of grassroots thinking going that could reform schooling is that we have large, vested interests profiting from schooling just exactly as it is, despite rhetoric to the contrary.

We have to demand that new voices and new ideas get a hearing—my ideas *and* yours. We've all had a bellyful of authorized voices on television and in the press. A decade-long free-for-all debate is called for now, not any more "expert" opinions. Experts in education have never been right; their "solutions" are expensive, self-serving, and always involve further centralization. Enough. Time for a return to democracy, individuality, and family.

I've said my piece. Thank you.

We asked Mr. Gatto if he'd write a few words on what had transpired since he delivered this speech. He wrote the following in reply. It's worth noting that, when he decided to stop teaching, he had no idea what, exactly, he was going to do to generate an income.

Dear Jon,

A year and a half after I gave that speech, I quit teaching (on the Op-Ed page of *The Wall Street Journal*, July 25, 1991). A week later, I was asked to speak to the engineers at NASA-Goddard Space Center, and a week after that, I was at the White House. Then in rapid order I was invited to open the full season at the Nashville Center for the Arts, be the keynote speaker for the Colorado Librarians Convention, and spend eight private hours with the comptrollers of the thirty-two operating divisions of United Technologies Corp. in Hartford, CT. From there to The Farm commune in central Tennessee, an Indian reservation in New Mexico, and a Christian homeschool convention in Atlanta.

All in all, since I quit teaching five years ago, I've given 522 talks and workshops in forty-nine states (missed Oklahoma) and six foreign countries. I don't advertise, but I go anywhere I'm invited as long as my hosts don't tell me what I have to say.

Being in an airplane seat about one day in every two has added eighty-five pounds, so I expect to translate to the spirit world momentarily—if I don't come up with a strategy—but in the meantime, I've met an amazing cross-section of fine and courageous ordinary people from every point on the political/social spectrum—enough to convince me an American renaissance is latent in the common folk of this country if we can figure out a way to restore the democratic promise.

I think we will. I have faith, as well as hope, that we can do it.

—JTG

John Taylor Gatto, a New York City public school teacher for thirty years, was named New York City Teacher of the Year in 1989, 1990, and 1991, and New York State Teacher of the Year in 1990 and 1991. He is the author of Dumbing Us Down, The Exhausted School, *and this year's* The Empty Child.

The Boredom Effect

by Ellen Ruppel Shell

As a child I loved a vacant lot we called "the woods." I went there alone, to read or to wander around. I went there with friends, to build tree forts. Sometimes, one of us would bring a magnifying glass to burn ants or to light little teepee fires. Sometimes, one of the boys would pee on the fire to put it out, and we'd laugh our heads off. Our parents knew none of this, of course, but that was the point. Back then, parents pretty much stayed out of children's business, which is to say they stayed out of our play.

Play went mostly unsupervised, and it was deliciously freeform. Our parents wouldn't have thought of making "play dates" for us, or cramming our schedules with lessons. After school and on weekends we hung out on the street until another kid showed up. If no one showed up, we bounced a ball off a stoop, or played solitary jacks, or lolled on the grass. If we had roller skates or a bike, we'd use them, If it rained, we roamed around the house, bored. But most of us avoided letting on that we were bored, for fear that our parents would find us something to do. I'm not talking about a trip to the amusement park or an afternoon of miniature golf. Something to do meant scrubbing the kitchen floor or mowing the lawn or washing the family car. So, unlike many kids today, we took charge of our boredom. According to child development experts, this was probably a good thing.

Last April, Ann O'Bar, president of the American Association on the Child's Right to Play told *The New York Times*: "There's nothing wrong with letting children be bored. Boredom leads to exploration, which leads to creativity." One day last spring I decided to put Ms. O'Bar's theory to the test.

My younger daughter Joanna, who's eight, was very, very bored. Her best friend was out of town, none of her other friends was free, and, to heap insult on injury, it was sunny outside. So rather than entertain her, I insisted she find something to do out of doors. I watched from the window, feeling a little guilty as she stomped, sulking, to the play structure in our back yard. She sat on the swing, scowling down at her bare feet (out of defiance, she'd refused to put on shoes). After a few minutes, boredom got the best of her. She had to do something. She twisted and twisted in the swing, then let go, twirling like a dervish. She did this a few more times, throwing her head back to study the cloudless sky. Then she climbed out of the swing and up to the top of the monkey bars, and peered over at the neighbor's parking lot. (We live behind a condominium complex.) She watched a neighbor scrub down his Honda for a while, until she spotted a squirrel. She followed the squirrel up a tree with her eyes, then did a skin-the-cat maneuver down from the monkey bars, back to solid ground. She gathered a bunch of pine cones and sticks, and made a tiny fort for her stuffed armadillo, Jessica. She got the hose and flooded the fort with water. She learned that stuffed armadillos can't swim. She charged into the house for her doctor's bag, then hustled back out-side just in time to bring Jessica back to life. I watched all this with one eye, my other trained on the Sunday paper. Gradually my guilt dissolved into pride. Clearly, Ms. O'Bar is onto something.

It seems to me that we've lost trust in our kids. We don't believe that they can navigate the world, so we try to navigate it for them. We muck around in the details of their lives. We load them up with lessons and orga-nized sports overseen by adults. We monitor their every move, demanding to know how and where and with whom they spend their time. And we sched-ule them so tightly that they lose their natural-born knack for spontaneous play. Put these over-scheduled kids in a room with crayons and markers and scissors and paper and, rather than dig in, they'll ask you what the assign-ment is. Stick them on a field with a ball, and they'll ask you about the rules. Put them in a room filled with blocks and dolls and trucks and they'll demand a television set or a video game, anything that will organize and structure their time for them.

I'm not sure why this happened, or when, but I am almost certain it has something to do with marketing. Making sure children are endlessly stimu-lated costs money—money that we are told we must spend if our kids are to be successful, productive adults. We are told that computer games will sharpen their minds, karate lessons will make them assertive, and that gymnastics classes will teach them "invaluable social skills." Many of us are ripe for this kind of argument. We are incredibly busy, juggling careers and community service and parenting like so many hot potatoes. We fear that if we miss a beat, look away for a second, the whole mess will come crashing down. We worry about our children wasting time, missing an opportunity that could, some day, help them get ahead, or even just get by. Most of us know intuitively that children need the opportunity to experiment, to fail. But we are afraid to allow them to do so for fear of their falling behind. In these achievement-oriented times, we parents want our kids to work as hard as we do.

Earlier this year, the Atlanta public schools eliminated recess in elementary schools. Other districts have turned to "socialized recess," where children are supervised in structured activities. Games that teach reading and math, frequently with the help of a computer, are encouraged, as is physical education instruction to "enhance motor skills." Many parents support this trend. We like the idea of our children spending all of the school day in structured learning situations. And we don't mind that new schools are being built without playgrounds. As one school administrator put it, you don't improve academic performance "by having kids hanging on the monkey bars."

I beg to differ. Half a century ago, Swiss child psychologist Jean Piaget identified play as critical to the emotional, moral, and intellectual development of children. According to Piaget, kids learn a whole lot while hanging upside down from their knees. They learn that gravity makes their blood rush to their heads. They learn that all that rushing of blood can make them dizzy And they learn that if they hang too long another kid will push them off. Play and the restless questing energy that provokes it, is, in a sense, childhood's greatest gift. As Susan Isaacs, a pioneering researcher in child development wrote in 1929: "How large a value children's play has for all sides of their growth. And how fatal to go against this great stream of healthy and active impulse in our children! That 'restlessness' and inability to sit still; that 'mischievousness' and 'looking inside' and eternal 'Why?' That indifference to soiled hands and torn clothes for the sake of running and climbing and digging and exploring—these are not unfortunate and accidental ways of childhood which are to be shed as soon as we can get rid of them. They are the glory of the human child, his human heritage. They are at once the representatives in him of human adventurousness and hard-won wisdom, and the means by which he in his turn will lay hold of knowledge and skill, and add to them."

The best play is spontaneous and unpredictable. Adults cannot control it, they can only sit back and let it happen. While we may spend hours building an architecturally correct structure, as pictured on the box of an expensive construction set, our children would rather brainstorm and build their own shaky pile of blocks. It is the *process* of creation, not the product, that naturally interests children, and it is this process that encourages their development as independent thinkers. But it's terribly easy to dampen a child's creativity, especially by insisting that there is a right and wrong way of doing everything, that life is a sort of multiple-choice quiz with adults holding the answer key. By forcing children to follow rules imposed by others, even during what is supposed to be their leisure time, adults can effectively discourage them from believing that they have anything significant to offer. They can turn them from confident and curious explorers, to cautious over-achievers intent on getting it right. Kids like this grow into adults who are edgy and averse to risk, adults who have difficulty thinking for themselves, difficulty creating. Adults like this make awfully good corporate cogs, because they do what they are told. But they don't make particularly good participants in a democratic system because they fail to grasp that "getting it" in the truest sense often has nothing to do with "getting it right."

And "getting it right" is often what "structured play" is all about—organized sports being a prime example. Last fall, Joanna enrolled in a local soccer league. Not surprisingly, neither she nor many of the other seven-year-olds on her team were terribly interested in the rules of the game. What they wanted to do was kick the ball around, schmooze with their friends, and pick three-leaf clovers on the field. But the coaches and the parents would have none of this. Girls whose attention wandered were called back to focus. Girls who stooped to pick a clover were commanded to keep their eyes on the ball. One father, a professor of mathematics who, from his appearance, has spent little time on playing fields himself, pulled his daughter onto his lap and barked in her ear "be A-G-G-R-E-S-S-I-V-E, AGGRESSIVE!" Another dad threw up his hands in disgust when his daughter kicked the ball into the opposing team's goal. Later I heard her promise that she'd "do better" next time. If kept to a minimum, this sort of adult meddling will probably do the girls little harm. But we're fooling ourselves when we gush over all the good such sessions can do for the pre-preteen set. Team spirit and competition are wonderful things, of course, but no thinking person would consider them essential to the psychic or moral development of a second grader. By projecting our own ambitions and needs onto our kids, by insisting, for instance, that kicking a soccer ball into a goal is more important than searching out clovers, we are making implicit judgments—judgments we may come to regret.

Which returns me to the concept of boredom. Maybe it's time we reconsider the concept. Perhaps boredom is not, as we often regard it, a symptom of neglect. Perhaps it's every child's natural-born right. Rather than supervise and coach and guide our children toward some predetermined goal, perhaps we should encourage them to follow their fancy to a goal we can't even imagine. Maybe it's time we gave childhood back to children. Maybe it's time we let them play.

Ellen Ruppel Shell is the author of A Child's Place: A Year in the Life of A Day Care Center, *a contributing editor to the* Atlantic Monthly, *and a frequent contributor to* Smithsonian *magazine and other publications. She is co-director of the Graduate Program in Science Journalism at Boston University.*

The Place of the Possible
by Sarah Putnam

On a beautiful summer day in 1952, Helen Lamb was sitting on the town beach at Oak Bluffs on Martha's Vineyard, Massachusetts, watching her three children cavort in paradise. Most overworked single parents on vacation might have breathed in the salt air and allowed themselves to delight in the scene. Not Helen. Instead, she was consumed with guilt. A speech therapist who worked with children in the Fall River cerebral palsy clinic, she was wondering what they were doing on this beautiful day, and she was afraid she knew. She suspected that, coming from poor communities and stressed families, they were shut up in dark tenement apartments, and she was outraged that they were not having the same kind of summer that her own children were. Next year, she vowed, would be different.

The following summer, Lamb rented a small gingerbread cottage on the old Tabernacle grounds at Oak Bluffs for a month, and convinced a high school student to help her bring sixteen children with cerebral palsy, six per week at the most, for the only vacation they had ever had. She knew she was also providing a much-needed respite for their parents. When she resumed her clinical work with these children during the school year, the positive effects of their summer adventure—both psychological and physical—were undeniable. And, always one to raise the stakes, Lamb determined to try it again the next summer, but on a larger scale. She placed an announcement in the *Vineyard Gazette*, asking if anyone knew of a slightly larger, better-equipped cottage that she could rent for a modest fee. The group's presence on the island the previous summer had not gone unnoticed, and the response to her request was a dream come true. The local 4-H club offered, rent-free, its Quonset hut, and its president, local businessman William Pinney, mustered the island community to donate goods and services. For the next ten years, the Martha's Vineyard Cerebral Palsy Camp—a cumbersome name for a freewheeling enterprise—accommodated a growing number of children each year. Helen's children began to take part in the work of the camp as soon as they could. Her son became a junior counselor at age fourteen.

Forty-four years after its founding, Camp Jabberwocky, as it's now called, welcomes children and adults with disabilities of all kinds, both physical and mental, and it is one of the most extraordinary summer camps in New England. Helen Lamb has long been known only by her moniker "Hellcat," a reference, it is said, to her driving style. She is a force to be reckoned with. Since 1965, the camp has operated on its own land—a gift from the local Episcopal parish—with buildings donated and built over the years by a wide roster of friends. Yet, Camp Jabberwocky is the ultimate anti-institution. The camp charges almost nothing for tuition, operates on a shoestring budget, and depends on the steady stream of contributions that flow in from both the island community and far afield, including ferry tickets, food, free rides on the carousel, and various invitations to sail, picnic, or otherwise indulge in the island's offerings. Jabberwocky houses about thirty campers and twenty counselors at a time. The waiting list for new campers is very long.

Hellcat Lamb, now eighty-three, is still an active and essential presence, but the camp is run by two of her children. Her daughter, Gillian Butchman, runs the July session, and her son, John Lamb, and his wife Kathleen, are directors of the August session. (In Gillian's session the age range is from six to fifty-three, with some campers returning for their fortieth summer. In John's session, the ages range from six to the late twenties.) A third generation of Lambs are also fully involved in the camp. John and Kathleen's daughters, Caitlin and Sarah, ages eighteen and sixteen, are both August-session counselors, and their younger sister, Dori, twelve, is an integral member of the community. "All the girls really love it here, but Caitlin really lives for it," says Kathleen. Caitlin, who enrolled in a school for occupational therapy last fall, has worked with the same camper, Michael Anderson, for the past four years. She has visited him at his home in Pennsylvania, and last spring, after Michael's most recent surgery for complications from cerebral palsy, she spent time with his family to learn his exercise routine so she could ensure that his physical therapy continues while he is at camp.

It was my first morning as a visitor to the August session, and I was disoriented and shy. I didn't know where to sit when I entered the dining hall for breakfast. No place looked very manageable in my pre-caffeine state. The choice of squeezing in between drooling wheelchair occupants who couldn't talk or hold a spoon, and talkative but hard-to-understand adolescents with Down syndrome, was not a comfortable one. So I ate standing up for a while, surveying the scene, before deciding to sit next to the six-year-old son of a counselor. I knew I could handle hanging out with a six-year-old; I had one of my own. By dinner time, however, my malaise of the morning would vanish as if it had never existed; as if it were a disability in itself from which I had been miraculously cured. None of the campers here are so lucky. Their disabilities are also, in many cases, progressive. But Jabberwocky offers them a cure of a different sort — a sanctuary, a fortifying of the spirit; bright moments of time in a beautiful place where they can simply have fun, and be themselves.

A torrential summer rain pounded the roof of the main building, muffling the din of the thirty campers at breakfast. Rael Gleitzman, Jabberwocky's pottery teacher, spoke to one particularly noisy group—the only table at which everyone could feed themselves. "Sitting around doing nothing is not where it's at, right? You guys gotta get organized to *do* something!" Breakfast had ended for these Down syndrome boys, and they were goofing around at increasing decibel levels, while other counselors were occupied as feeders at those tables encircled by wheelchairs.

Although the camp is aptly named—a very different world through the looking-glass—Jabberwocky's current physical facilities are classically camp-like. Nestled in the woods at the end of a residential street in Vineyard Haven, its presence is announced only by a rectangle of cracked asphalt abutting the street. A volleyball net is strung casually across the court, and a low basketball hoop hangs at the far end. A driveway curls uphill to the camp's hub, a long, gray wood building housing kitchen, dining hall, and infirmary, with a large porch in front. Wheelchairs and walkers proliferate, and for those still in doubt of their whereabouts, a gold-leafed sign proclaims "Camp Jabberwocky, Martha's Vineyard."

On a pole, a cluster of hand-decorated pointers splay out to the woods behind, where eight cabins perch with thematic names like Mimsey, Slithy Toves, and Galumphing, a reference to the Lewis Carroll poem. Scattered peripherally around these cabins are the art studio, the computer cabin with costume room (which occasionally serves as counselors' trysting room), the "studio" (a large performance and dance hall, with stage), a yurt, a couple of staff cabins, and the many tents on platforms that handle overflow. All buildings are linked by webs of asphalt path and long wooden ramps leading back to the hub. Even brief visitors to the Vineyard are likely to be aware of Camp Jabberwocky. "Napoleon," the big red school bus that is the camp's flagship, trundles everywhere over the island, carrying its raucous consignment to a multitude of daily destinations. Impossible to miss, with a wonderfully monstrous winged dragon, Jabberwocky, painted on the hood, and various characters from Alice in Wonderland cavorting along its sides, Napoleon also doubles as a rolling musical instrument and an inside-out drum. The mere touch of camp director John Lamb's foot to the accelerator precipitates a rousing and specially-tailored repertoire of old sixties songs ("Yellow Submarine" frequently segues into "Rudolph the Red-Nosed Reindeer," a perfect August-on-the-Vineyard tune). The only alterations to the bus are its crimson coat and Wonderland decor, the removal of a couple of rows of seats in the back, and the installation of floor clamps for securing wheelchairs. "People keep offering to donate ramps," says the ever-practical John Lamb, "but they just don't work out. They break, and it's faster to load by hand, and you can fit more people in if the ramps aren't taking up room."

The loading and unloading of Napoleon is an apt metaphor for the camp itself. The bus embodies the notion that any destination is attainable. The traffic jam of wheelchairs waiting to be loaded, and the slow progress of people with braces or crutches, inching themselves up the steep stairs, reveals the will and enthusiasm of the campers to attempt anything and everything. The bustle and joshing and brawn and teamwork of the counselors as they puzzle the logistics of loading, and hoist occupied wheelchairs four feet up into the back of the bus, are the WD-40 of the camp. They are the facilitators who make all activity possible.

With the exception of the cook—and the nurse during the August session—who are paid a small stipend, all Jabberwocky staff are volunteers. This includes the camp directors, the physicians (who do morning rounds and are on call while they are vacationing on the island), the instructors who lead activities, and of course, the incredible corps of counselors. There is a nearly one-to-one ratio of counselors to campers. The counselors learn from each other and brainstorm together when issues arise. During my first night at Jabberwocky, the counselors called a midnight meeting, requesting that the director not attend, to tackle two problems: the feeling that some newer counselors weren't carrying their weight, and concern over a lack of sensitivity to some campers. The latter was solved by pledging not to always load the heaviest camper on the bus last, realizing that it hurt her feelings. The former problem was left open to ongoing discussion of more specific ways to help orient new counselors and clarify expectations. "We're just trying to get to the next level," says one veteran. "We don't want to just sit back and say 'this is great.' So we were asking 'what would it take to make this place even better?'"

Most of the counselors at the children's session are in their teens and early twenties. At an age when most of their peers are chafing at authority they're thrown into authority roles, bearing all the responsibility for major and minor decision and tasks. Most have no training or experience in working with the disabled, save for the few who have siblings or close friends with disabilities. But there is nothing so potent as on-the-job training, and Hellcat, in typical fashion, puts it this way: "I don't want counselors to have any training, because I want them to use initiative. If they can't use initiative, and if they don't have any initiative, they're no good, they're dead wood. If a counselor came to me and said 'What can I do?' I'd say 'Look, I don't care a damn what you do. You can stand them on their head! You can't make them any worse than they already are, so go and do something.... It's up to you.' This was the best thing I could have said, because it made them think for the first time in their lives."

Beyond teaching new recruits how to load and unload wheelchairs into the back of the bus without damaging their own backs, John Lamb gives counselors little direction during the brief orientation before camp starts. "I tell them that it's very hard work, that you never have, and never will, work as hard. That it is twenty-four hours a day with no time to go pee. If I started out by going into the nitty-gritty of personal care, they wouldn't stay!"

But stay they do, with few exceptions, and then return, summer after summer. It begs the question of why anyone, especially in late adolescence, would choose to come to one of the most beautiful spots on earth at its prime time, knowing that not only would they be unable to personally indulge in the bounties of a Vineyard summer, but that they would be worked to the bone for twenty-four hours a day with no pay and scant opportunity to tend to their own basic needs. (The camp record for counselors going without a shower is twenty-four days, and it is challenged annually.) They sign on for anywhere from one to four weeks of this because a friend or family member has enthused convincingly that it would be the greatest experience of their life—or they have seen the Jabberwocky contingent while they were on the Vineyard, and been captivated by the spirit. But not everyone can hack it. Some people leave—or are asked to leave—within the first week (this goes for counselors and campers alike), but those that survive the trial-by-fire are passionate about this community.

"There's just nowhere else I'd rather be," says counselor Jen Oelberger, returning for her third year. "It's just a magical, magical place. I wish I could be here every day of the year, but I can't, because you don't get paid. But it's better that way because it means that everyone is here because they really want to be. We live in such a fairy tale here, and we're reminded every time we go into town of how these kids' lives must be the rest of the year. At Jabberwocky it's not like you meet disabled people—you meet the people, you deal with the disability, and understand the people."

"You know how we all clap and cheer at every little thing here at Jabberwocky?" asks Laurie Murray, who's been a counselor for ten years. "Like 'Yeah, you blew your nose!' (clap, clap, clap), and stuff like that? When I first got here, and the red bus pulled up, and I saw all these wheelchairs, and saw all the drooling and cheering, I thought 'Oh my god, what have I gotten into?' But you're able to look through all the hardware after a couple of days, and just look at the person, and try to get to know them without all the external stuff interfering. It's an amazing moment of revelation. It only happens that first summer, but it's reinforced every year."

There is a liberation in not having time to be self-absorbed, in not being consumed with personal worries about school, or job, or being too fat or too thin, or boy- and girl-friends. And there is a solid inner reward. The poise and grace that is common ground to all these young adults springs from an inner sense of confidence and value. It is a parents' dream to have their teenagers grow into such human beings, and Camp Jabberwocky offers a crash course in personal growth. In fact, many of the counselors arrange, like Caitlin Lamb, to visit with campers during the winter, taking them out to the movies or to dinner, or just staying in touch, the way friends do.

Two decades older than most of the other counselors, Jack Knower has returned to Jabberwocky for seventeen years. During the school year, Jack works with mentally retarded junior-high kids in Rochester, New York. He considers Jabberwocky a sabbatical, and he saves enough out of his paycheck throughout the year to pay himself for the month he volunteers at camp. This summer he brought his six-year-old son, John, with him for the first time. I tell him that I can't quite believe anyone can do this kind of demanding social work year-round, and not burn out. He laughs. "If I had a boring job I'd get burn-out! This is fun! We're in it for the fun."

Not *just* for the fun, it turns out, because it's a place to learn and experiment, and stretch his own professional expertise. "There's always someone dropping in at camp with different ideas, methods, and tools," he says. "You can pick their brains about doing special-ed differently It's a safe environment to try things out that you might not get the chance to do at school because your boss might be a 'behavior mod' [modification] guy.... Our job is to make this the best month of their year for the kids, and when it's over, there's this incredible bond, this magical wonderland."

At Jabberwocky, the deepest kinds of friendships form. (Kathleen Lamb met her future husband when she was a counselor at the camp.) Campers form invaluable friendships very different from those they have at home. During the rest of the year, many campers, mainstreamed in schools, cannot escape the fact that they are always the minority, always different. To be in a place where disabilities are both the status quo and the rule can be mind-blowing. Some campers resist at first, feeling that camp is like confronting a mirror they don't want to see. But for most, through the looking glass they go, only to discover that the central reason for their presence at Jabberwocky—their disability—is not the defining aspect of their lives while they are here.

"I hated my first time at camp," says Lorry LaDouceur, who has spina bifida, and is in a wheelchair. "I was nine years old, and I thought my parents had abandoned me." This year, Lorry is a counselor for the first time—the only one with a disability. "The thing I was most afraid of when I was little was that people would see my disability and not see *me*. I'd been the only disabled person in my town, and I never thought I was different. So I got to camp and didn't want to be like 'these people.' But I got to know so many great people—some of my best friends I met here—that I just didn't care how I was perceived. I wanted to give something back to this place, and I wanted to prove to myself that I could do it. If I could do this job, I knew I could do anything." She can't help lift chairs into the van, but she challenges any other counselor to better her at cleaning cabins, helping campers with personal care, or mentoring.

Last summer, first-time camper Kara Johansen heard ad nauseum about

Becca Larko, a camper who, like her, has cerebral palsy, and is in a wheelchair. This summer the two girls finally met, and instantly became best friends. Though neither girl can talk, they speak worlds with their eyes. A quick flash up means yes, a dart to the side means no. With the occasional help of Becca's counselor, Laurie Murray, and Kara's aide, Toby Packard, who accompanied her to camp, conversation between the two has been nonstop. At fifteen, Kara is two years older, and when they met, she was anxious to teach Becca how to use the alphabet board that she brought with her as a communication tool. It's a clear plastic board with large letters printed on it, through which she spells words for her aide with her eyes. Becca learned quickly and now the two are talking with everyone else, as well. Even when Laurie and Toby are not at hand, the two girls giggle and chatter on with flashing eyes. They are completely tuned in to each other, and delight (there's no other word for it) in each other's presence. Each always seems to know where the other is in the room, and constantly checks in to see how the other is doing. At rest time, they ask to be put next to each other on the bed, and their flashing eyes never close, though the rest of the cabin snoozes. Girl talk.

For many kids here, the camp session is the carrot on a year-long stick. "Kids come from homes or institutions who tell them to be 'normal,'" says counselor Jack Knower. "After a week here, everybody loses self-consciousness." Camper Bethany Chandler, a six-time returnee, was mainstreamed in high school, and felt discriminated against. "Here at Jabberwocky [my cerebral palsy] feels usual," she says. I feel more a part of the community." This summer, her younger brother Ben joined the camp as a first-year counselor.

Kirk Wittman lives at home and works at a sheltered workshop. He earns money for camp tuition by recycling cans, and he always saves pocket money to bring with him so he can take his friends out to dinner and bowling. For those kids who are mainstreamed in school, some of their best friends are the ones they make at camp because they share the same experiences. At Jabberwocky, there's no getting left behind at recess.

Jeremy Long spends a lot of time in front of the television at home. He has multiple complications from cerebral palsy. The first day or two at camp, he is quiet, sitting in his wheelchair watching the spin and buzz of camp life around him. But by day three he has become Mr. Motor Mouth, teasing counselors relentlessly, cracking lame jokes, raising his hand for any activity proposed. He's hanging out on the porch one night after attending a production of *A Comedy of Errors* with the rest of the camp. "How was the play?" I ask.

He grimaces, so I'm not sure if he means thumbs up or thumbs down, but then he arches back in his wheelchair, throws his arms up in a V, and roars. As he slides back down into his chair he grins slyly and says, "Awesome! It was awesome!"

"Awful?" needles Rael. "That's too bad."

"No! Awesome!" Jeremy bellows. Rael laughs, and Michael Harrison hears him and yells out "Da" and "Da" again between giggles. Rael tells me that the first time Michael saw Rael he grinned, brushed his hand over the top of his head and said "Da." Rael, like Michael's father, is bald, and thus earned this parental nickname. Jabberwocky is family.

With a mixture of dread and delight, the campers' usual first question upon arrival is "What's the play this year?" The play is always a musical extravaganza, a Broadway hit tailored to Jabberwocky standards by John Lamb in his role as script-master general. This year, the camp will stage *Annie*, and following breakfast on that rainy morning, John assembles the campers in the studio to watch the movie version.

Afterward, John steps to the podium, and the business of casting begins. There's no audition here, but nerves could not be tighter. It's one of the few hard and fast camp rules that everyone must participate in the play. There are only two weeks until the performance, which will be attended by family members, former counselors (who make a point of returning for the event), and various members of the island community. It's a big deal. For the next two days, John will retreat to work on the script, various crews of counselors and campers will be assigned to props and scenery, songs will be rehearsed, and the script, when it is finally written, will be learned. It is natural here, at Jabberwocky, that the script be written after the casting; John has to write according to the speech and movement capabilities of each performer.

The lead is quickly assigned to Rebecca McCrow, a die-hard Tom Petty fan, who had played the lead in two previous camp productions. She is as cool as any seasoned pro, commenting that she's already played this part in a performance at the Perkins School for the Blind in Watertown, Massachusetts, and knows it cold. She whispers knowingly to me that she thinks the camp version is going to be a lot more fun. The casting proceeds. The camper who wants to play Sandy has to demonstrate that he can bark, and he works hard to show his stuff. When another camper calls out that he wants to be an orphan, John quips, "Does your mother know about this?" Another volunteers to be the orphan Molly. John balks. Molly has more lines than this camper would be able to remember. "How about you be Tracy?" he asks.

"No, no! I have to be Molly, I just *have* to be!" is the teary response. John is unmoved and insistent, and just when it threatens to become a major dramatic moment, a voice pipes up from the back row, "Why don't we just switch the names? Nobody in the audience will know or care."

That problem resolved, John realizes that he has yet to cast the role of President Roosevelt. "Who wants to be the President?" he asks, looking pointedly at anyone in a wheelchair. Phillip Kellem leaps to his feet from the front row, where a group of Down syndrome kids are sprawled on the floor, and yells "Me!" John hesitates, asks if anyone else wants to be FDR. Phillip jumps up on stage, gets on his knees, and begs relentlessly for the part. "OK," says John, "I get it. Everybody is in wheelchairs *except* the President!"

Few activities engage the campers as pottery does, with the tactile quality and responsive nature of clay. Artist Rael Gleitzman has been volunteering as pottery instructor since 1986, when he visited his daughter—then a counselor—and was asked to give a pottery demonstration. He was hooked. "It just felt so right," he says.

One night, long after the campers are in bed, and as counselors congregate in the dining cabin, the lights are on in the pottery studio. I wander over to find Rael working like a madman, glazing a series of bowls that Kirk, a prolific potter, wants to enter the next day in the island's agricultural fair. (Jabberwocky pottery won first prize.) Rael is enthusiastic about the work, and it's easy to see why. The clay bowls lined up before him are freeform, organic, and textured with stamped and overlaid clay. When Rael applies the colored glazes, they seem to throb. "Kirk is really excited by the process of making pottery, but he's severely limited by what he is able to do. So I work with him, and his excitement carries over into what I do in my own work.... I have to find untraditional ways to work with people, because they don't have traditional abilities."

The next morning, I see this in action. Of the activities offered today— including candle-making, music, and drama—pottery was in such demand that two shifts were hastily organized. The table in the studio is crowded, and the clank of wheelchairs jostling for position sounds like jockeys at the starting gate. Rebecca McCrow exclaims excitedly as she presses the clay into a mold to make a bowl. Danielle Austin, a seasoned camper in her twenties with multiple disabilities—of which Down syndrome is the least—gets right to work with no comment. In the past day or two, she has seemed to be either fussy or staring vacantly at her hands. It is a transformation to see her so utterly absorbed in creating a Medusa-like sculpture from rolled pieces of clay. I can't help but wonder if what she envisions in her mind is anything like what she is building so deliberately. No matter. She is clearly pleased with her work, and it rivals the force of any abstract work I've seen.

At the far end of the table, Rael is working closely with Kara, who, because of her cerebral palsy, usually has no control of her limbs. When she's enthusiastic about something (which is most of the time), her arm will suddenly shoot out, and anything in its path is catapulted across the room. Yet when Rael works with her, helping her to roll coils of clay with her feet, she melts back into her chair, and one can feel the unwinding as the coils of energy in her body relax. When she smoothes the clay into a round medallion (a present for her aide back home), pressing it flat on something that looks like a pizza stone, she is so focused that—remarkably—her limbs obey her will.

After lunch, which is pure, noisy mayhem, the announcements begin. A staff member runs through the options for afternoon activities, which almost always entail an expedition. A trip to the beach for sunbathing and swimming, to a nearby stable for horseback riding, an invitation to go sailing, or a trip into town to get ice cream. A number of campers work each day at Chilmark Chocolates (always a favorite), and the day's assignments there are made. Following the official announcements, the floor is open to comments from counselors and campers alike.

Liam, a counselor and the pianist for the play, goes first. "The piano was really treated roughly this morning. There was drool and stuff all over it. It was really gross, so please treat it well, or better yet, keep away from it." Anna, a camper, jumps up, tears filling her eyes. "You are like friends to me—you are great people. We are lucky to have this camp. Please don't ever cancel." Her friend Gracie is called upon to sing a song. After two lines, Phillip jumps up. "All this family here is so special. Thank you!" Anna gets up again. "I want to tell you the reason I've been sad. My uncle is dying; he's a great guy and we're just waiting for him to die." She runs from the cabin in tears, followed by a counselor. There is a moment's stunned silence, and Phillip, irrepressible, jumps up again. "I want to say the cabins must be kept nice and clean. President Roosevelt has spoken."

He raises both arms up and bows. Hoots and hollers and cheers fill the dining hall, and then the clatter of crutches and wheelchairs as campers head out, island-bound.

At the end of a busy afternoon, campers and counselors straggle back, hungry and tired, and gather on the porch, catching up on each other's day and waiting impatiently for the dinner bell. After the meal, Napoleon and the two grey vans load up and head for a strip of beach along Vineyard Haven harbor. The small crowd that has assembled around a group of drummers on the beach is suddenly more than doubled by the arrival of the Jabberwocky contingent. The drummers are in their own head-space, and don't miss a beat as this noisy, clumsy group swells their ranks. A whispering passes through the crowd, "It's the kids from Jabberwocky." There are smiles but, perhaps because of embarassment at the mayhem of this arrival, nobody looks directly. Wheelchairs are pulled bumping over the sand, counselors grunt and strain. Bodies are lifted, carried, and deposited on blankets quickly spread to receive them. I can't repress a quick mental flash of film clips of the allied forces crawling up Omaha Beach. Unintelligeable greetings are barked and howled at Rick, one of the drummers. He grins and nods in reply. The counselors continue their relay of bodies from bus to beach until finally the toting completed, they collapse in the sand to catch their breaths.

But their rest is short-lived. Bodies on blankets and in wheelchairs begin moving to the beat, and soon they're being lifted in the arms of counselors, and supported in bearhugs as the dancing starts. A conga line takes shape, snaking through the blankets and coolers and the few who remain seated. The crowd on the beach becomes a single organism, moving to the primal rhythm of the drums. This is a laying-on of hands, a goofy relaxed intimacy clearly illustrating how large a part touch plays in the dialogue at the camp. By necessity there is license to be physical, and it is a healing and cathartic thing. Hugs happen all the time. The drumming and dancing go on as the sun slowly sets and the waves lick the shore. The mosquitoes come out and the gulls wing home, and finally, so do we. Back at camp, the bus is unloaded in the dark, and campers straggle along the web of ramps to their cabins.

The parents of any toddler would be sympathetic with the time required to get campers to bed, but the labor-intensity of this endeavor would be beyond even their ken. As if the past twelve hours of hoisting and toting were a mere warm-up, the counselors now go into high gear. Getting a single camper undressed and bathed, into pajamas, teeth brushed, to the bathroom, and finally into bed can take at least an hour. Most of us would have to crash immediately thereafter, but for the counselors, this is the only pocket of time in a twenty-four hour cycle that they have for themselves or friends, and they don't waste it on sleep.

Camp Jabberwocky is no Shangri-La, no island of perfection and ever-flowing peace and harmony; it is simply a group of people assembled together with a common goal. But as with any group, there are all the dramas of human nature—bad moods, jealousies, personal intrigues. It is precisely because it makes room for the flaws and rough edges of our natures, and laces them with love and laughter, that this is so potent a place.

"We celebrate the imperfect," says Gillian Butchman. "For most of us, people with disabilities are like living art. By that I mean you are forced constantly to do things in a new way, to see things in a new way. I think that's what all good art is; something that helps us see things in a slightly different way than we have before. That's why some of us are addicted to these summers. It draws us out of ourselves, it improves and expands us, and encourages us to become really creative in our activities and in our thinking." Jabberwocky is a place of possibilities.

Hellcat initiated horseback riding for her campers during the first year of the camp. At a time when the handicapped in this country were kept out of sight, she dared to take them horseback riding. "They had such lousy adductors that I thought it would be good for them. And it works!" Using muscles they don't normally use, it is wondrous to watch those who cannot sit up straight in their wheelchairs—even when strapped in—sit astride a horse. It is especially wondrous to watch children, who cannot make their own legs work, smoothly covering distance in this way, daringly taking the small jumps in the center of the riding ring.

Tall and elegant, Allison Ashmore, who is in her early twenties, has the cool regard and cheekbones of a 1930s Hollywood star. She never stops talking, and she peers directly into your eyes, closely monitoring your reaction as she recounts in minute detail the plots, characters, costumes, and casting of fairy tales she has dramatized. She holds tightly to your hand while describing stage direction and actors' gestures. "In my play *Rumplestiltskin*," she says, "I play the princess, and I wear a long gold dress made of golden thread, and my baby wears a turquoise party dress with layered ruffled skirts." Or, "I've decided to change the ending to my play *Dracula*, so that when I get bitten on the neck, I get better, instead of turning into a vampire. It's much happier that way, don't you think?" There is no escape, no casual walking away, and anyone who enters her sphere is a potential captive audience. It is something to watch when strangers, drawn by her articulate charm and grace, begin to realize that they have been led into the outer reaches of a far galaxy of the human mind.

It all changes on the day that Allison goes riding. Her poise falls away and her dreaming and staging are suddenly gone. The horse is large and alive. Reluctant and fearful, she whimpers repeatedly that she doesn't want to get on. The counselors are tough, and they ignore her pleas. As she sits in the saddle waiting for the stirrups to be adjusted she wails, "I'm scared. I want my mommy." But the horse is led off with Allison aboard, a protective cordon of counselors surrounding her. Within minutes, at the far end of the ring, I hear a more familiar ring to Allison's voice as she calls out to anyone who will listen, "Look at me! Don't you think I'll be ready for the U.S. Equestrian Team soon?" She is sitting tall in the saddle, both arms outstretched, looking for all the world like one of her own heroines.

Sarah Putnam is a freelance photojournalist whose work has been featured in Time, Ms., Yankee, Parenting, Forbes, Fortune, and The New York Times Magazine. *She is a children's book reviewer for* The Boston Herald.

My Mother Is a Rodeo Queen
by Tonja Evetts Weimer

My mother is a rodeo queen. If you ever met her, you'd know it right away. Her Stetson hat, western shirt, skin-tight pants, and elaborately stitched cowboy boots are her everyday wear. The back of her belt has sterling silver letters that spell out her name, ALMA. But it is the enormous diamond-and-ruby studded belt buckle that she won in the rodeo that is the true sign of her authenticity. When she rides out into the rodeo arena, the roar of the crowd sounds like someone hit a home-run in the bottom of the ninth at the world series. My mother is seventy-nine years old.

My mother's journey is a remarkable one. I remember a time when I was in high school and reading Steinbeck's *Grapes of Wrath*. My mother asked me about it and when I told her, she said plainly "I don't need to read that. I lived it." My father always thought my mother looked like the movie star Loretta Young. (Of course, privately, he thought he was Clark Gable.) They came from Oklahoma to California in the 1930s to escape the poverty of the Dust Bowl. She was seventeen, he was nineteen, and neither had graduated from high school. To survive, they went to work in the cotton fields.

My mother was neither large nor particularly strong, but my father and family friends say she could pick 500 pounds of cotton a day in the hot sun of the San Joaquin Valley, out-picking all the women and half the men. She never quit until the last man in the field hauled his sack to be weighed.

I knew when I was young that my mother was not like anyone else's. When she came to my elementary school, all my friends would say "Ooh, Tonja! Your mother's so pretty!" She would sit shyly and quietly with the other mothers, shrinking into the background, saying little. But I knew another side to my mother. When she fixed on something she wanted, she could become terrifyingly fierce. You somehow felt if you got in her path, she'd run over you in her pickup truck. She played a little basketball in high school, but she was not athletic and did not participate in any other sports. Aside from dancing to soulful country music with my father, I never saw her doing anything requiring physical skill.

In our family you had a horse before you could walk. My father had a passion for roping in the rodeo; my sister was California Barrel Racing Champion; and my brother became a World Champion Team Roper. But whenever any of us had our horses out, my mother stayed way, way back and just took pictures. From her early childhood, she was terrified of horses. When she went with us to a rodeo, she sat in the car and sewed. She was almost fifty when she suppressed her fears and climbed on a horse for the first time. She said she was just tired of being left out.

In professional rodeo, there is one event, the barrel race, specifically for women. It is a timed race around three barrels set in a cloverleaf pattern. Horses are trained for years to charge the barrels, turn on a dime, and cut those corners as close as possible. Rider and horse lean sideways into the barrels at impossible angles as they turn. They're trying to shave tenths of seconds without knocking one over and getting a five-second penalty. The riders are usually young, athletic, highly skilled women. It's fast and it's dangerous.

My mother's first rodeo was in Chowchilla, California in 1965; she was forty-nine. She didn't win, but she didn't embarrass herself either. She said all she hoped for in that first race was to not fall off. She didn't. She began to enter rodeos and local "jackpots" every weekend. Slowly, she began to win a little.

In 1974, she won the barrel-racing championship at the California State Rodeo in Salinas. The rodeo newspaper carried the headlines in the boldest print you've ever seen: "ALMA WINS SALINAS!" The world that knew my mother was overjoyed for her. In 1983, she entered the Chowchilla Rodeo again, her original starting point, and won first place at the age of sixty-seven.

In 1987, my husband, Vik, and I got to see my mother ride in the Santa Barbara Rodeo. Since we lived in Pennsylvania, it had been years since I had been to a rodeo. Seated in the grandstand, I remembered how nervous I used to get when my mother first started to ride. Back then, she looked so precarious on her horse; I was always worried that she might get hurt. Now I watched as Mother entered the arena on her little black mare, one rider away from starting. She pulled her hat down tight in anticipation of her run. Her horse danced sideways, trembled and snorted, and strained to break loose to run. It was nothing compared to what I was doing; I could hardly stay in my seat. I thought of my mother's arthritic back and crippled hands, her bruises and the permanent dents in her shin bones from hitting the barrels, and her concussions and broken bones from her horse falling in slippery arenas. For all of her years of riding, she still looked too precariously perched on that horse.

Mother edged her horse to the starting line and the announcer proudly bellowed, "Here she is folks! Alma Evetts! She might not look it, but she's old enough to be drawing Social Security! Everybody's favorite champion— the barrel racing grandma!"

The flag dropped, Mother started her run, and my heart was in my throat. Tears filled my eyes as my husband and I and the crowd of thousands sprang to our feet. Around the first barrel, just a little wide, and the crowd cheered, "Come on Alma!" Around the second barrel, a little bit closer, and they all screamed, "Come on Alma!" Around the last barrel and into the final stretch, everyone yelled, "Alma! Alma! Alma!" I wanted to run up and down the aisles and yell, "That's my mother!"

I returned to Pittsburgh and plunged back into my work and my life. I reflected on the enormous frustration I occasionally felt at not accomplishing the goals I had for myself and my business. I had just closed my schools of creative movement for children, and launched a small publishing company for my children's folk song albums. I had left the comfort of the known and entered the murky waters of the unknown, and at times, I felt I was drowning. But then I thought of my mother's wins, and how she had worked twenty and thirty years for some of them. In my mind, the rhythm of her horse's hooves was like a cadence that kept time to the words: "You never give up, you never give up, you never give up!"

My mother is nearing her eightieth birthday. My dad bought her a new saddle for Christmas last year. She is, of course, still riding in the rodeo.

Tonja Evetts Weimer is an educator, entertainer, and motivational speaker who writes books for parents and teachers, and performs song and dance concerts and albums for children and adults.

Indian Giver
by Kimberly Ridley

When she was thirty years old, Rebecca Adamson, a part-Cherokee single mother, cashed an unemployment check and bought a plane ticket from South Carolina to New York City. Armed with a long list of addresses but little else, Adamson canvassed the big foundations to see if they might be interested in funding her new project to help Native Americans—the poorest ethnic group in the country—become more self-sufficient. She rarely made it past the reception desk. But that didn't stop her "When people were saying no, I was thinking I needed to explain it better," Adamson says.

That was 1980 and Adamson—already a veteran organizer in a movement that won Native Americans the legal right to run their own schools and other programs—was accustomed to plowing ahead, despite rejections. And she was convinced that her approach of encouraging self-sufficiency was the right one. So, she kept knocking on doors in New York. Finally, someone listened. A $25,000 grant from the Ford Foundation put Adamson in business.

She moved to Fredericksburg, Virginia, and used the grant to launch what has since become the First Nations Development Institute—even as she battled uterine cancer. Adamson beat the disease and drew up a ten-year plan for an organization that would support economic development on Indian reservations, not by imposing solutions from the outside, but by seeking the answers from within Native American communities. And she committed herself to making it work without government money.

To test her ideas, Adamson headed straight for the poorest place in the United States: the Oglala Sioux's Pine Ridge Reservation in South Dakota, where the average person makes about $3,500 a year. Her pilot project, a traveling exhibit of artwork by reservation children, raised about $20,000 to enable the reservation's Little Wound School to purchase such necessities as warm winter coats for its students. But Adamson wasn't satisfied with this one-shot-deal, because without the funding to train a successor, the project ended when she left the reservation.

She returned a few years later to discover the roots of poverty on Pine Ridge and to find a way to grow the economy from that point. Collaborative studies by First Nations and local groups soon revealed that eighty-five percent of the reservation's gross income went directly to the towns bordering it because there were so few places to spend money locally. Subsequent research revealed that fewer than fifty formal businesses on Pine Ridge were run by Native Americans.

Yet Adamson sensed a source of hidden opportunity in this dun-colored landscape of rolling prairies and arid badlands. With First Nations funding, graduate student Richard Sherman found it. His study uncovered a vibrant economy built on home-based businesses. People living on Pine Ridge were engaged in more than 100 moneymaking activities—they welded scrap metal into iron crosses to sell to the cemetery; mended fences, broke horses, babysat, made beadwork. And with a little help, Adamson argued, they could become more self-sufficient. One woman wanted to cater lunches at the Bureau of Indian Affairs (BIA) but needed a little cash to buy sandwich material. One man had taken a locksmith class, but couldn't afford the tools and materials he needed to bid on a job at the BIA. "I said, we want to make loans to these kinds of people," Adamson recalls.

The result was the Lakota Fund, one of the first microenterprise loan funds in the United States—and First Nations' first big success. Developed in partnership with Adamson's organization, the Lakota Fund has now distributed more than 300 loans to nurture small businesses on Pine Ridge, and kindled a spirit of new self-sufficiency among the Oglala and Lakota Sioux. In a move that was at once anti-corporate and classic "Becky," Adamson decided in 1992 that the fund should become independent from First Nations.

Far beyond the borders of Pine Ridge, Rebecca Adamson's kitchen table project has become the only Native-American-controlled organization in this country that distributes grants and loans to support culturally-appropriate economic development projects on Indian reservations. First Nations has awarded nearly $3.1 million in grants to tribes, which, combined with a

$1 million revolving loan fund, expertise in technical assistance, and policy work, add up to a powerful force that is helping tribes find their own solutions to poverty. And that, Adamson says, is the whole point of effective economic development. "We're preparing indigenous people for development on their own terms so they can control their economic futures."

But her work is not just about creating businesses. Adamson argues that, given the opportunity indigenous communities have much to teach the rest of the world about building truly sustainable economies through a shared value she calls "enoughness." Many tribes have traditionally emphasized sharing, rather than accumulating, excess wealth through basic laws and certain ceremonies including the potlatch, in which the wealthiest members gave away food, clothing, and possessions to the poorest ones. Adamson argues that such economies were not only vital, but that they could also serve as a conceptual model for everything from restructuring the economy to rebuilding communities. "We can never create an economy that's sustainable if we focus only on accumulation and growth, and don't focus on how to share the wealth," she says. "What this means is that very rich people are no better for the economy than very poor people. They have more than they can use and it doesn't circulate, it accumulates."

Adamson's ideas are attracting attention outside Indian Country. An economist and philosopher by training, she is a bridge-builder whose ideas have been sought by such diverse entitites as the International Labor Organization for International Indigenous Rights, the President's Council on Sustainable Development, and the Calvert Social Investment Fund. And as her ideas gain currency, she is beginning to draw recognition. A 1996 *Ms.* magazine Woman of the Year, Adamson has also won national awards for creative grant-making and for her contributions to the Native American community.

Her faith in the ability of indigenous peoples to determine their own destinies by drawing on their culture and values—combined with her organization's commitment to teaching them how to gain control of their assets—is proving to be an effective approach time and again, from the American Southwest to the Australian Outback. Those who know Adamson say her ability to see the big picture while working at the community level makes her a rare kind of leader. Says A. David Lester, a national authority on economic development on Indian reservations, "She has always taken the approach that a river is made up of a zillion raindrops."

Rebecca Adamson brings a unique set of strengths to the difficult business of economic development on Indian reservations. Born near Akron, Ohio, in 1949 to a part-Cherokee mother and a Swedish father, she has always traveled in two worlds. And she has searched to find her place in both.

A quiet, dark-haired girl who spoke little in school, Adamson was on the road by the time she was a teenager. She developed an early penchant for hitchhiking, a pursuit that drove her parents wild with worry and gave her a first inkling of the inequities between the suburban life of greater Akron and the impoverished world of her Cherokee relatives in rural North Carolina. On school vacations, Adamson would hitchhike more than 500 miles, down to her grandparents' place near Lumberton, North Carolina. She would spend hours in the woods with her Cherokee grandfather, from whom she learned an appreciation of nature and stillness that she says helps sustain her strength and spirit to this day. But in that small community, Adamson also witnessed her Cherokee cousins' poverty and lack of educational opportunities. When she returned to Akron, she felt more alienated than ever.

After studying philosophy at the University of Akron, and law and economics at Piedmont College in Georgia, Adamson dropped out of school and hitchhiked to the West Coast. She was twenty years old. She soon found her way to the reservations, where, in the late sixties and early seventies, a Native American movement was starting. For the first time, Adamson felt that she truly belonged. On the reservations, young, college-educated Native Americans from the cities were joining forces with those who had preserved the traditional ways. It was a time of consciousness-raising: rekindling traditional values—like respecting the land, valuing kinship, and nurturing community—and examining the painful aftermath of generations of economic dependency and destruction of Native people and culture.

Adamson's travels soon took her to the Nez Perce reservation in Idaho, where she was hired as a planner to help the tribe find money for economic-development projects. For the first time, she witnessed the disconnection between U.S. government funding and culturally appropriate economic development. The Nez Perce wanted to build a ranch to breed their famed and beautiful Appaloosa horses. Adamson and tribe members applied for a grant from the federal government, which was then the main source of funding for economic development on Indian reservations.

Federal officials rejected the application because, at the time, they were more interested in building industrial parks on reservations. With no funding, the Appaloosa plan was shelved. That made no sense to Adamson, who could see a powerful resource—a reservoir of cultural pride and knowledge that, with support, could help the Nez Perce begin to pull themselves out of poverty "I knew you should start with what you had and what you wanted to do," Adamson says.

As she became more aware of the problems on reservations, Adamson joined other Native Americans in a new movement to wrest control of Indian schools from the U.S. government and the Christian religious groups that had been running them for more than 100 years. Generations of Indian children had been taken from their families and sent to Indian boarding schools, where they were not allowed to speak their own language or follow their tribes' cultural and spiritual teachings. Isolated, alone, and miles from their families, some children were physically, emotionally, and sexually abused.

In 1972, at the age of twenty-three, Rebecca Adamson became director of the Coalition of Indian Controlled School Boards, a national group based in Colorado. She was jailed three times for peaceful protests as she helped more than thirty Native American communities around the country win control of their schools. In the midst of her organizing work, Adamson was married and, in 1975, gave birth to her daughter Neva (Cree for Snowbird). The following year, the grassroots movement for which she had worked so hard saw to the passage of the Indian Self-Determination Act.

But, in a painful epiphany, Adamson soon realized that although this law gave Native Americans the right to run their own schools, agencies, and programs, the effort would be hampered by the fact that someone else held the purse strings. She recalls sitting through negotiations with the Bureau of Indian Affairs in South Dakota after the legislation passed, watching ideas for new curricula getting knocked down because the bureau wouldn't fund them. The solution quickly became obvious: "I realized we needed to decrease our dependency on federal dollars," Adamson recalls.

For the next several years, she worked as a consultant to help tribes out West determine their communities' needs and develop appropriate programs. Adamson's marriage dissolved, and she traveled with her young daughter from project to project. Everything she saw confirmed what she had witnessed on the Nez Perce reservation, and again in South Dakota. She was determined to find ways to help Native Americans gain greater self-sufficiency from government dollars. Back then, she was pretty much free to experiment and, as she likes to put it, "tinker." As Adamson tried out fund-raising ideas at the United Tribes Educational Training Center in Bismark, North Dakota, she met A. David Lester, an Oklahoma Creek and then Commissioner for Native Americans in the Carter administration's Department of Health and Human Services.

"She was bright, creative, and idealistic," says Lester, who is now executive director of the Colorado-based Council of Energy Resource Tribes. "She was not well-experienced in those days, but she was willing to try anything." Adamson wanted to find a way for students to earn money for their school by making and marketing a mix for fry bread. "When most people ask 'How do you raise money?' they are looking for a donor who can write a six-figure check, or an event that will bring in a half-million dollars," Lester says, noting that such success is rare. "But she was thinking, even then, 'How can I sell a two-dollar package of fry-bread mix?'"

Though Lester doesn't recall whether the fry-bread venture ever got off the ground (and he chuckles as he talks about it), he says that over the years, Adamson's ideas have convinced him that starting small can work. "She has always looked at development in small steps...involving local initiatives and local leadership that, when taken as a whole, become something larger," Lester says. "That has broadened my understanding that economic development can start with the question, 'What can you do today?'"

Adamson's continuing work in Bismark and elsewhere gave shape to a larger vision: an organization that would grow the grassroots talents of Native Americans living on reservations by providing technical expertise and funding from outside sources. Along the way, she fell in love again, then suffered a tragedy: The man she loved was killed in a hunting accident. In 1979, Adamson moved back East to start the Native American Financial Self-Sufficiency Project, which would evolve into First Nations.

Creating an economy on an Indian reservation is no small undertaking. "Indian Country," as the nation's approximately 300 reservations are collectively known, is like an archipelago of poverty in a sea of plenty. Native Americans have the lowest per capita income, highest unemployment rate, worst health, and shortest life expectancy of any minority in the United States. Of the nearly two million Native Americans counted in the 1990 US, census, about half live on reservations. On most, it's hard for anyone to find a job because there are so few businesses. It's tough to start a business because there are almost no banks to lend money. And it's nearly impossible to get a loan elsewhere, because few Native Americans on reservations own much in the way of conventional collateral.

Yet tribes need to gain control of their economic destinies perhaps now more than ever: The Bureau of Indian Affairs, the federal agency created more than a century ago to manage tribal assets, is in shambles. The BIA is supposed to collect fees from the leasing of tribal land for such activities as mining, timbering, and grazing, and disburse it to Native American landowners. Today, $2.4 billion in tribal money remains unaccounted for, and the BIA is unable to track down and pay one in six Native American account holders. President Clinton recently appointed Paul Homan as Special Trustee for American Indians to sort out the BIA's accounting problems. Homan, an independent bank consultant, told a National Public Radio reporter, "This is the worst operational trust mess I've ever encountered."

Meanwhile, casinos aren't making life any better for most Native Americans. Of the 100 or so tribes that run gaming operations, only about ten percent are making money, according to Adamson. With casino dreams on shaky ground and the BIA in a state of chaos, a growing number of tribal leaders have contacted Adamson's organization for help.

The projects First Nations helps fund and advise share one thing in common: Each is built upon a tribe's unique culture and the resources at hand to work toward a more stable economic future. For example, the Hopi Foundation in northern Arizona employed the traditional teaching *itam naap yani*, which means "we're responsible for our own destiny," to create a Hopi-controlled solar energy project that supplies 300 pueblo homes with electricity. The InterTribal Bison Cooperative in South Dakota united tribes that are working to bring back a creature that supplied everything from food to clothing to spiritual sustenance to the tribes of the Great Plains. The Menominee Tribe in Wisconsin drew upon traditional values of community ownership and sacredness of the land to develop and expand its forestry operation, which won the President's Council on Sustainable Development's 1996 Honors Award.

Some of the projects Adamson's organization has supported have led to lasting changes in Indian Country. For example, the Saginaw Chippewa tribe in Michigan regained control of tribal trust funds and invested $10 million in a partnership that is building affordable homes for needy families. In addition to creating the Lakota Fund, community members on the Pine Ridge Reservation built their own health clinic. In New Mexico, Ramah Navajo weavers have revived their beautiful churro wool rugs and found markets for them. In Oregon, the Umatilla tribes have begun rebuilding their fractured land holdings in a process that is a model for efforts on other reservations.

As First Nations has grown, the child of the Ohio suburbs who reconnected with her Native American roots has gained respect in both worlds. Foundations trust her talent for finding Native American economic-development projects that are worthy of support. And a widening circle of people in Indian Country have come to value her commitment to honoring their perspective, helping them create their own solutions and find reliable financing. Observers say Adamson's from-the-ground-up approach has been a revelation to those working on economic development for Indian reservations.

Her organization has catalyzed a shift in thinking—away from searching for ways to bring big businesses to reservations, and toward appreciating the cumulative power of nurturing many small ones. "Rebecca Adamson brought another view to the table," says John Echohawk, a lawyer and director of the nonprofit Native American Rights Fund, which has raised millions to represent Native Americans in legal battles. "We were forgetting what was already there. In essence, what First Nations is doing is empowering people at the grassroots community level. That's going to help us economically, socially, and politically."

Although Rebecca Adamson's organization has helped inspire a new spirit of self-sufficiency among Native Americans, some of her ideas have cost her dearly. In addition to personal regrets (she names missing much of Neva's growing up as a big one), she has endured the occasional but inevitable failure of some projects First Nations has supported. She has alienated funders and lost grants for defending her belief that economic development projects must originate from within Native American communities. Adamson has also faced professional jealousy and growing scrutiny. When First Nations launched its Eagle Staff Fund, which raises big grants from outside foundations and redistributes the funds to Native American projects, some residents of Indian Country accused her of hoarding resources and being a gatekeeper to foundations.

But John Echohawk, who witnessed the accusations, is quick to come to Adamson's defense. At the time, he was a member of the Coalition for Indian Development, a group of Native American organizations that united to explore funding sources. "People felt [First Nations] was preempting local efforts to solicit funds," Echohawk says. "But if Rebecca didn't raise the money, they probably couldn't have done it themselves. It's a very difficult task, and Rebecca performed a great service by doing the heavy lifting."

Another admirer of Adamson's work is Wayne Silby, founder and president of of the Calvert Fund, the nation's largest socially-responsible mutual investment company. He met her at a Calvert Group Social Venture Network conference in the early 1990s, and soon invited her to join Calvert's seven-member board. When Adamson learned of the kinds of companies Calvert supported—solar energy firms and the like—she had one question for him: "What about the poor people?"

That simple challenge altered Silby's thinking, and soon, Adamson proposed investing one percent of the fund's portfolio in community groups that made loans to microentrepreneurs, who, like those on reservations, were cut off from conventional credit sources. The shareholders approved, and Calvert has been investing in poor communties ever since. "Our focus shifted, with her presence, to the underserved," Silby says. "She came from where people are...right on the ground."

The woman who appreciates the river for the raindrops has seen small successes grow into larger ones. The Lakota Fund that her organization helped launch has itself spawned other enterprises on Pine Ridge, including a tribal arts center (located in a new building with space for other businesses), a business library, and training center. In collaboration with other community groups, the Lakota Fund is planning a pilot project to build ten houses, creating jobs for Sioux carpenters, contractors, and others, and providing decent homes for prospective owners who complete a training program.

More than twenty years after Adamson tried to help the Nez Perce find funding for an Appaloosa breeding program, a grant application from the tribe landed on her desk at First Nations. Delighted, she committed her organization's support with a grant. Today, the Nez Perce are developing a new breed of Appaloosa horse, and reconnecting their young people with their heritage through the Nez Perce Young Horseman Program.

First Nations has nurtured many other small successes that, taken together, add up to a larger one—a new sense of hope and confidence among Native Americans that they can begin solving the problems that underlie the alcoholism and social ills plaguing their reservations. Adamson continues to be inspired. "I'm always moved by what we could be," she says. "I haven't spent time fighting against things, but working to build them."

Many of the development issues facing Native Americans are shared by indigenous people the world over. With First Nations firmly established in this country, Adamson has begun turning her attention to struggles elsewhere.

As the U.S. delegate to the Indigenous and Tribal People's Convention in the late 1980s, she made sure that positions on land ownership and other rights were included in the convention, a statement that nine nations are enforcing to help indigenous peoples resist pressure from multinational corporations and governments. Last year, she rallied support for the Khwe Bushpeople of Africa's Kalahari Desert, who face eviction from land their ancestors have lived on for thousands of years—now a Botswanan game reserve. Adamson is now working with the Khwe to secure title to the land their ancestors have lived on for an estimated 60,000 years.

In addition to helping tribal people secure land that is rightfully theirs, Adamson has also begun exploring ways of assuring their ownership of another powerful asset: intellectual property rights. Last year she boarded a bush plane and flew to remote settlements to meet with Australian Aborigines. She initially set out to discuss ways of raising revenues through cultural tourism, but after talking with the tribes, Adamson came up with another idea involving the upcoming Sydney Olympic Games. "When you think about Australia, you think Aboriginal art," Adamson says. "The whole look of the Olympics will be Aboriginal."

In collaboration with Australian natives, Adamson is in the process of negotiating payment for the use of Aboriginal art in the marketing and merchandising of the Olympics, a strategy that she says could generate upwards of $30 million. This sum, in turn, would finance the creation of a new independent First Nations Development Institute in Australia. If these efforts succeed, the new organization would be the first non-federal entity in Australia to fund Aboriginal projects, and it would represent the first step toward Australian natives' independence from federal dollars.

Whether she's working overseas or in her own back yard, Rebecca Adamson continues to challenge conventional thinking about economic development as a process devoid of culture, beliefs, and human values. And she argues that the Native notion of enoughness provides an important philosophical starting point for building economies that are truly sustainable.

Can human beings ever have enough? Adamson makes her point with an exercise she often uses to open her lectures and presentations. "I tell people, 'Take a deep breath, the deepest breath you can take...hold it as long as you can...let it out. You're taking only what you needed. You give back when you let out. You could not take in more than you could use.'"

Kimberly Ridley is Editor of Hope.

No Fear of the Dark

by David Eskes

....

It is almost over now. One more pitch to go before summiting. Hans has already scrambled over the top. So has Jeff. And now Sam. Three thousand feet below, the frigid Merced River snakes its way through rugged Yosemite Valley and its shaded campgrounds, meadows, and shouting children. Erik can't hear the children anymore. They are too far away, shut out by winds that buffet the impassive granite face of El Capitan. Up here, the nearest sounds are the eerie jetlike "whoosh" of birds as they career past. Winged reminders of whose place this really is.

Within an hour, twenty-seven-year-old Erik Weihenmayer will clamber out of the vertical wilderness he has clung to for four days. He will discard the canned soups, the apples, and blueberry bagels. He will shed the carabiners and camming devices, climbing ropes, and other gear hanging from his "rack," and start down the trail toward home. He will leave behind Cathedral Rock and Half Dome, the gear-filled cabin, and camaraderie. It will be back to Phoenix Country Day School, his fifth-grade students, and quiet moments with his girlfriend, Ellen Reeve. He will remember "El Cap" as long as he lives, but in a different way than his Team HighSights climbing partners. Erik doesn't see with his eyes, so there will be no snapshots, no visual flashbacks to the towering rock face looming over the valley. Only the remembered feel of granite in the August heat, the taut ropes, and cooling breezes; the voices floating up from far below, the secure tug of anchored cams, the reedy irony of Hans playing "Three Blind Mice" on his harmonica, and his own fleeting panic under the "Great Roof." But all that is in the future. Erik has only one thought now: "Ten minutes to go. Just don't let anything go wrong." It does not occur to him that he began climbing El Cap long before he ever set foot in Yosemite National Park.

Ed Weihenmayer suspected something was wrong when he held his infant son and the boy's eyes shook. "Is that normal for a baby?" he asked his wife, Ellen. "Don't worry about it," she replied. But Ellen wasn't as nonchalant as she seemed. She, too, was concerned and took the baby to the doctor. The visit ushered in a seemingly endless round of examinations. Doctors shook their heads in bewilderment. Speculation abounded. Eventually, Erik was diagnosed with retinoschisis, a rare disease in which the retina is gradually destroyed from the center outward, like an eclipse starting in the middle of the sun. What lay ahead, the Weihenmayers were told, was steadily dwindling peripheral vision ending in total blindness. Nothing could be done.

As Erik grew into boyhood, retinoschisis proved more of an annoyance than anything else. He didn't consider himself different. After all, he could see almost as well as his pals. And what he couldn't see, he worked around. Erik was too busy being a boy. Too busy carving out a niche in the sighted world, which was what his parents wanted. "We didn't want him in a blind school," Ed reflects. "We thought he could operate with assistance in a regular school." But when a public school in Florida balked at mainstreaming Erik, his mother found a private school. At the time, Erik, who wore ultra-thick glasses, had to weld his face to the page in order to read—a practice that often left smudges of ink on his nose. But he prevailed, mainstreaming through schools in both Florida and Connecticut with assistance from technology and teachers.

"His dad allowed him to do things most parents of blind kids wouldn't," recalls Chris Maggio, a boyhood friend from Connecticut. "Like riding a bike. I'd lead and he would follow behind. Same thing when we went sledding. He hated people treating him differently, and created systems so they wouldn't know he was losing his sight." Such ruses included smuggling a telescope into movies, and lingering after school so his classmates wouldn't see him board the station wagon for handicapped students. Sometimes, he skipped the station wagon altogether. Erik fit in so well, Chris says, that it was easy to forget he was, basically, blind. It still is. There were occasions, however, when the truth couldn't be finessed.

When he was eight, Erik developed a passion for basketball. Since he could not see objects directly in front of him, his teammates bounce-passed the ball to him and played zone defense, permitting Erik to cover a defined area rather than a single player. One time, his father recalls, Erik wrestled the ball away from an opponent and dribbled haltingly downcourt, where he unleashed a shot. "He didn't even aim in the right direction," Ed says. "It was sad. I don't think he scored a basket in all the games they played." Erik was crestfallen. But instead of holding a wake, father and son returned to the court and studied how best to use the painted circles for gauging where the backboard was. Find solutions. It was an approach Erik learned early.

Meanwhile, doctors warned the Weihenmayers that rough-housing, especially blows to the head, could hasten disintegration of the retinas and accelerate the onset of total blindness. Erik ignored the advice. Rough-house or not, pieces of retina kept breaking away forcing him to adjust to increasingly lower levels of vision. As basketball faded Erik found a new passion—wrestling. It was perfect. He was in physical contact with his opponent almost from start to finish. It was "do-able." Erik didn't waste time grieving over basketball. He cut his losses and went to the mats. "He never once complained to me about being blind," Chris Maggio says. "He was always happy, always funny." And always hopeful—a family trait.

By age twelve, Erik's vision had deteriorated to the point that he was having difficulty finding the homemade wooden ramps he and his friends jumped their dirt bikes over. Once, he missed the ramp entirely and rammed into a tree. He sustained only cuts and bruises. But, rather than forbid him to jump again, his father painted the ramps bright orange. His older brothers, Eddie and Mark, demonstrated their confidence by lying down between the two ramps. This time, Erik cleared them. But success was short-lived. After a while, he couldn't even see the orange. During the same period, Erik, who had begun seeing double, misjudged a dock at his grandmother's lakeside home in Florida and fell into a boat. Once again, he wasn't hurt, but it was becoming painfully clear that the inevitable was just around the corner.

Erik's initial response was to step up the denial. He refused to use a cane or to learn Braille. He refused to take the station wagon for handicapped students if he could get away with it. The way his father saw it, he was "less concerned about going blind than in losing his sighted friends." Once, leaving Chris Maggio's house—a route he had memorized—Erik tripped over a misplaced rock in the driveway and injured his arm. Rather than seek aid from the Maggios, he walked home. In the midst of all this denial, an epiphany occurred. The station-wagon driver, apparently irritated by Erik's constant carping about not being handicapped, slammed on the brakes one day and grabbed a basketball. "I think he was a coach of some kind," Ed says. "Anyway, he said, 'Here, catch this,' and threw the ball, which hit Erik squarely in the chest. Then he said, 'You're blind. Face it!' He told Erik he was going to throw the ball again and to put his hands out when he yelled 'Catch!' Erik put out his hands and caught the ball. 'You see,' the driver said. 'Let people help you. Don't keep fighting everybody.'"

Erik realized that the driver was right. If he didn't shift gears, his life would get worse and he wouldn't be able to do the things he really wanted. So he reluctantly accepted the cane, started to learn Braille, and turned his full attention to wrestling. Ironically, now that he was officially blind, doctors gave him the green light to let it all hang out. Erik posted a two-ten (win-loss) record in wrestling his freshman year. By his senior year, however, he was thirty-three-three. In between, he was elected captain of his high school team and represented Connecticut in the National Freestyle Wrestling Championships in Iowa. ABC's "20/20" even sent a crew to do a segment on him. Later, Erik would wrestle at Boston College and be inducted into the National Wrestling Hall of Fame, as the recipient of its first Medal of Courage.

In the summer of 1985, just as things were beginning to jell, Erik's mother was killed in a car accident. The shock and loss were sudden and shattering. Erik, who was away at wrestling camp, was sixteen years old. "Our parental roles were stereotypical," Ed reflects. "Ellen provided a lot of tenderness and love, while I was probably a little tougher. I had to go up and tell him—he thought I'd come early for his tournament. It was the worst moment of our lives." Chris Maggio remembers Erik as being very close to his mother. "That was a big part of his life. It is to this day. He was in shock the day after it happened. But he just sucked it up. Later on, we talked about how it would have been nice if his mother could have been there for his high school graduation. But he's reserved. He doesn't show much on the outside." With Ellen Weihenmayer's death, Erik's life would change dramatically.

Day One on El Cap

The plan is for Team HighSights to climb the 500 feet—about four pitches, or rope lengths—to Sickle Ledge, a huge coin-shaped indent, leave haul bags and water, then secure ropes and rappel down for one more night in the cabin. Jeff Evans, twenty-six, the paramedic from Colorado, goes first, followed by team leader and professional climber Hans Florine, thirty-two, teacher Sam

Brigham, thirty, and Erik himself. They are taking the "nose route," pioneered in 1958 by Warren Harding, a legendary climber of psychedelic proportions. Harding, a character out of a Ken Kesey novel, crafted a reputation for being unruly, anti-establishment, and absolutely fearless. His Motto—"Just do it!"—preceded Nike ads by thirty years. Harding, now a pudgy, silver-haired septuagenarian, had come by the cabin before the ascent to meet Erik, and to wish the team well. Today, looking straight up the "nose"—a million-ton snout, really—Harding's feat seems incredible. Its mass defies perspective, and its sheer face brings to mind the most commonly uttered observation by tourists as they squint upward: "Those guys are crazy."

Accompanying the climbers today is Jonathan Chester, an Australian photographer and leader of TerraQuest—an online adventure "magazine"—which is providing live coverage on the World Wide Web. Team HighSights members, all of whom except Erik are sighted, will maintain contact with the ground via cellular phones. The burly, bearded Chester nimbly works his way up the rope, pausing occasionally to train his big Nikon lens on team members. Also temporarily joining the group is Hans's climbing partner, Steve Schneider. Erik seems shaky at first, as he tries to gain hold on the granite slabs, but he soon gains confidence. "There's a foothold about two feet to your right," Steve says, standing on a narrow ledge. "That's right.... Excellent." Later, Erik takes a turn at belaying, in which he feeds rope cautiously to his teammates while they work their way upward. He is Grand Central Station, a study in total concentration, as he pulls rope here, releases it there. Hans shouts down, "Mine's the purple one," then corrects himself. "I mean, the thin one." It's easy to forget.

Before his mother's accident, Erik remembers that his father's daily routine was one of leaving home early and getting home late. Ed Weihenmayer had segued smoothly from Marine fighter pilot in Vietnam to head of human resources for the Hong Kong operations of a pharmaceutical conglomerate. Later, he moved to Wall Street investment firms in a similar capacity. Erik's mother had her own career importing antiques for her Westport, Connecticut, store. Now, though, it was just Erik and his dad. The older kids—Mark, Eddie, and Suzanne were gone. Ed made an effort to get home early whenever possible—even cook on occasion. He became, in Erik's words, "Mr. Mom." Suzanne, married and living in New York, sometimes invited Erik down on weekends for his favorite meal of meatballs and tomato gravy. "We became close," Erik says of his sister, who left home when he was seven years old.

"She called often, and still does."

Meanwhile, Erik became a latch-key kid, struggling not only with his mother's death but the lingering trauma of going blind. Moreover, he was paying the price for his earlier refusal to learn Braille. In his freshman year, he was forced to take Algebra by listening to a tape of the textbook. "I didn't do so well," he admits. "Sighted people learn to read over twelve years. I had to learn Braille in two." On the other hand, Erik had no problem typing Braille. Teachers spoke aloud what he could not see, and he banged it out on his laptop. A special resource teacher, who came by for one period a day, helped tie up any loose ends.

In 1987, Erik entered Boston College, where he majored in English and Communications. Later, he would earn a masters degree in middle school education from Leslie College, also in Boston. In his spare time, he honed his skills in rock climbing, his latest love. Chris Maggio, who matriculated at William and Mary College in Virginia during the same period, recalls going pub-crawling with Erik and Wizard, his first guide dog. "Some bars would refuse to let him in because of the dog," Chris says. "Erik would call the police, who would come down and force the matter. It was his legal right to go in the bar. He cares what other people think, but he's strong-willed. He's got a temper." When meeting women, Erik was prone to fudge a little, telling them he had lost his sight in a skydiving accident—admittedly, a more glamorous pitch than the clinical, "I had retinoschisis." He and Chris also devised coded handshakes to rate potential dates. Once, Erik entered a Best Body contest on a whim and won. The audience didn't realize he was blind until Chris led him offstage. On the other hand, life wasn't all fun and games. Once, for example, a young woman was forbidden by her parents to date Erik, presumably because he was blind. They refused even to meet him. "It got to him," Chris recalls. "They only knew what they'd seen of other blind people. There was nothing he could do."

Yet this seemed inconsequential compared to Erik's experience when he arrived on Nantucket Island one summer to assume a job at a hotel desk. The job had already been arranged. When the supervisor saw that he was blind, she quickly told him the job had been filled. "It was a bad scene," Erik recalls. "This lady was crying and upset, but she still wasn't going to hire me. So I thought, what's the easiest job to get? Dishwashing; there are tons of restaurants around here. I hit almost every one. People were astonished I would even try. It was as if a Martian had walked in and applied for a job." Excuses sprouted: The kitchen was too big; it was too small; the pots were too hot; he would bump into things. In desperation, Erik volunteered to rake yards, move furniture, whatever. But everything turned up snake eyes. He went home early that summer.

"The thing that blew me away" he says, "was—a dishwasher!—I knew I could do that. It made me mad that ignorant people could stop me from doing something I knew I could do. It scared me to think there were things in life I might not be allowed to do." The experience seared Erik, who had rolled over stereotyping until then. "I don't think people purposely discriminate against the blind," he says. "And I don't think it's the liability issue. It's a lack of understanding, an unwillingness to take risks. It takes a courageous person to say 'Hey, this guy's got something to offer. I'm going to give him a try.' "

The next fall, Erik hit the same wall, applying several times for a job as manager of a weight room. He got no response. Meanwhile, he noticed the place was closed frequently—twenty-seven times, by his count. So he wrote the owner a letter. "I told him I thought he blew me off because I was blind. I told him if I had been working there, the place would've been open all those times." Erik got the job.

Day Two on El Cap

Things start off badly this morning. Only Hans arrives on time. The other members are late and aggravate the situation by forgetting a haul bag at the cabin. Steve drives back for it at warp speed. Erik leads off today's climb, demonstrating by his stamina why Sam refers to him as a "mule." He gets to hoist the haul bags, a.k.a. "pigs," with Hans. Erik is philosophical: Haul bags, he says, are "part of life" on El Cap. Full of gear and food, they are essential to the climbers. But Sam is less charitable—he likens them to capital punishment. It is hot today and things go slowly, very slowly. "Logistical problems," surmises Jonathan Chester. A pair of British climbers above Team HighSights seems stuck, as if on flypaper. Higher still, another team inches its way up the nose. "Looks like nasal congestion," Steve cracks. Morning wears into afternoon. Nobody seems to move.

By 3 PM, Team HighSights is three hours behind schedule, and Hans takes the lead in an attempt to catch up. As he moves swiftly up the rock face, he is economy in action, eating up big chunks of rock, rope drooping, before securing himself. He uses his camming devices hand-over-hand, thrusting them into cracks like suction cups. It's easy to see why he holds the speed record for the nose: four hours, twenty-two minutes. Hans reaches a tiny ledge and, grunting and wrenching, raises the haul bags. Sam follows, then Erik and Jeff. Then Hans is off again. Things look up. They're "caterpillaring" now. Meanwhile, the British pair rappel down in defeat. They trudge out of the woods silently, the man staring straight ahead and the woman following with her head down.

Team HighSights is more than a thousand feet up, specks to the naked eye. Only powerful spotting scopes and heavy-duty telescopic cameras can pull them in. Tourists stop in the meadow to gawk. "A blind guy's up there? No kidding!" The afternoon wears on, softening into twilight, then night. The sky is littered with stars and dusted by the Milky Way. Ed, Ellen Reeve, and Sam's wife, Sherry, wave their flashlights in an impromptu light show for the team, which is still inching up El Cap somewhere in the darkness. Seigo, Erik's guide dog, snoozes in the grass. At 9:45 PM, the climbers call down by cellular phone. They've reached their goal of El Cap Towers, a narrow ledge where they will bivouac, or "bivy," sleeping fitfully in sleeping bags on foam pads while harnessed to the wall. Hans and Jeff keep working until midnight, securing ropes on Boot Flake, some one hundred feet above, in preparation for tomorrow's climb. Hans, the professional, does not want a repeat of today's ordeal. Finally, after eighteen hours, the team collapses into sleep. Erik doesn't know it, but tomorrow holds a reality check for him. It's called the Great Roof.

. . .

With Erik's mother gone, Ed Weihenmayer sought ways to keep the family members bonded. Why not take them on adventure treks? he thought. Suzanne was otherwise engaged, but Ed's sons were available, and all were athletic and competitive. Mark, the oldest, was a standout football player, while Eddie, the middle son, was a champion weightlifter. Erik, of course, was game for anything. Since then, the Weihenmayer clan has trekked over the Boltera Glacier in northern Pakistan, explored the Pamir Mountains in Tadjikistan, followed the Inca Trail to the fabled ruins of Macchu Picchu, and chopped through the dense New Guinea highlands with Yali tribesmen. This Teddy Roosevelt ideal of the strenuous life dovetailed nicely with Ed's conviction that sensible physical risk-taking would build Erik's confidence—that it would pay off in everyday challenges, whether those challenges involved walking into a restaurant or punching keys on a word processor. He came to believe that too many parents of blind children stunt their offsprings' emotional growth by being overprotective. "Life itself is a risk," he says.

Ed chose treks that were educational as well as physically challenging. They encountered famous places and endangered cultures. In northern Pakistan, the Weihenmayers visited Hunza, the mountain valley used as the model for James Hilton's fictional Shangri La. In the Karakoram Mountains, they learned of an army garrison stationed at 19,000 feet, where oxygen-deprived troops had to be relieved every two months. "They even had a fire-fight at 21,000 feet with the Chinese," Ed says, still in awe. In New Guinea, they found naked headhunters who stalked birds 125 feet up in trees and who started fires with sticks. They lived in the natives' huts and sampled native food, which Ed judiciously describes as "staples." Three members of the party contracted malaria. In Erik's case, the disease incubated for nearly two years, popping up on the eve of another trip to the former Soviet Union. His father retained a doctor to temporarily suppress the malady, then "permanently fix" it upon their return. Overall, the treks served to arouse in Erik a thirst for adventure. To become, as he says, an "experience hog."

Day Three on El Cap

Team HighSights "oversleeps" this morning and doesn't get off the dime until 8 A.M. This is the last full day of climbing before summiting. The objective is to bivy tonight on Camp VI, about 2,500 feet above the valley floor. It is another hot day, but morale is high. By mid-morning, the team is crossing the "Gray Bands," an area of black diorite riddled with little cracks and gouges that ensnare ropes and haul bags. At one point, Sam has to rappel down and free the ropes. Otherwise, progress is surprisingly good. Hans hopes to over-take the Oakridge team, two pitches (about 250 feet) above. The possibility arises that the Oakridge team will claim squatters' rights to Camp VI, leaving Team HighSights to bivy at Camp V or the Terraces, a series of skimpy ledges just above. But progress is slow and the team is unable to catch up.

By mid-afternoon, Hans is making the first pitch across the Great Roof, a huge concave umbrella. As he moves swiftly, hanging from the ceiling, Erik awaits his turn and chats via cell phone with his dad. "It's hot," he says. "We've pretty much had our faces to the wall." The haul bags gave him a "pretty bad cramp" in his left arm yesterday, but it's okay now. Water is getting short. There is mild concern about running out before Camp VI, where Hans and Steve stashed a gallon or so on a climb last week. Within thirty minutes, Hans has traversed the Great Roof and Erik cautiously begins to make his way across, removing anchors from the crack behind him as he goes. Midway, he stops inexplicably. He is absolutely motionless. Long minutes pass. Finally Hans rappels down. Erik has lost track of procedure. He is temporarily confused about the proper sequence. Hans talks to him, sets him straight, and he procedes. "I became discombobulated," Erik later admits. "It was a panicky moment." On El Cap, there is no margin for discombobulation.

. . .

After Erik received his masters degree, he applied for a position at Phoenix Country Day School, a private institution in Phoenix, Arizona. His grade point average of 4.0, and his background in sports gave him instant entree. Ellen Reeve, a sixth-grade teacher there, noticed him right away. "He was at ease with the kids," she recalls, "and they responded to him. They were curious about him—about his dog, Seigo, and his Braille computer. I told my boss, 'If there's anybody we need here, it's that guy.'"

Erik quickly settled in, teaching English and math, and coaching the wrestling club. As it turned out, he and Ellen had a lot in common. Both had degrees from Leslie College, both were athletic, and both were staunch environmentalists. They started scuba diving together, hiking, even skydiving, where Erik used a spotter on the ground to advise him by two-way radio. When scuba diving, Ellen tapped coded messages on his wrist to keep him updated on the air supply. Erik, in turn, introduced Ellen to rock climbing. Ellen calls their friendship "chemistry.... When we're not together," she says, "we miss each other."

It was Erik's friendship with Sam Brigham, a fellow Phoenix teacher and climber, that really ignited his climbing career. Sam looked past Erik's blindness and focused on his considerable skills. He knew Erik was capable of conquering more than just local rock faces. "When I tie my boots in the dark," he says, "my fingertips are collecting information and my mind is arranging it. That's what Erik does all the time—from tying shoes to setting anchors on a cliff." When Sam suggested tackling Alaska's Mt. McKinley—at 20,320 feet, the highest peak in North America—Erik was ready. After teaming up with Jeff Evans and Ryan Ludwig, associates of Sam's from Denver, they set about financing the venture by securing the sponsorship of the American Foundation for the Blind (AFB). Erik began a fundraising drive, as did his father, now a fulltime AFB volunteer. Manufacturers donated climbing gear. In a semantic nod to the AFB, the climbers dubbed themselves Team HighSights. They chose Long's Peak in Colorado and Washington's Mt. Rainier—both of which exceed 14,000 feet—for field training.

Erik would not be the first blind person to climb McKinley, as a fifty-year-old blind woman had accompanied a team of climbers just a year or two before. But Erik was determined to be an equal member of the team, and to pull his own weight. He would not be a burden. More than eighty climbers have died on McKinley, and many of them are still entombed within its deep crevasses. There is little room for charity on its icy flanks. The prep time spent on Long's Peak, where winds reached 100 miles per hour, and on the heavily glaciated Rainier, yielded valuable lessons, such as the need to keep roped together, especially in high winds, and to keep track of gear at all times; to work things out before a climb. On Rainier, for example, Erik found he couldn't set up tents with his gloves on and had to ask for help. It was humiliating. Once back in Phoenix, he practiced every day until he got it right. Meanwhile, he and Sam sprinted up and down the stairs of Phoenix's forty-story Bank One building wearing fifty-pound backpacks. They tested themselves in the nearby Superstition Mountains and on Flagstaff's Humphrey's Peak (12,633 feet).

On June 9, 1995, Team HighSights began its ascent of McKinley at the 7,200-foot level with two Park Service guides. They leapfrogged their way up, caching food one day and "traveling" the next. In effect, they climbed the mountain twice. Katie Couric of the "Today Show" conducted a remote broadcast from Anchorage that morning. Tom Brokaw's "American Closeup" and ESPN were also on top of the story. As they climbed, Erik's teammates gave him verbal glimpses of the terrain—"sound clues," as Sam calls them. Otherwise, he trudged ahead, poking for footprints with a ski pole and fingering the rope for directional shifts. His teammates found that in describing things to Erik, they sharpened their own perceptions and became more focused. Surprisingly few adjustments had to be made to accommodate him.

At 17,000 feet, the team ran into a fierce storm and spent three days sitting it out. Other climbers—American, Dutch, Swiss—were also stuck. Jack London-style tales crackled in the subzero temperatures—about hunting, fishing, and canoeing in the Brooks Range. Sometimes, Eric turned on a tape of Ellen telling stories and ribald jokes. Finally he turned it off. "It made me miss her too much," he recalls. The storm cleared on June 27, and Team HighSights made for the summit. They crossed "The Auto-hahn," a stony ridge where several German climbers have died. Then came Summit Ridge, which drops off for thousands of feet on both sides. It was the final challenge to the oxygen-hungry climbers. Weary and nauseated, they shuffled to the top. As a plane circled overhead carrying Erik's father, brothers, and Ellen, Team HighSights held up a flag bearing the letters "AFB." Ed Weihenmayer caught it on video. As Erik jubilantly waved his ski pole, Sam nudged him. "It's pointed the wrong way" he said.

Summit on El Cap

Last night, bivy was on the Terraces below Camp VI. Penthouses from hell. Erik dreamed of motion, of "endless pitches and climbing, climbing." It didn't matter. This morning he was invigorated. Pumped up. He would lead the roof pitch for himself and Sam, while Jeff and Hans went on ahead. The roof pitch, where El Cap flares out in a forty-five-degree lip just below the summit, would be Erik's fourth pitch, out of twenty-six total, and the grand finale to the El Cap adventure.

Now, as Erik dangles 3,000 feet in space from bolts drilled by climbers going back to Warren Harding, Sam moves past him to join Hans and Jeff, who have already topped out. He is the only one left. The cheering gets louder as he grips sloping rock and moves methodically up, then over the rock face and onto level ground. They're all there—his father and friends, Seigo, the TerraQuest team, the press—they'd hiked the relatively easy eight-mile trail to the summit. Even the Oakridge climbers, who have waited three hours to witness this moment, are there. Erik has made it. He stands on the summit, the first blind climber to conquer the face of El Capitan. But it is Ellen's soft "Hi, Erik," in the midst of the applause and excitement, that catches his ear.

Making it in a Sighted World

Erik Weihenmayer tells you he isn't a blind person, but a person who happens to be blind. It isn't just semantics. Erik's world is the sighted world. It always has been. He believes people who are blind should seize life, not languish in the shadows. He dislikes euphemisms such as "visually challenged," preferring the unadorned "blind." "It's not the word you have to change," he says. "It's the association behind it."

Eric first linked up with American Foundation for the Blind (AFB) in 1993, when the organization asked him to do a public service announcement.

Since then, he has given more than thirty presentations to such organizations as the Dial Corporation, AT&T, and the National Industries for the Blind. His fundraising for the McKinley climb raised more than $125,000 for AFB. It is Erik's way of giving back. Working with the AFB, he emphasizes, is not his profession. "I want to make it in a sighted world," he says. "After all, if you're black, that doesn't mean you have to work for the NAACP." Erik's primary concern within issues of blindness is the seventy percent unemployment rate. "Most people don't know what blind people can do," he says. "Society doesn't have to do a backflip to accommodate them."

To achieve success in his own life, Erik has learned to ask questions, delegate duties, and memorize situations. "When he goes into a new house," his father says, "he quickly cases the joint. 'Okay, here's the bathroom, and a few steps to the right is the bedroom. Back up to the hallway and straight down is the kitchen.' He does it pretty well whether it's a house or a city." In the classroom, Erik delegates students as co-teachers. It sounds Pollyannish but it works. "Mr. Weihenmayer counts on us to behave ourselves," explains one student. "There's that trust between us."

"They get to do everything," Erik says, "from writing equations on the board to filling Seigo's water dish. In return, I have to communicate with them as clearly as possible. Other teachers involve kids to keep them interested. I involve them because I need them." As coach of the wrestling club, Eric takes the same approach. He either gets on the mats himself to monitor his charges, or he delegates his best wrestlers to describe what's happening, so he can give instructions. Delegating runs parallel with asking questions. "If you don't ask, you won't get anything," says Erik, who regularly solicits help in supermarkets and restaurants. "People are nice," he says. "They want your business."

For Erik, climbing not only provides new experiences but also new perspectives. "Erik's pretty driven," says Ellen. "He's got a lifetime filled with goals. He doesn't accept 'no' for an answer." And each goal is carefully considered. El Capitan was thoroughly researched before it got the green light. "If I fail at something," Erik reasons, "people will equate that failure with blindness." Would he risk failure on Everest? "Maybe." How about K2? "I'd probably get killed on K2."

"One of the more interesting things Erik is trying to do," Ed Weihenmayer says, "is establish a camp for blind boys. We're working on it together." The camp would duplicate Erik's recipe for success by rigorous development of mind and body—the goal being to instill confidence. "Normally," Ed says, "the son is inspired by the father. Here, I think, it's the other way around."

David Eskes is a freelance writer whose work has appeared in newspapers and magazines around the country. He is a regular contributor to Arizona's Phoenix magazine.

Reading Lesson
by Edith Pearlman
....

She is called Felicity. A name less apt is hard to imagine. I have seen her high on drugs and drink, I have seen her quieted by medication, but I have never seen her happy. But she remembers better times—a few years spent in an orphanage run by nuns, and a stint in a foster home, which ended abruptly when the foster mother died.

She is about thirty. She is tall—my height—with cropped dense hair, a coffee complexion, a sway back, and drooping shoulders. Her sagging abdomen recalls her many pregnancies. She has never terminated a pregnancy, and she turns thumbs down on a tubal ligation. It's not disapproval; it's that she's terrified of hospitals, medical apparatus, social service personnel, even the angel-faced nurses who come to the Boston soup kitchen where I work and Felicity hangs out. So she carries her babies to term and enters the hospital only to deliver and relinquish them. How many? She's lost count. A grimace creases her petal-soft cheek. Her diet and habits should have ruined her skin, but all that estrogen keeps it smooth.

We are on first names here. But Felicity addresses me as Countess. She knows that I am incurably middle class. But she senses my secret fondness for the nobility, democrat though I claim to be.

"Countess, read to me," Felicity said.

I was scraping carrots, the only carrot scraper that day; the other workers were browning beef or quartering potatoes or plunging toilets. We were running behind on meal preparation, but carnelian flakes were mounting in my bowl, and little logs of carrots were piling up on a stainless pan.

"Which book?" I asked.

Though the basement kitchen was warm, Felicity was wearing a tweed coat and a wool helmet. A mittened hand held out a picture book. *Amazing Grace.*

"You read that to me," I suggested.

"Can't."

"Try."

She took off her mittens and stuffed them into the pockets of her coat. She opened the book over the bowl, leaving a narrow crescent for me to scrape into.

I knew the picture book; I had often read it aloud in the Children's Room of our facility. Amazing Grace is a black child living with Nana and Ma. Grace loves stories. Detailed watercolors show her enacting favorite tales with the help of homemade props and costumes. She's a pirate with a cloth macaw on her shoulder. She's an explorer in a turban. She plays Joan of Arc, Achilles, and Mowgli. (The little kids are mystified by these names. "A leader of her country. A fierce warrior. A boy brought up in the jungle," I explain.)

Amazing Grace is aching to get onto real boards. She wants to play Peter Pan in a school production. Her classmates mock this grandiosity. Peter Pan is a boy. He's white! But Nana and Ma won't tolerate this narrow-mindedness. Nana takes Grace to a ballet in which Juliet is danced by a Trinidadian. Grace, emboldened, auditions for and wins the part of Peter Pan. Nana gets the last words, encouraging though ungrammatical: "If Grace put her mind to it, she can do anything she want."

In the steamy kitchen Felicity began to read. At first she faltered over the simplest of words, but a grunt from me kept her going. She had once been taught reading, but her phonetic skills were rusty and her idea of context had vanished. "Excited" in the text became "exited" in Felicity's mouth—approximating the syllables but ruining the sentence. "Excited," I offered. She gave me an ungrateful look and continued.

"'Grace went to battle as Joan of Arc,'" Felicity read.

"Do you know who..." I began.

She turned the page. "'She sailed the seven seas with a peg leg and a... and a...and a carrot!'" She turned the next page. "'She was.... She was...'"

"'Hiawatha.'"

"'...sitting by the.... Shining Big Sea.... Waiter.'"

And now it dawned on me that context didn't matter to Felicity. Even story didn't matter. Felicity wanted only to get most words nearly right so as to present those words to me. Occasionally she did need to make sense of a phrase. When the teacher in the story said, "We'll have auditions next week," Felicity, after some breathy starts that I could not only hear but feel, for we were, by then, standing very close, tried, "We'll have audios." I let it go. "Audios?" she inquired.

"Auditions," I said. "Try-outs."

"I know," she said. "Countess, I know."

She knew something, all right. She stood shoulder to shoulder with me, this warm, malodorous, drugged, probably pregnant young woman. My favorite aunt had taught me to read, had listened to my eager stumbling through the "Just-So Stories," had shown me the way to exaltation. Reading surpasses any other pleasure I've yet tried: sex and laughter and even smoking. For Felicity, at that moment at least, reading to a trusted woman beat sex and laughter and shooting up, too. She was almost happy.

She flagged a little during the episode of the ballet, which flung hard words like matinee and tutu at her. But she rallied when Amazing Grace got the Peter Pan role, and she had no trouble with "fantastic," and she hung up only briefly on "success."

"'If Grace put her mind to it, she can do anything she want,'" Felicity concluded.

We were now leaning against each other. I was shredding my finger into the bowl.

"I did good, Countess, didn't I?" she said.

And, although it is my policy to respond to ungrammatical constructions with grammatical ones, to say the thing right, this time I managed instead to say the right thing.

"You did real good," I told her.

Edith Pearlman is a writer and volunteer in a Boston area soup kitchen. She is the winner of the 1996 Drue Heinz Prize for Literature.

Chance
by Alexander Chee

Three years ago a psychic told me a story about a saint who worked with Native peoples in South America. He was a missionary, and his teachings with the people would soon lead to the expulsion of him and his brothers on the orders of angry Spaniards, but in the meantime, the saint had to worry about the other monks. Jealous of his popularity with the tribes he was teaching, disturbed by the rumors of his miracles, they took him out of the fields and put him to work serving food in the dining hall. He took his reassignment without complaint, but soon there was a problem. Every time he went to set down a plate, the Lord would levitate him to the ceiling. The monks, hungry, soon reassigned him to his regular work.

"I felt I had to tell you that story," the psychic said, and she took my hand and opened my palm with her fingers. "I don't know why." I thanked her. I hadn't told her I was a waiter, but she added, as she looked at my palms, "Two things: One, you have a saint's hands. Two, whatever you do for work, you should be around as few people as possible." I smiled, and paid her with some of the cash I had earned the night before, on a dinner shift where I had served over forty people myself.

Waiting tables is an occupation of little miseries, wants that are not yet pain but that make of themselves a little suffering. "Could you do this when you have a chance?" people ask. Chances are actually my job. "Can I have this or that?" people ask, as if they are in someone's home, and not a place where they are paying for everything I will bring to the table. They face me with how much they have never had brought to them in just asking for a soda. Their misery (hunger, thirst) becomes mine (get the salad, the steak, the drink), their satisfactions, my living. Fifteen percent of what they spend on dinner in a night, over three hundred days, becomes one hundred percent of my income.

These hands the psychic held have held thousands of plates balanced in a wing-up position that allows me to carry the charred steaks and potatoes for five guests across a dining room, up the stairs full of drunk guests, and then across what my restaurant calls "the mezzanine," a seating area the size of a loft apartment set for dinner with seventeen tables. I then set that dinner in my arms down in front of the five very hungry people waiting. The steaks weigh several pounds each, the potatoes a pound or more, and the dishes also weigh several pounds, all requiring me to lift weights to work in this busy midtown steakhouse here on the island of Manhattan. We serve 300 to 500 people a day. Sometimes we have served 500 people in a single night's dinner. I am part of a crew of thirty-five waiters, called "servers" here. We are well-treated, in some ways: we get health insurance and paid vacations, for instance. We have flexible schedules. But we still make a shift pay of $2.90 an hour, the legal national minimum wage for a tipped employee, leaving us at the mercy of stingy businessmen and those foreign visitors who live in countries that think to pay their waiters enough to live.

I recall a recent patron who complained of the price of the baked potato. "Four-fifty," he said, in mock horror for the benefit of his friends at the table. I said, "Sir, Where are you?"

He looked to his friends. "I am in New York," he said.

"This potato," I said, "is from Idaho. In order for this potato to get from Idaho to midtown Manhattan, baked, and placed on this table and linen in front of you, at least seven people had to touch it. And they all had to get paid."

His friends laughed. "I see," he said. "I'll have the baked potato."

If my year's pay was included in the cost of the potato, I knew, it would cost him six dollars. Maybe seven. But as I left with their order I knew I'd already said too much. No one likes to labor-talk in restaurants. I work twenty to twenty-five hours a week, and before taxes I bring home enough to have a home and to write in that home. But everything I live on, I pick up from a black bill-charger left behind on the table.

You are in my restaurant. You order a bottle of the Haut-Brion '88, two tomato salads, and two New York Strips, one *au poivre* and one charred rare.

I take this order. The order rests lightly inside my mind, in alignment with the knowledge that the souffle cake for the table next to you, table 52, has ten more minutes, and that table 50, behind you, will be reset for a four-top that has waited for forty-five minutes and their wine, first bottle, is to be comped for the wait. While doing this I run through the last conversation I had with the line, in which the cooks told me about something they saw on television about gay gangs and how violent they are and how surprised they were about that, and as I grab the Haut-Brion from my wine captain and begin the walk to your table, I see my manager about to pick up a set of hot plates from the line, where no food is allowed to wait, and so I hand the bottle off to him. "Table 51," I tell him, "position 2," meaning you, who will taste the wine, and I grab the plates and note which goes where and set off across the room, to put them down in front of strangers, in another station, not mine, who ask me for a Diet Coke, and didn't we have creamed spinach? Which we, the restaurant, have never, ever had. And so I head off to order your tomato salads and find their waiter to tell him about the Diet Coke.

This job is not for everyone. You have to be a diplomat with the kitchen cooks and salad and dessert prep line, all of whom are from as many different countries as there are dishes served in the restaurant, who don't always understand you, and haven't seen their wives in years. You have to be nice to the bartender after he ignores you in the service station while you wait for drinks only he is allowed to make, so that later, when you need him to close your checks, he won't ignore them as well, keeping you there for as much as an hour after the last of your tables has gone home. When someone yells at you about a price or how something has been cooked, neither of which is anything you can do anything about, you have to smile and let them think what they want to think. Because it isn't that the customer is always right, so much as the customer is a customer, and it's not your job to educate them.

Last summer, a man was choking. He stood up in the dark, small, private dining room, and turned to face me, already red, his mouth open. I thought he was enraged at first. I had just set the steaks down, and sometimes, these men, they get angry about their food. Everyone with a barbecue grill thinks they know what a real medium rare is. But I soon realized from his face that he was afraid. I turned him around and as my thumb crossed his ribs, I traced the way to his solar plexus and my hands assumed a position I had never held before. I yanked towards my chin through the distance of his body, from his solar plexus towards my face. I felt something in him slide loose. Heard it hit the floor. I made sure he was okay and then got a manager. Men choking in restaurants often, out of pride, hide in the bathroom, where they die, unable to receive aid. Or they pass out, requiring you to Heimlich an unconscious person, a difficult thing to do. I was glad I'd caught him right there.

I left the room and continued with the night. He handed me forty dollars as he left. "I guess that's what his life was worth," said my manager, who has done this much more than I have.

I wasn't disappointed. I understood. What is the best we are all capable of being to each other, if not the rescuer and the saved? As the cash crossed my hand, neither one of us liked the look of it there. Money's not what life looks like, ever.

Alexander Chee works in New York and writes for Salon, Out, POZ, *and* Publishers Weekly *magazines.*

Crossing Delancey
by Jane Braxton Little

Gerald Miller is describing his ski trip to Lake Tahoe over afternoon coffee at a downtown San Francisco waterfront restaurant. Sipping from a china cup, he smoothes an invisible wrinkle in the white linen table cloth and aligns a silver knife at a perfect right angle to the table edge. His dark conservative suit is immaculate, his tie a stylish mauve abstract print knotted over a flawlessly pressed white shirt. On his neck is a six-inch scar.

"Knife fight," Miller says.

He is here, in this restaurant on a boulevard lined with palm trees, instead of prison. So is the waitress who pours our coffee and the waiter practicing his French during a lull in the afternoon clientele. This is Delancey Street, where Miller and 11,000 others have crawled out of past lives as crackheads and junkies, pimps and prostitutes, carjackers, burglars,and murderers. Some talked their way through the wrought iron gate at 600 Embarcadero Street. Others came straight from prison. All arrived from lives at rock bottom.

At Delancey Street they are starting over. And they are doing it entirely by themselves—without staff and without a penny of government funds. In the process, these offenders, whom society has labeled losers, are proving that simple self-help and hard work can transform lifestyles of violence and crime to ones of integrity, purpose, and success.

"It's hard-core responsibility," says Mimi Silbert, a fifty-four-year-old criminologist and psychologist who co-founded the Delancey Street Foundation in 1972. "We are lunatics on taking responsibility for everything—not just self, but neighbor and community as well. If we want it to work we have to *make* it work."

Something is working at Delancey Street. Despite the residents' pasts, there has never been one incident of violence. An episode or two of spitting, says Silbert, but never a fight. No one has been arrested at Delancey Street in its twenty-five years of operation.

Most graduates of the program never return to prison. The success rates range from seventy-five percent to ninety percent—a direct contrast with the sixty-seven percent of inmates released from prisons who end up being reincarcerated. But Silbert calls the statistics "silly counting games." What's important, she says, is that most Delancey Street participants stay out of prison.

Delancey Street alumni graduate into society as taxpaying citizens who work as lawyers, truck drivers, contractors, realtors, and retail business owners. They have been elected to the San Francisco Board of Supervisors, served on the San Francisco Housing Commission, and as deputy sheriffs. Delancey Street's success is no mystery, says Stephanie Muller, a program spokeswoman who has been a resident for years. "It's just hard work. We do it ourselves. It's life."

Gerald Miller holds open a gate outside the Delancey Street restaurant and, with Stephanie Muller, begins our tour of the Mediterranean-style complex. Handsome three-story brick-red stucco buildings surround a spacious quadrangle complete with a small swimming pool. Pink and red geraniums bloom from pots decorating the windows of the second-floor dormitory rooms where the 500 residents live.

A middle-aged man sweeping the terra cotta courtyard greets Gerald and pauses to lean on his broom, his eyes suddenly vacant. He's a new resident, probably still kicking drugs, says Stephanie. A pair of burly laborers cross the quad in green coveralls with Delancey Street's triangle logo on the back. They work across the Embarcadero at Pier 36, headquarters for Delancey Street Movers, the program's cross-country moving company.

Inside a freshly sheet-rocked space on the ground floor, a crew of residents is building an espresso bar. This is Delancey Street's latest enterprise, a cafe, art gallery, ice cream, and book store. "It opens when we're done," says Muller. "Soon." Just beyond the hubbub of construction, a woman who does not look up silently clips an edge of grass in a serene courtyard where a mourning dove perches in a fig tree.

Delancey Street runs on the work of its residents. No one receives a salary, not even Silbert, the president, who is clearly in charge of the entire operation. All of the labor is provided by residents, from food services and maintenance to administration, business, and financial management. To generate income they run a bevy of outside enterprises: print and copy shop, automotive service center, Christmas tree sales and decorating, movie screening, catering, paratransit services, and roller blade rentals. These businesses net around $3 million a year. All are solely owned and operated by Delancey Street Foundation.

In addition to raising the money that feeds, clothes, and houses the residents, the twenty-five commercial enterprises provide vocational and business training. Delancey Street is less a recovery center or experiment in rehabilitation than an educational institution, says Stephanie Muller. Everything is about learning.

The curriculum starts with personal maintenance: how to make a bed, plan a day, get along with people. The first work most new residents do is cleaning. The next semester is training in the restaurant or one of the other in-house enterprises. Everyone at Delancey Street is required to complete vocational programs that give them skills in three areas: business, labor, and working with people.

Along with these three basic skills, no one leaves without the equivalent of a high school diploma. "We even make you go to opera, theater— everything. How to have a classy conversation. This is a total re-education of   everything. We want you to be a good person, or at least act as if you are until you begin to believe it," says Stephanie.

Soon, some residents will earn college degrees. Delancey Street recently became chartered as a campus of Golden Gate University, offering classes in a four-year bachelor's degree program. The campus has its own college shield, a double triangle emblazoned with the Latin "Vertere Vertute."

"We made it up," says Stephanie with a giggle, "but it's very real. It means 'To Transform Through Courage.' That's us!" She and Gerald are both members of the freshman class.

While education and vocational training are the tangible preoccupations at Delancey Street, beneath them is a bootstrap operation so fundamental and so personal that most new residents don't believe it is possible. No one expects them to—not at first, says Silbert.

"We have a saying, 'to act as if.' We say if you walk around saying 'please' and 'thank you,' you will become a person who talks that way. If you act as if you believe in yourself, you will."

And if you act as if you are a community that can build a $30 million upscale residential complex a block from the San Francisco Bay Bridge, you will. That's how, in 1990, the residents got their block-size triangular center on land leased from the city's redevelopment agency. Instead of hiring outside crews, they did everything themselves—for half the cost, says Silbert. "We walked around the construction site acting as if we could pull down buildings and raise girders. Pretty soon we began to believe it ourselves."

The construction, she says, reinforced one of the program's fundamental lessons: "You're building your own foundation here. If you make a mistake with a wall or a joint you tear it down and rebuild it. That's what we're doing here at Delancey Street for ourselves—tearing down bad crooked things and replacing them with good straight things."

Named for the section of New York where immigrants assembled at the turn of the century, Delancey Street sees the felons and addicts it houses as new arrivals in another America where they must learn the language, social values, and employment skills of success. The average resident has been a hard-core drug addict for ten years and in prison four times. Many have been gang members. Most come from families trapped in poverty for several generations.

Delancey Street is the place where their jig is finally up—where everybody has already heard all the excuses, all the stories, and all the lies because they have told them all themselves. This is where the life of lies ends and they begin building new lives. They don't call it rebuilding because most never had real lives before Delancey Street, says Stephanie Muller. "We're all people who would be dead or in prison for the rest of our lives," she says.

A vivacious forty-two-year-old with warm brown eyes and a throaty raucous laugh, Stephanie Muller stumbled into Delancey Street from the streets. "I blundered myself in. I was a homeless bag lady. No clothes. No money. I slept with anyone who had money, and I'd rip 'em off."

She had been "shooting dope" since she was thirteen years old. The daughter of a middle-class California family, she was kicked out of school in the tenth grade. "I hated the way I was. I did degrading things and I felt guilty. I couldn't think about it, so I shot dope so I wouldn't. I did not care what happened to me."

At Delancey Street, Muller saw a way out. "I saw people just like myself—acting, looking, just like me. I saw a chance to be able to...well, *hope*—a chance to hope."

Muller moved from waiting tables to painting and decorating the new building; she is in charge of the foundation's Christmas tree sales program. Since 1989 she has worked as Silbert's assistant in the president's office, a series of carpeted rooms with framed watercolors on walls above desks strewn with the paperwork of managing a 500-unit residential complex. Stephanie juggles two telephones nearly buried in a functional mess of file folders and loose papers. And hats—a stack of them careening on a shelf beside her office chair. "We had Hat Day," she says. "Someone got a bad haircut so we all wore hats to make her feel better."

Gerald Miller, who's forty, arrived at Delancey Street from prison, where he had spent thirteen of his last fifteen years. A towering man with an imposing presence, he speaks with careful deliberation. Like seventy percent of the residents, he wrote a letter of application to Delancey Street from his cell. "I told a bunch of lies about how I wanted to change my life. A couple of residents came and interviewed me and I was accepted."

Gerald was facing twelve years in prison for drug-related crimes; Delancey Street offered a two-year program. "It was a mathematical choice," he says with a beguiling smile. "I was out of it, but not *that* out of it."

What looked like a cruise compared to prison, however, became the hardest thing Gerald had ever done. He faced the daunting task of getting a life. And all those lofty goals—all those "lies" in his application letter—came back to haunt him.

"You hang yourself with your own lies," Muller says with a laugh as Miller nods his head and grins agreement. "You say all these things—just like Gerald—and we use them against you. Because even if it's a lie, it's *your* lie. You wanted to come here. We didn't make you. You have to take responsibility, even for your own bullshit."

And that was what was hardest for Miller, he says: taking responsibility. He began by simply getting up in the morning, getting dressed, and cleaning his room. His first job was setting a table. It took him a week.

"It felt like a week, learning where all the spoons go. In prison the table is already set. Before that I just never learned—didn't pay attention, I guess."

From setting a table, Miller moved to an espresso bar. He worked in the foundation warehouse, then ran it; he did maintenance, then supervised the crew of new maintenance workers. Next he worked with the program's advertising gift specialties, where he sold imprinted items. "It was hard," he says. "I didn't want people to know how much I didn't know. And it's hard to be responsible for everything that comes out of your mouth. It's not easy to live like a decent human being."

Miller had hardly begun thinking about the possibility of becoming a decent human being when he was given responsibility for a new arrival fresh out of prison. Everyone, even an addict only a month off drugs, has something to offer, according to Silbert. The Delancey Street program depends on the principle of "each one teach one." A person who reads at an eighth-grade level teaches someone at the fifth-grade level.

"That was hard, too," says Miller. "I wasn't ready to show someone else how to do anything. I was just learning myself. But I did, somehow."

Appearance is part of changing a resident's self-concept. Silbert calls it the "outside-in" approach to personal transformation. If you dress as if you are a successful person you begin to believe that you can be, Silbert says.

Stephanie Muller walked into Delancey Street wearing "little hussy clothes, about this big," she says, pinching her forefinger against her thumb. "I thought the only way people would like me was looking like that." She made the obligatory trip to the Delancey Street boutique. "They put me into a dress with a frilly collar, then a business suit. I felt so awkward."

For Gerald Miller, it was a suit and tie. "I'd never worn a necktie in my life. I had no idea people got up every morning and wore ties everyday. Now I do it," he says with a broad smile, which crosses his face and bursts into a laugh. "You change. I started seeing I could live life a different way. I didn't have to be a drug addict or a convict."

Gerald Miller and Stephanie Muller are among the approximately 9,000 of Delancey Street's 11,000 participants who have put crime and drugs behind them. The program's success in reshaping the lives of drug addicts has been recognized with a wall full of awards. It has been hailed as the most successful program of its kind in the world. But, although government officials have studied its unorthodox mix of in-your-face realism and ambitious idealism, no state or federal agency has incorporated it into a publicly-funded drug treatment program.

"We do everything differently" says Silbert. Instead of hiring professional staff to "bend down and help the poor, sick, crazy, nasty people," Delancey Street uses its own residents, she says. Instead of isolating problems into bureaucratic categories such as welfare, crime, literacy, or skills problems, Delancey Street deals with the whole person. "If you don't do everything, none of it will end up working."

Government officials who respect the successes of Delancey Street say they use some of the same methods to treat hard-core drug addicts. Numerous state and federal programs create a similar therapeutic community where clients have to earn privileges by taking more responsibilities, says Fred W. Garcia, deputy director of the Office of National Drug Control Policy.

California's Amity program at the R. J. Donovan prison, for example, provides intensive substance abuse treatment for inmates during the last nine to twelve months of their prison commitment. Many states offer treatment instead of prison for first and second offenders, who are processed through drug courts and given a chance to kick their habit. These programs result in a seven-dollar savings for every one dollar invested, says John Erickson, chief of California's Office of Substance Abuse.

But the current public push to "lock 'em up and throw away the key" has not favored rehabilitation, despite its proven success. In 1993 Silbert worked briefly with Lee Brown (then President Clinton's federal drug czar) to establish a national drug rehabilitation program. Their approaches were simply too different, she says.

"They all look at you and want to pigeon-hole you. When government thinks about replicating our model, it loses sight of what makes it work: common sense and not a lot of abstract theories," Silbert says.

Delancey Street has replicated its own San Francisco model in North Carolina, New York, New Mexico, and Los Angeles, where, in 1993, the foundation bought the abandoned Midtown Hilton Hotel to accommodate 200 residents. At these five centers, approxiinately 1,000 drug addicts participate in the program at any given time.

In response to the deluge of requests for advice, the foundation launched a training program in 1994. The Institute for Social Renewal accepts trainee applicants willing to live at Delancey Street and participate in residential life for two days to a week. Some arrange to stay longer.

"Living here is the only model I have," says Silbert. "If you don't do it, you can't teach it. If you can't teach it, nobody's learning." Participants at the training institute have included school kids from Amherst, Massachusetts, homeless people from Detroit, members of the Arizona Board of Corrections, and Maoris, the indigenous people of New Zealand. What they take from Delancey Street and how they apply it are still complete unknowns, says Silbert.

For Gerald Miller, life at Delancey Street does not allow him to forget the life he left behind. One of his regular jobs is in the criminal justice department, visiting the prisons where he once lived. He interviews applicants for Delancey Street who are candidates for court-ordered probation. If assigned to the program by a judge, they must comply with all of the terms of their probation or return to prison.

Although a judge approves the assignment, Delancey Street residents decide whether to accept a candidate. Gerald looks for the worst of the applicants, the ones who have hit bottom and want something else. Delancey Street is as selective as Harvard, says Silbert, but instead of seeking the top two percent of applicants, it chooses the bottom two percent.

Once they have been accepted, residents spend their first thirty days without any contact with their families. Then they are allowed to write and receive letters. After six months they earn one telephone call home.

For the families outside, the wait without communication is excruciating, says the aunt of a current resident who requested anonymity. "He had to prove that he was worthy of just speaking to his mom," she says. But after watching her nephew's life go downhill in a slurry of alcohol and drugs, Delancey Street seemed his only chance. "It's his hope. Without it my sister figures she would have to write off her son. Gone forever. Like dead." When her son had successfully completed one year, the mother was allowed to visit him at Delancey Street. "It was awkward," the aunt says. "She wanted to say 'good for you,' but it's not a cheerleader sort of deal."

Most Delancey Street residents reach a point in their stay when the months of acting "as if" suddenly sink in, says Stepanie Muller. "You've been b-s-ing your way through everything when you see that you are actually going to make it. At some point you say 'Shit! This is real.' When that moment finally comes, other people help you. And you need them."

Not everyone makes it. Some are unable to keep their commitment to stay at Delancey Street for two years. "They just leave. It's not like we have any locks on the doors," Miller says. If they are on court-ordered probation, someone from Delancey Street notifies the probation department. Others do just fine. "They leave here and just have regular lives," he says. Delancey Street keeps no statistics on residents who leave, but Silbert estimates that between ten and twenty-five percent of the 11,000 accepted revert to drugs and return to prison.

Despite its odd collection of tenants, Delancey Street is a small town whose residents know all about one another's warts. Like small town neighbors, they respond to one another's needs. "Everybody works together, lives together, yells together, cries together," says Silbert. "All these gang members sworn to kill each other—they become part of a completely integrated community here. Ultimately, they know they need each other to make it."

It may be the intimacy of this community interaction that is responsible for the remarkable lack of discipline problems, says Stephanie. The rules are simple: No drugs or alcohol. No physical violence. No threat of physical violence. And sex? "We're very old fashioned," she says. "You have to date here, and everyone's always in your business.... The program works because this is our home. It's just like family. We develop a certain loyalty to it and to each other. People here are saving lives."

After five years as a Delancey Street resident, Gerald Miller is beginning to look forward to a life outside the residential complex. He has stayed longer than the average of four years. When he does graduate, it will be a decision he makes with the fellow residents he has grown to love and trust. "Ultimately, the choice is up to each individual, but you make it the way a family does when a child leaves home," says Miller.

Miller hasn't decided what his work will be. "Something constructive. Something I'm comfortable with that generates an income." And his life beyond work? "I'll have a family. I'll drive home from my job in a car," he says with a gaze toward the bay which takes him far beyond it. "I used to care what kind of car it was—had to be a Cadillac or something really nice. Now it's just a car that takes me home to a wife and a couple of kids. I'm a decent, responsible, caring human being."

The Woman Behind Delancey Street

Mimi Silbert drives a bulldozer and teaches Shakespeare. She ties rebar (steel reinforcement rods used in construction) and holds a double doctorate in psychology and criminology. She is a former high school cheerleader and student of existentialism under Jean-Paul Sartre.

As president and CEO of the Delancey Street Foundation, Silbert uses everything she ever learned, and every inch of her five-foot frame to bootstrap drug addicts into productive, crime-free lives.

"I've been at this twenty-five years—my entire [adult] life, really. I have this silly, absurd notion that if I could just get the entire United States to sit still, and talk to them about what we're doing here, I know they'd understand. It's just plain common sense.

Silbert started Delancey Street in 1971 with four drug addicts in a San Francisco apartment. Her partner was John Maher, a former felon. They shared a vision of a center for criminal rehabilitation, and vocational training run by ex-convicts for ex-convicts. It would be entirely self-sufficient, they agreed, with no outside funds, and everyone working to support the group.

In late 1972, Silbert, Maher, and around 100 former felons pooled their incomes to buy an old mansion that once housed the Soviet Consulate in fashionable Pacific Heights. To mollify the neighbors, who were less than thrilled with the purchase, Silbert and Maher volunteered the residents for neighborhood chores. The first request came from a society matron who needed her living room cleared of furniture for a benefit. That job inspired Delancey Street Movers, one of the first of the businesses owned and operated by the foundation.

For Silbert, Delancey Street is a duplication of the immigrant neighborhood of her childhood near Boston. Her father owned and operated a corner drugstore. Both her parents matched the poverty of their neighborhood with a deep sense of justice, she says. "Everybody looked out for everybody else. We were all struggling upward. It was like holding hands climbing a mountain together. Together we rise or together we fall. That's what it's like here at Delancey Street."

After majoring in English and psychology at the University of Massachusetts, Silbert earned doctorates jn criminology and psychology from the University of California at Berkeley. It was during her intern work as a prison psychologist that she began questioning the penal system. With everything provided and paid for by taxpayers, it is no wonder criminals emerge from prison feeling no different than when they went in, she says.

At Delancey Street, residents do everything for themselves. But Silbert has built more into the program than responsibility and skills. In the midst of her success as a prison consultant—in a moment of flush over the joy of helping people—she had a flash of what it would be like not to know the power of giving. She made the experience of personal success a cornerstone at Delancey Street.

"No one should be in the position of only receiving. That's depressing. It's enough to make you feel violent or give you a victim's view of life," she says. "Everyone should get to feel terrific because they are helping people."

Silbert and Maher fell in love and lived together for ten years, helping one another raise twin sons from an earlier marriage. In the mid-1980s, Maher, a recovering alcoholic, began drinking again. A few years later, he resigned from the organization. He died of a heart attack in 1988.

If Silbert has one regret about Delancey Street, it is that she cannot include more people. Turning applicants away is painful, she says. She hopes her Institute for Social Renewal will inspire others to launch their own programs tailored to their own skills and the particular problems they want to solve.

Meanwhile, Silbert devotes her energy to the Delancey Street operation, which last year raised $12.3 million in revenues. She negotiates new programs, helps solicit around $3 million a year in product donations, participates in conferences with drug rehabilitation professionals around the world, and scolds a construction crew outside her office, where her long working hours require three secretaries operating in shifts. In a system based on role models, Silbert is the ultimate role model.

"It takes me a long time before I say something is working. I have no idea what will happen when we come to the real test. But I've been doing this for twenty-five years—smashing my head against a brick wall. The bricks are beginning to move. I can feel it."

Jane Braxton Little is a freelance writer whose work appears in newspapers and magazines around the country.

Why Lawyers Get No Respect
by Harvey Schwartz

My name is Harvey. I'm a lawyer, a trial lawyer. No, this isn't the introduction to a twelve-step program. I'm proud of what I do, but I'm saddened by what lawyering has become. My kids know all the lawyer jokes. They tell me the latest about lawyers crawling under snakes and I smile and moan but it really doesn't feel very good. I don't like my own kids putting down what I do with my life. I'm proud of being a lawyer. What is most frightening, though, is acknowledging that there is some truth in lawyer jokes. Maybe we lawyers should accept some of the blame for the public perception that the first place to look for a sharp lawyer is under a damp rock. As an example of how far things have gone astray, let's look at a nursery rhyme from a lawyer's point of view.

> Humpty Dumpty sat on a wall,
> Humpty Dumpty had a great fall,
> All the King's horses
> And all the King's men
> Couldn't put Humpty together again.

If you're a lawyer—or even if you're not—take a moment to reflect on what your first thoughts might be were the Widow Dumpty to show up at your office and recite this tale of woe.

"Must have been a problem with the design and construction of the wall that caused this great fall. We'll need an architectural expert to testify about the poor quality of the mortar holding the bricks together."

"Great fall, huh? You can only have a great fall from a great wall. Just how great was this wall? Sounds like the wall owner is a deep pocket. How do we sue him? Could that Great Wall be an attractive nuisance?"

"What's all this with the King? Might be a sovereign immunity problem. Can we sue the king's men in their individual capacities? When is the deadline for notifying the king about the widow's claim?"

"Horses? What were they doing using horses to put him together again? This could be a med-mal claim. Do we need a veterinary expert?"

"I wonder if Dumpty suffered before he fell to pieces. That could boost the value of this case."

"How much can I make on this case? Will I make more if I keep it, or refer it to somebody in the city?"

Would it enter most lawyers' minds to tell the grieving Mrs. Dumpty that she doesn't need a lawsuit at this time in her life, that she should stop looking to blame others and just admit that she was married to a guy with an eggshell skull who should have known better than to sit on high walls?

How much business should a lawyer turn away because he or she thinks the case is silly—even though there is money in it? Or do we find those two concepts to be contradictory, that a case that can make us some money is by definition not silly?

There was a time when lawyers were considered counselors-at-law, wise persons to whom others turned for advice and guidance about difficult problems. Now we are often seen as hired guns who have a license to threaten to do unpleasant and even horrible things unless our target pays the person who hired us lots of money. Could it be that we are not regarded as respected professionals because we aren't acting like professionals?

Professionals exercise discretion and judgment. A gas station doesn't hire a professional to pump gas. It hires a kid who'll pump the same gas into every car that stops at the pump. If we are to be professionals, we have to do something more than just pump out litigation for every person who shows up at our offices with a tale of woe, money in hand, or a deep-pocket defendant in sight.

I had a long conversation the other day with a lawyer I greatly respect. She was referring a case to me—a man who had been fired by a large corporation. We discussed his situation and she and I concluded that he had no legitimate legal claim. And then this well-respected attorney suggested that we write to the corporation's general counsel and propose negotiations about a settlement.

"They'll give him something to make him go away," she told me. "They'd rather pay him than pay their big law firm. Let's see what we can get for him."

I declined, but I'll freely admit that from time to time I've gotten settlements for clients on some pretty precarious claims. And I'll admit that she was probably right and I was probably wrong.

I was wrong because we could have gotten some money for this poor fellow who'd lost his job, and probably needed the money more than his former employer did. The corporation most likely would have paid him something to make him go away—actually to make me go away. And it would have been a wise move for the corporation; it would have cost less to pay him than to pay its lawyers to defend a lawsuit. This sort of decision-making has become bread-and-butter legal practice for lawyers on all sides of these issues.

But I really wonder how this situation differs from extortion, differs from the gangster telling Mom-N-Pop grocers that, for a little protection moolah, they should buy "fire insurance" from him? It would make as much sense for Mom-N-Pop to simply pay up as it would for the corporation to settle a frivolous claim cheaply.

"Joe the Legbreaker" made his demand in order to line his pockets, as do we attorneys. Of course, what we do is, by definition, legal, while what the gangster does is frowned upon, and because of that we run little personal risk in making our demands.

But speaking theoretically for a moment—is writing a demand letter "just to see if they'll pay something" a totally different creature from suggesting a payment of protection money to avoid something undeserved-but-awful happening to your business?

Of course, this doesn't apply to legitimate claims, real harm, real violations of law, real cases where writing an initial demand letter is just being polite, and one intends to go the full route if need be. We should pursue these cases, vigorously. We should still be conscientious and creative, venturing into what William Schwartz, a former professor of mine at Boston University Law School, used to call "the idear frontier."

Such cases don't lead to lawyer jokes. What I'm talking about are the cases brought "to see what we can get." Extortion cases.

If we are to be "counselors at law," one of my favorite letterhead phrases, shouldn't we be doing more counseling and less gunslinging? Just because our licenses and skills enable us to get money for a client (or to assist a client in avoiding paying money) shouldn't we instead consider counseling the client to back off, and not do what he proposes to do?

There was a time, not too long ago, when this country was run by lawyers: lawyers as lawyers and judges, lawyers as legislators and mayors and governors, and lawyers as business counselors, the people you went to when you had a sticky problem. Lawyers sold (or gave away) wisdom. Lawyers told business people when not to do something wrong (not how to do it and get away with it).

We need to do more counseling. We need to tell the people who come to us for our wisdom not to do something that we know is wrong, instead of working our hardest to help them get away with it so long as there is some money in it for us, too.

I had a client once who told me my job was to tell him just where the line was...and then how thick it was, because he wanted to shove his toes right up to the far edge of legal behavior. We used to laugh about that.

Looking back, however, what I should have done was tell him to put his shoes back on and back off from the line. Maybe he wouldn't have made that last nickel, but he wouldn't worry about whether he'd danced over the line when I wasn't looking. I should have counseled him about doing good, not advised him about how he could be as bad as he could be without getting caught.

We can be a great force for truth, justice, and honesty in society. Most of what many lawyers do is pretty noble. And while they can hate us and joke about us, society is, in fact, better off with us. People who complain the loudest about lawyers often want representation by Genghis Khan, Esquire, when they get into trouble.

The way law is practiced today contributes to much that is wrong with society. By empowering victims, primarily, we encourage a victim mentality. By creating excuses for everything, we absolve people of responsibility for anything and everything. By taking money or making money to do whatever our clients ask us to do, we prostitute our professionalism.

Years ago, I received a telephone call from Igor, a Russian emigre taxi driver. Still new to this country, he had already learned about personal injury litigation.

"Harvey," he said breathlessly. "Got big case, worth million dollars. I was standing on curb and truck came by and almost killed me, just missed me by one inch. So what you think, big case?"

"Igor," I replied. "Almost got killed...almost big case. Nothing happened to you."

But this wasn't Igor's first foray into the tort system. He'd learned the language. Undaunted, he dropped what he thought was the big one.

"Emotional distress, Harvey. I've got so much emotional distress."

"Igor," I said. "If that truck had hit you, then you would have no more emotional distress ever again. Until then, you're going to have emotional distress every day of your life. Live with it. Forget the emotional distress. Instead of suing somebody because they almost killed you, take your wife out to dinner and celebrate that you're still alive."

That was the last I ever heard from Igor. I expect somebody else settled his emotional distress claim for him for some amount, a token amount, but enough for Igor to pay for dinner with his wife.

There's nothing wrong with saying no to a client. No, I won't file this suit just because it has some settlement value and you and I can make some money. No, I won't drag this plaintiff through years of humiliating discovery just to wear him out for a settlement. No, I will not help you get around this law, which protects people, but costs your business some money.

If lawyers are to regain respect, we must act more professionally. We are, after all, officers of the court, and that means something. We are given powers and abilities far beyond those of "mere mortals."

With a stroke of our pens we can compel people to drop what they are doing, come to our offices, and answer endless questions. We can force people to give us their most private records. We can command deputy sheriffs to go to peoples' doors and deliver threatening documents to them, demanding a response within twenty days.

Our licenses empower us to extract huge sums of money from the wealthiest corporations. The most humble of us can compel the U.S. government itself to come to court and answer our allegations.

Lawyers are made different by the power society bestows upon us. Lawyers have been given these gifts, these powers, because, historically, lawyers have been wise in their use of power. Lawyers wrote the Constitution and formed this country. Lawyers sat in Congress, made up the presidents' cabinets, advised and counseled titans of industry. Lawyers earned the authority society gave them.

But the system has broken down. Those in business now view lawyers as gumming up the works instead of lubricating the gears of commerce. We are like the archetypal heroes who misuse their special powers. Some say we have succumbed to the dark side.

We can work our way out of this hole. We can begin to advise our clients that they should obey the law even when they are not likely to get caught breaking it, as silly as that may sound. We can advise people to take responsibility for harm they have brought on themselves, rather than blame everybody else for the hand that life has dealt them.

If we are professionals with at least a modicum of responsibility to society, we can decline a few opportunities to make money just because they present themselves to us.

Respect for the legal profession—which translates into respect for lawyers—can be restored. We can put our Humpty Dumpty back together again. But we won't do it by blaming the king's men and the king's horses. We'll do it by accepting the blame for what we've done to ourselves, acknowledging the role of conscience in our work, and changing our own behavior.

Harvey Schwartz is a Boston civil rights lawyer and a partner in the law firm of Schwartz, Shaw, and Griffith.

A Day in the Life of the Hole in the Wall Gang Camp

by Bob Tedeschi

In 1985, when it became clear that Paul Newman's salad dressing business was actually generating a profit, the actor hatched the idea to create a camp for kids with life-threatening illnesses. The mission, he said, was to give them a space where they could relax, forget about their medical conditions, and "raise a little hell."

Three years later, the first kids arrived at the Hole in the Wall Gang Camp in Ashford, Connecticut. Since that time it has grown internally and expanded its reach.

Beginning this summer, there will be four Hole in the Wall Gang Camps, with two more on the way. The Barretstown Gang Camp in Ireland, The Boggy Creek Gang Camp in Orlando, Florida, and the Double "H" Hole in the Woods Ranch in upstate New York are running, while The Silver Lining Ranch in Colorado and L'Envol, in France, are in development. The camps rely on each other for assistance, but each camp is ultimately responsible for its own administration, medical programs, and fund-raising. Each receives part of its funding from Newman's Own, the actor's food business, from which all profits are donated to charity, and which is a story in itself. Sometimes misidentified as a camp exclusively for kids with cancer, the Hole in the Wall Gang Camp serves children with a wide range of medical conditions, from hemophilia and bone tumors to HIV and Sickle-Cell Anemia. Campers who have recovered from their diseases are also included in the mix. They range in age from seven to fifteen years.

Over the course of three months each summer, more than 800 children visit the Ashford camp alone, in sessions that last as long as nine days. The camp is free, as is the medical treatment they receive there. The medical staff is comprised of pediatric specialists who run a state-of-the-art facility housed in a building dubbed the "OK Corral."

The fifty camp counselors—mostly college students and recent graduates—are assisted by about twenty-five volunteers each session. The job is both inspiring and exhausting. Several of the younger counselors know this all too well: they were among those campers in the late eighties who were scampering around, doing their personal best just to raise a little hell.

This is how a typical session works:

Early Morning

Friday, dawn. The first things that move at camp are the animals. The cocks crow; the goats stir. At the pond, a blue heron leaves its leafy roost, hops into the water and stands motionless. Two snakes slide onto a high rock at the pond's western edge.

The oldest campers, the fifteen-year-olds in cabin two, lay deep asleep. They'll have to scurry up the hill to make the 8:30 breakfast bell. But across the cabin green, Alonzo, Ricky, Allen, James, and David rise in cabin nine. It's 6:30, the eight-year-olds are ready to get going, and three counselors gather them for an impromptu nature walk. Alonzo is the spirit of this group, an affectionate, engaging, hip-high hip-hop boy who was born with HIV. Of the others, three have finished their chemotherapy treatments long enough to regrow hair, and one is in full remission. The fourth has hemophilia.

On the walk through the woods toward the pond, the boys fill the air with chatter, especially Alonzo. They're on the way to see the fabled "Snake Rock," in their minds a mottled pit crawling with lethal vipers. "I'm gonna catch a snake in my hand!" Alonzo boasts.

Yak yak yak. "Zo," who has seen only the wildlife of his Los Angeles neighborhood, pushes through the bushes to the waterfront and scans the rock. Nothing. As the others reach the clearing, the heron flaps into a low branch nearby. "Look at that giant bird!" Ricky says.

"That's not so big" Alonzo says. At that, the heron unfolds and lifts away its wingspan twice as long as Alonzo, who whispers "wow" as the bird floats slowly across the pond.

There's a commotion at the rock, where David has spotted the two snakes. The boys gasp, move closer to the counselors and push them toward the rock.

For five minutes, the boys stare. When the others move on, Alonzo remains for a long moment, fixed and silent, his grip closed on a counselor's shirtsleeve, an awestruck smile upon his face.

Breakfast

Andre is at breakfast in the camp's dining hall. He is one of a circle of 150 people seated at fifteen tables, surrounding a smorgasboard of cereal, pancakes, and fruit. Andre has barely put a dent in his bowl of bran flakes and prunes. He's too busy dispensing witticisms, too busy listening to everyone around him; too busy taking part.

His eyes look straight ahead at nothing, and he blinks a few times. The conversation has hit a soft spot, so he munches a spoonful of bran. Noise erupts from the corner. "Hey! What's goin' on?" he calls to anyone.

"Dave is drinking everyone's cereal milk."

Andre grins widely "That's gross."

While fighting leukemia for half of his thirteen years, Andre has sacrificed much physically. Radical chemotherapy paralyzed him from the waist down, but drove the cancer into remission. The next time, the treatment took his eyesight. That was a year ago, when he met a counselor named Marcus, who has become one of his closest friends. They are a perfect pair. Bright, funny, and vigilant against negativity.

"Hey Marcus," he calls. Marcus moves his shiny shaved head closer. "What's up?"

Andre pulls him close. *Sotto voce*: "When are we gonna talk to some girls?"

Marcus smiles, puts his arm around Andre. "In a little bit. You gonna show 'em who the mac daddy is?"

"Yup," he grins. Marcus pats his back. Andre kisses him on the cheek.

"But you gotta finish your food first," Marcus says.

"We need those prunes. Otherwise we can't get unplugged."

Andre frequently refers to himself as "we." It seems fitting. No one could do what he does, purely alone.

After a few minutes he's finished most of the bowl. He makes a bad face when he bites into a prune, but he never complains about this, his everyday breakfast.

He puts his spoon down firmly. "Gotta go," he says, and two counselors lead him to the bathroom. They pick him out of his "hoop-dee," as he calls his wheelchair, and help him onto the seat. The entire time, he's chatting about home life, cracking jokes about school, and giving matter-of-fact directions on how to handle him. He is completely unguarded.

Leaving the dining hall, one of the campers is pushing Andre's hoop-dee. Another is waiting his turn at the wheel. Andre rolls away surrounded by people who are quietly amazed by him, as he sets his mind to scoring some points with the girls.

Morning Activity

Milton is a sweet ten-year-old who, because of his brain tumor, has lost much of the mobility in his right side. The tumor has also taken the edge off his hearing and speaking abilities; but he can express himself just fine, thanks to a pair of enormous brown eyes that dive into yours when he's got something to say, which he often does.

If Milton laughs too hard he loses control of his bladder, which can be a problem, because he is always laughing. The trick is to know his threshhold. So a counselor named Alex, who shares Milton's quirky, ridiculous sense of humor, spends most of his time one-on-one with Milton. The two are together again for morning activities.

On other mornings, Milton's group will ride horses, write poetry, climb ropes, make crafts, swim, fish, play sports, or play in the theater. This morning they are in the woodshop. Milton and Alex search through the box of pine shapes. There are teddy-bears, birds, cars, and squares onto which campers can sketch and paint. Milton grabs the teddy bear, and Alex helps him secure it in the vise.

Across the workbench stands a smaller girl, also with a teddy bear shape. The first step for both of them is to file the splintered edges. Milton tries to file, but his hands don't comply. He stops and frowns.

He spots a saw, smiles and looks at Alex. "Go to it, Big Man!" Alex says. Milton puts the saw to a leg. The girl across the table smiles and shakes her head. It takes Milton five minutes of intense sawing, but finally the leg gives way. Milton howls and high-fives Alex. He immediately goes to work on the other leg. Next comes the left arm. Gone. When the right arm hits the floor, half of the woodshop stops and cheers. Alex frees the poor bear from the vise.

"You want to paint it now?"

"No!" Milton shouts, barely able to contain his joy "Do the head!"

Milton saws gleefully into the neck. Finishing the job, they both laugh so hard that Alex has to squelch his high-pitched giggling, lest Milton laugh too hard.

As other kids finish their wood projects, they stack them in a corner to bring home and remember camp by. The amputee bear is in the garbage. Milton is mauling another piece of wood, lost in his work.

Lunch

Back to the dining hall, where the five units (each with twenty-five or so campers) line up according to unit color and sing the unit cheers. Once inside, music director Leo Loginov plays a synthesizer/drum machine that sounds like a well-amplified five-piece band. Pop singer Amy Grant, who has come to hang out with the kids for the day, steps to the microphone for grace, and sings "Amazing Grace."

The dining hall has a circumference of about 120 feet, and rises to a spire perhaps 40 feet high; Grant's crystal voice rightly consecrates this space, the spiritual center of the camp. The walls are draped with banners each unit has painted with slogans like "Green: See How We Grow!" and "Welcome to the Purple Planet!"

The rainbow of units is separated by color while the kids eat, but for a half hour after every meal the colors mix like spin-art. Kids and counselors sing at the microphone, and in the middle of the room everyone else dances.

Leo breaks into "La Bamba," and a conga line of 150 people hops, crutches, and wheels through the dining hall. As usual, some kids and adults arrived at camp a bit shy about dancing and singing in public. You can see them now locked into the conga line—and you can hear them, unabashedly off key, louder than a pop star.

Rest Hour

It is 1:30 P.M., and Zephyr, Jamaad, Shamar, and Mike are playing cards. This is the time of the day referred to as "rest hour," but no one rests—especially not these boys, the oldest kids at camp.

The rap song "Juicy" plays in the background. It's the anthem of the week, the most popular song in the clubs, and it plays twenty-five times a day in cabin two. It's about a kid who breaks out of the ghetto through rapping, and showers his mom, daughter and friends with luxuries. "Don't let'em hold you down," they sing. "Reach for the stars."

These are some of the oldest living people born with HIV. (Zephyr is fifteen years old.) Jamaad is fourteen, a playful soul, maybe five feet tall with chocolate brown skin and a small, round face given to huge smiles and exaggerated expressions. He wears his baseball cap backward.

Abdul, a tall, muscular kid, walks by and flips Jamaad's cap. Jamaad scowls. "Cut it out Abdul," he says. Abdul does it again. "I ain't playin', Abdul," he says, louder. Abdul walks by once more and before his hand can touch Jamaad's cap, Jamaad is up, face-to-chest with Abdul. They glare at each other. "I said I ain't playin'!"

Their friends look alarmed, and start to move toward them. Jamaad flips Abdul's cap, looks at the others and winks. Abdul laughs, too. Jamaad was playin'.

Afternoon Activity

At 3 P.M. the temperature reaches 102 degrees. The entire camp, it seems, has chosen to flee to the pool for afternoon activity. Gregory has brought half of his cabin with him. He's a twelve-year-old with a slightly caustic sense of humor and a sweet smile that turns to tears when he leaves at the end of the session. Cancer has taken much of his right leg, so he'll pilot brightly-painted crutches until he's old enough for a prosthesis operation. He leaps into the water, where he's as fast as anyone.

In the glare of the water, chaos reigns. Wacky Noodles form makeshift rafts. Beach balls fly, kids tangle near a basketball. In the deep end, a pair of bald shiny heads glisten and bounce in the waves. One of them belongs to Marilyn, a reed-thin, cheery fourteen-year-old who recently finished chemo. Gregory and Marilyn bounce near each other. They haven't met. He looks the other way then splashes her face with water. She yelps and retaliates.

Soon, the boys and the girls are warring in various splash factions. In a few minutes, when they call a truce and rest at poolside, they'll know more about each other. And when one of them enters the hospital for a bone marrow transplant after the summer, cards and letters from these camp friends will fill the hospital room, and the campers themselves will visit, as well.

Dinner

Dinner starts with announcements. A seven-year-old named Emily sprints to the podium to tell everyone how many fish the red unit girls caught today. Her unit goes wild, and she claps as she runs back to her table. Other announcements: Six campers learned to swim today, four caught their first fish. Two rode horses for the first time.

Dinner is served. Kids feast on chicken fingers and fries, scorn the sweet corn. By this time in the session they've had it up to here with Newman's Own lemonade, but the alternative is water. They go for the sucrose.

Tucked behind the main eating space is a circular walkway with low ceilings and less noise than the rotunda. Mike, a counselor, and Sam, a camper, are on a bench there, having a little talk. It seems Sam wants to launch his corn at the purple unit, and when told he cannot, he has tried to bolt the dining hall. Twice. Mike lays down the law, while Sam stares at the floor, his yellow hair half-covering a troubled expression. Mike looks a bit frazzled himself.

Five minutes later, he corrals Sam at the door again. Mike takes his hand and leads him back, shaking his head. Much of a counselor's job involves setting boundaries, to keep things relatively orderly and safe. Even with volunteers to help the staff, the tasks can overwhelm.

The meal is finished and Leo plays a camp favorite called "Humpty Dumpty," a series of nursery rhymes sung to a rap beat. Kids head for the microphone, counselors line up on a bench and perform a synchronized hip-hop routine, while everyone else hops and twists in the middle and sings along. Every able-bodied counselor has a kid on his or her shoulders; almost everyone else has a child's hand. Near the middle of the floor, a blond head bounces up and down, seven feet high, as his "ride" twists along with the tune. It's Sam, arms waving overhead, singing. He's on Mike's shoulders.

Evening Activity

Tonight's activity is Stage Night, where nearly every kid will get up on stage and perform. Perform. One hundred and twenty kids in various states of adolescent and pre-adolescent insecurity, many of whom are used to shuffling in the shadows with their disease or appearance, will stand in front of their peers and do things other kids wouldn't do at gunpoint. Call it what you will; it seems a lot more than performance.

The little ones, true enough, eat this stuff up. Alonzo and the boys prance and pose through a rendition of "YMCA," while the seven- and eight-year-old girls adapt a song and dance from *The Wizard of Oz*, which leaves most of the adults in the audience thinking adoption.

The older the kids, the more tentative their entrances. Johnnie takes the stage with the lyrics to "Lunchlady Land" in his head and perhaps three guitar chords in his hands. This is his first time before an audience this size.

His legs shake, as does his voice, but he delivers his lines with a huge smile spread across his face. As he strums to a stop, the campers stand and scream.

For a full ninety minutes, the acts come. Some are funny, some are ridiculous, some are simple and moving. For the finale, sixteen-year-old Marie takes the stage alone to sing "Colors of the Wind." In the back corner seats, two of her longtime counselors, Lisa and Lauren, fall silent and lock arms. When they first met her she was a short, skinny, quiet kid. Now she stands tall and graceful, if still a bit skinnier than she should be.

Leo strikes the song's opening piano chords, and out of Marie's mouth pour the sapphire sounds of a woman, with full-throated volume and sage softness. No one in the crowd moves for three minutes. She finishes with her head up, smiling humbly; there's a half-breath pause, followed by an eruption from the crowd. When the house lights go up, Lisa and Lauren have their faces buried in each other's shoulder. Then they run backstage.

Cabin Chat

Every night ends with a cabin chat. The kids lie in their beds, the counselors sit on the floor, everyone looking to the candle in the center of the room. Most of the time the kids just talk about what's on their minds from the day. Sometimes the counselors will pose a question for them to address. Once, we asked our youngest campers, "If you were stuck on a desert island, what three things would you want with you?" The responses: "A can of soda, a wash cloth, soap, a bag of Doritos...."

Tonight, I'm the only counselor in the cabin. Zephyr, Abdul, Shamar, Jamaad, Mike, Juan, Peter, and Jason sit up in bed. I ask them to talk about one person in their lives who has helped them out in a time of need. I figured the discussion would settle on role models.

Zephyr, as usual, speaks first. He is the acknowledged leader of the group; an intelligent, proud, thoughtful young man who could pass for a twenty-year-old. "I think about my mom" he says, whispering. "She passed a long time ago. Whenever I needed anything, no matter what, she was always there to help me out."

Abdul follows. Identical response. Same with Shamar, and Jamaad, and Juan—each of whom lost both parents to AIDS. They talk about how much they miss their moms; no melodrama, no interruptions. When they share, the air thickens, and words move slowly. After each has had a say, Zephyr blows out the candle.

They will stay up late tonight, just as they did last night and the night before. Only this time, they won't puncture the night with giddy howls and barbs that send the counselors scurrying to keep the peace. Tonight they talk quietly and listen respectfully. The counselors barely hear their whispers, smiling like proud parents in the next room. They sound nice, those whispers. Like young men working together in fair weather, building a proper shelter for their days ahead.

Bob Tedeschi, a journalist and a counselor at the Hole in the Wall Gang Camp, teaches writing at the camp and at Norwalk (Connecticut) Community Technical College.

On Larks
by Paul Newman

Newman's Own began as a lark—a joke more or less—and became a challenge. I had no idea that the salad dressing would out-gross my films—which is a humiliation almost beyond repair—but that's the way it happened. Today there's an entire generation that may know me more for popcorn than for movies.

I wish I could recall with clarity the impulse that compelled me to help bring this camp into being. I'd be pleased if I could announce a motive of lofty purpose. I've been accused of compassion, of altruism, of devotion to Christian, Hebrew, and Moslem ethic, but however desperate I am to claim ownership of a high ideal, I cannot.

I wanted, I think, to acknowledge Luck: the chance of it, the benevolence of it in my life, and the brutality of it in the lives of others; made especially savage for children because they may not be allowed the good fortune of a lifetime to correct it.

But whatever the impetus, the place exists. It wasn't so much built— it simply exploded into operation out of other people's generosity. It magically collected everything: canoes, a swimming pool, volunteers, architects, doctors, fishing tackle, nurses, a pig, snakes, an amphitheater, food, loyalty— an endless list.

From the introduction to I Will Sing Life: Voices from the Hole in the Wall Gang Camp, *by Larry Berger, Dahlia Lithwick, and Seven Campers, with photographs by Robert Benson,* © 1992. *Reprinted with permission from Little, Brown and Company.*

The Gilligan Cure
by Nancy McCallum

When I give thanks to whoever or whatever it is that created life, I now give thanks to some lesser deities. Mary Tyler Moore comes to mind. I thank her and Rhoda, and Murray and Lou. And Samantha and Darrin. Well, Darrin not so much. I do have some standards. My television friends saw me through a bad time. I was struggling with depression, which had started in my early teens and seemed to worsen as I grew older. I could point to various childhood experiences as root causes, but the important fact is that I did not know how to live happily as an adult. Old feelings of loneliness and hopelessness were being played out in self-destructive ways, including addictive relationships. I would meet a woman, then throw myself completely into the relationship, obsessing over every interaction. Unfortunately, I always chose partners who were emotionally unavailable. Four years ago, the last in a series of hurtful relationships sent me whirling down into the thickest depression ever. There were moments when I wondered why I was even living.

Watching comfort shows from childhood was one of the many small steps I took to feel better. Television's "Nick at Nite" was the first piece of everyday life that I was able to use in a therapeutic way. (And I'm sorry to say, when you're depressed, PBS just won't do.) It was free, it was soothing, and so far, non-addictive.

That night several years ago when I accidentally came across Mary on the tube, I found myself smiling and laughing for the first time in ages. This old show, which I had watched faithfully as a child, was familiar, comforting. I marveled at the feeling; it felt good to feel good. I wondered: Is it weird that this makes me happy? Then I decided: No, but it's weird that it is so hard for you to let some lightness in.

It was the beginning of an important shift. The depression had felt so complex, so dense, that it didn't seem possible that simple little acts could bring relief. I discovered I was wrong.

When you feel bad, it seems that the only thing that can help is an epiphany, a *big change* that suddenly takes you to higher, happier levels. But what I learned about earth-shattering change is that it can arrive quietly, piece by piece. It is quite a lesson for someone who is impatient. It meant I had to trust that doing new things would bring new results.

I call my "Nick at Nite" discovery the first step in my "one hundred little things" program. It's something I created rather naturally, spontaneously, haphazardly, and at times, somewhat desperately, to feel better—to be better—always. The program to happiness for me was the program that came from me. No trademark involved. When I have moments of gratitude, I think of all the little things that helped me pull the pieces of myself—my true self—together, to become whole.

One hundred is a rough estimate. Maybe it was 1,000 or maybe it was 78. Doesn't matter. Each time I did something that helped me feel happy, whole, alive, I opened up even more to the possibility of a good life. I began to think: Something good might just happen today. And if it does, I will recognize it. And if something bad happens, it's not the beginning of an end. It's just a bad thing.

This year I turned forty and I am happy now. Not "I-just-joined-a cult" or "I'm medicated-for-life" happy. Happy at my core. Happy enough to have an occasional funky day and know it will pass. Happy enough to spontaneously sing an ABBA song in public.

So starting with "Nick at Nite," here are a dozen steps that helped me. Even when it felt like the thing I was doing was so small, I took the leap of faith that doing something was better than doing nothing. Such tiny acts add up if the message behind them is consistent: Take care—take good care—of yourself.

I took my sitcom discovery, **step one**, and used it as needed. Mornings had been the worst part of my day, so I started off with a dose of pure comfort. Instead of waking up and starting that depressing "why go on, life is so pointless" loop that played in my head, I tuned into Andy Griffith, and even Gilligan. One morning someone called, and I said: "I"m sorry, I have to call you back. Ginger thinks she's Maryanne and Maryanne thinks she's Ginger." This was a good sign. My true self, my silly self, was returning.

At the risk of sounding even more shallow, I'll call my Martha Stewart moments the **second step**. Trolling around the tube one rainy Saturday morning, I saw Martha for the first time. In her cool, vaguely superior manner, she was extolling the virtues of various herbs. I thought, rather critically: This woman has nothing better to do than focus on a flavor. Then it hit me: And how much better that is than focusing on a debilitating emotion. Rosemary vs. Despair. Thyme vs. Futility. Tarragon vs. No Self Worth.

I was awestruck. I asked myself—where are my flavorful herbs? Where is my sun-filled kitchen?

Thanks to Martha, I became acutely conscious of my surroundings. I couldn't afford to actually live the Martha Stewart lifestyle, but I did begin to organize and purge with a vengeance, enroute to creating a home that would carry my own stamp. The therapeutic value of purging—**step three**—cannot be overstated. I felt lighter and lighter as I disposed of unwanted items, especially the gifts from exes who were long gone. Who needs sweaters and books and furniture from people you want to forget?

This led to **step four**. I started creating rituals. It arose quite naturally, probably out of some basic human desire for order and meaning. Nothing serious, no sacrifices or piercings involved. But one night on a full moon I went to the beach and built a fire (which is against the law, but I was giddy with purpose and my new-found interest in living happily) and burned things I did not want: love letters and old journals filled with old despair. As I lit the match I realized that I was living more consciously, that I was feeling more powerful.

I must mention another T-word here—that's therapy, not television. I went to therapy as my relationship deteriorated because the pain was intolerable. I could barely afford it, even though I found a woman who had a sliding fee scale. But it was crucial that I talk with someone who could offer some insights that friends could not. Seeing a therapist who said to me, over and over, "Nancy you deserve to be as happy as anyone else," truly helped me. I went for a year and a half, and I started to get it.

Although some days all it would take to send me into a deep gloom was the mention of my ex's name, I came to understand that it really wasn't her, but that she was a trigger, a symbol of a larger, older grief. The therapist helped me understand that. So I would remind myself that the bad feelings would pass, and that the good feelings I also had were just as real as the bad. An amazing shift.

As I chased away bad energy in my life, I replaced it with good—**step five**. I began my day with another little ritual. I lit a candle, and sometimes lit some pinon incense, which is supposed to banish negative energy from your space. Then I read from a book of daily meditations that told me I was okay, imperfections and all. Soon my day started having a real rhythm: Candle, meditation, journal writing, Andy, Aunt Bee, Gilligan, Skipper. It's what I call a balanced life.

Step six was a continuation of my mission to bring good vibes into my life. One day when I was looking for some tax records in the cellar, I found boxes full of my grandmother's stuff. My Memere was the kindest person I had ever known. She thought I was wonderful. I looked at these things that held her essence, and thought, What am I waiting for? These remembrances of her happy spirit need to be in my rooms for me to see.

Now Memere's things are part of my life. The flower-painted garbage can with a foot pedal is under my desk, the TV tray that held Memere's evening meals now holds my articles in progress. The fake fruit that intrigued her grandchildren now intrigues my visitors, and only one has attempted to bite into it. Martha might not approve of this faux fruit and faux flower look, but I never said I was a Martha clone, just an admirer.

Step seven—I recovered some long-lost selves, including my inner athlete and my inner rock star. I bought a basketball and got my hook shot back. When I'm stressed I shoot hoops at the rec area, pretending I am up against the Chicago Bulls, all by myself, with one shot left to take at the buzzer. I always win.

For my fortieth birthday, I bought an electric guitar, something I'd wanted since I was thirteen. Now I'm looking for bandmates, preferably three other forty-something women who know all the words to "Jumpin' Jack Flash," but I'll settle for three boys who'll let me be in their garage band. Yeah, they might call me Mrs. McCallum and it might be weird playing high school dances, but you've got to start somewhere.

As I started feeling better about myself, I flirted with incredible self-indulgence, **step eight**. For example, I got a really short hair cut and loved the attention. Well, it's true some of the attention included questions like, "Are you Sinead O'Connor?" But I felt like I was being noticed. When you are depressed, most of the time you skulk around, preferring to not call attention to your miserable self. I took the temporary narcissism as a good sign. I even subscribed to *Self* magazine. I smelled a perfume ad in there I liked—Calvin Klein's "Be"—and spent $55 for it. I wore it every day even if I was only traveling to my desk to work.

I have come back to center somewhat—the hair is a little longer (now people think I'm George Clooney), and the *Self* subscription has expired. But I'm still spraying that "Be" like it was cheap toilet water, and I've got my eye on some "Obsession" body mist.

For **step nine**, I did something really outrageous. I took a month off: August of 1995, which had a record twenty-eight sunny days. My routine: get up, pack iced tea, apple, and protein bar, bike to beach, sit and look at water, wonder how many shades of blue there are, write a little in my journal, read *Self* magazine, smell perfumes, walk along the water's edge, lie down. Put living expenses on my credit card. Still paying for it. Would do it again if I needed to.

I think this may have been the biggest piece of healing I did. Because at that time I needed to be outside, to breathe, to be still, to think about all I had gone through. It made me feel powerful to buck the culture that told me to hurry up, fax it, e-mail it, or overnight it. It was a major visit with Mother Nature, and she was a lovely hostess, indeed.

On the other end of the spectrum, when I was sad I said, "God, I'm sad," and rented a movie to either laugh or sob my way through the feelings, which was **step ten**. *Uncle Buck* is good for laughs; *The Way We Were* is a five-Kleenex experience. It was much better than sitting and holding the sadness inside for days. I learned sadness could pass through, but it did not have to move in for the weekend.

Along the way I kept a few self-help books bedside, which was **step eleven**. Yes, those pop culture self-help books. Some are effective. My psychology books offered a sane voice when I needed one. They reminded me that I wasn't the only person in the world to feel depressed. Books about re-framing the way I thought were the most helpful, because they showed me how my thinking was askew, how I often automatically leapt to the worst conclusions. Like, when things didn't go my way I figured it was because: a) I was doomed; b) I should never expect much; c) I was possibly insane and didn't know it, although everyone else did.

Step twelve—I started taking my career seriously. Using the principles learned from Martha Stewart, I spruced up my home office with new file cabinets and shelves, and got really organized. It's actually easier to find things when they aren't thrown in old milk crates. I became pickier about the writing assignments I accepted, and decided I would be more valued if I valued myself more. Hey, guess what? It worked. My income has doubled since those miserable days when I did not want to get out of bed. I'm still a few steps away from *Fortune*'s 500, but you never know. A few more spritzes of "Be," one more Mary Tyler Moore marathon, and Nancy Inc. may make that list.

So there it is. Life is good, although I still have stuff to work on. But I have learned not to simply act on my impulses, and to call friends when in doubt. They remind me to move slowly, to look for and to heed red flags.

In so many ways, I know I am better—way better. I know this because in the morning I am eager to slide back the shutters that I once kept tightly closed to keep out the light. Because I get up three hours earlier than I ever did. Because I always feel like writing. Because I will sit and watch a chickadee outside my window and notice the black cap and the white feathers and the black iris of his eye.

I never could have done that before, because I was never that present. I was inside my head, hardly drawing a breath, waiting for the next wave of pain. I am almost thankful now for that last hard relationship because it was the kick I needed to start living.

I am alone at the moment and in no hurry to be in a relationship. If someone comes along, great; I will consider it the frosting on the cake. But cake alone is rich. And the fact is, I don't have a lot of time right now, what with my hook shot, my music career, my writing. And, come 10 PM, "Nick at Nite." It's a little thing, but it makes me smile.

Nancy McCallum is a writer and a teacher who lives in Maine. She collects music from the seventies, verbs, and stones.

The Cellist of Sarajevo
by Paul Sullivan

Among all the musical experiences I've had in recent years, one in particular has changed my life forever. I'm a pianist, and in April, 1994, I was invited by cellist Eugene Friesen to perform with him at the International Cello Festival in Manchester, England, where, every two years, a group of the world's greatest cellists gathers for a week of celebration. It's not a competition, nor simply a string of performances, but a true celebration of the cello, with workshops, master classes, concerts, seminars, recitals, and parties all day and evening for a week. It evokes a tremendous feeling of fellowship and friendliness, as well as inspiring an incredibly high standard of musicianship. The patroness of that year's festival was the Duchess of Kent, and the general tone of the event was a natural, easy blending of royal formality and relaxed camaraderie. By any measure, it was an extraordinary event.

Every evening, the entire group of 600 or so participants gathered in the Royal Conservatory Concert Hall for the day's major concert. We sat in the same seats every night, so that by the end of the week we knew all of our neighbors, and it felt a little bit like the Great Lodge at a scout camp. My seat was on the aisle not twenty feet from center stage, so I had a perfect, unobstructed view of all the proceedings. And what proceedings! Each note that rose from that stage was the polished, burnished work of a master. One after the next, the greatest players in the world came out, took a simple bow and proceeded to astound us with unimaginable lyricism, poetry, precision, and virtuosity.

The opening-night concert consisted of works for unaccompanied cello only. There on the great stage in the magnificent hall sat a single, solitary chair. No pianos, no music stands, no conductor's podium. Just a single, waiting chair. This was to be cello music in its purest, most intense form. Furthermore, the concert was to be performed by several cellists, each playing only one piece, so the atmosphere was supercharged with anticipation, concentration, and focus. If ever a chair could be properly called a hot seat, that chair was it. Yet even with all the intensity and the nervous anticipation, we had no idea just how deeply moving this concert would be.

Yo Yo Ma was one of the performers that night, and the program notes about his piece related an amazing story:

On May 27, 1992, a bakery in Sarajevo—one of the few that still happened to have a supply of flour—was making bread and distributing it to the starving, war-shattered people. At 4 P.M., a long line stretched out into the street. Suddenly, a shell fell directly into the middle of the line, killing 22 people instantly and spattering flesh, blood, bone, and rubble over the entire area. Not far away from the gore of ground zero lived a 37-year-old man, a musician named Vedran Smailovic. Before the war he had been the principal cellist of the Sarajevo Opera—a distinguished and civilized life, no doubt, and one to which he deeply and patiently longed to return. But when he saw the carnage from the massacre outside his window he was pushed past his capacity to absorb and endure any more. Driven by his anguish, he decided to take action, and he resolved to do the thing he could do best. He made music. Public music; daring music; music on a battlefield.

Every day thereafter, at 4 P.M. precisely, Vedran Smailovic put on his full, formal concert attire, took up his cello, and walked out of his apartment into the midst of the battle raging around him. He placed a little camp stool in the middle of the crater that the shell had made, and he played a concert. He played to the abandoned streets, to the smashed trucks and burning buildings, and to the terrified people who hid in the cellars while the bombs dropped and the bullets flew. Day after day, he made his unimaginably courageous stand for human dignity, for all those lost to war, for civilization, for compassion, and for peace. Although the shellings went on unabated, and death and destruction stalked the streets, he was never hurt; he seemed to be protected by a divine shield, even during his darkest hour when his beloved cello was itself destroyed.

The news wires picked up the story of this extraordinary man, sitting in his white tie and tails on a camp stool in the center of a raging hell—playing sweet music to the empty air and deserted streets. An English composer, David Wilde, was so moved by the story that he, too, decided to make music. He wrote a composition for unaccompanied cello, which he entitled simply, "The Cellist of Sarajevo," into which he poured his own feelings of outrage, love, and brotherhood with Vedran Smailovic. And it was this piece that Yo Yo Ma was about to play for us that evening.

Yo Yo came out on stage, bowed to the audience, and sat down quietly on the chair, dressed in his white tie and tails. Quietly, almost imperceptibly, the music began, stealing out into the hushed hall and creating a shadowy, empty universe, ominous with the presence of death, haunting in its echoes. Slowly it built, growing relentlessly into an agonized, screaming, slashing furor, gripping us all, before subsiding at last into a hollow death rattle, and finally back to the silence from which it had begun.

When he had finished, Yo Yo Ma remained bent over his cello. His bow still rested on the strings. No one in the hall moved, not a sound was made for a long, long time. It was as though we had just witnessed that horrifying massacre ourselves. Finally, still in silence, Yo Yo slowly straightened in his chair, looked out across the audience, and stretched out his hand toward us. All eyes followed as he beckoned someone to come to the stage, and an indescribable electric shock swept over us as we realized who it was.

Vedran Smailovic—the cellist of Sarajevo himself, rose from his seat and walked down the aisle as Yo Yo came off the stage and headed up the aisle to meet him. With arms flung wide, they met each other in a passionate embrace just inches from my seat. The drama was unbelievable, as everyone in the hall leaped to his or her feet in a chaotic emotional frenzy: clapping, weeping, shouting, embracing, and cheering. It was deafening, overwhelming, a tidal wave of emotion. And in the center of it all stood these two men, still hugging, both crying freely. Yo Yo Ma, the suave, elegant prince of classical music worldwide, flawless in appearance and performance. And Vedran Smailovic, who had just escaped from Sarajevo, dressed in a stained and tattered leather motorcycle suit with fringe on the arms. His wild long hair and huge moustache framed a face that looked old beyond his years, creased with pain and soaked with so many tears. Through my own tears, I stared at them, wanting to capture and remember every single detail, so that one day I could describe it to my son, and say "I was there!"

Then I thought about the audience—all the jewels, perfume, and sophistication—now utterly meaningless and forgotten. We were all stripped down to our starkest, deepest humanity. What a triumph for all of us! A triumph for dignity and compassion. Beethoven's Ninth Symphony pales next to the emotion in that hall that night. And what a triumph for the cello! Here was a room filled with people whose lives had been largely devoted to that simple and unassuming instrument. Here were the bowmakers, collectors, amateurs, historians, even varnishers, and, of course, the great master players. They came from all over the world to celebrate the cello together for a week. And here, on the very first night, they encountered this man who shook his cello in the face of bombs, death, and ruin, and defied them all. It was the sword of Joan of Arc. It was the mightiest weapon of them all.

A week later I was back in Maine, playing for the residents of the Penobscot Nursing Home, where I've played a concert/sing-along every month for the last five years or so. I sat there that evening in the pale, humming fluorescence of the ceiling lights, playing a piano that, like most of the audience, had seen happier, healthier days. And I couldn't help but compare this concert to the splendors I had witnessed only a week earlier. I was struck, surprisingly enough, not by the enormous contrasts, but rather by the profound similarities. With his music, the cellist of Sarajevo had defied death and despair and celebrated love and life. And here we were, with a chorus of croaking voices and a shopworn piano, doing exactly the same thing. There were no bombs and bullets, to be sure, but there was real pain, and dimming sight, and crushing loneliness, and cherished memories, and all the other trophies and scars that we accumulate in our lives. And still we sang and clapped and listened, like Scouts around a bright campfire on a dark night.

It was then that I realized that music is a gift we all share equally, whether we create it or simply listen to it. It's a gift that can soothe, inspire, and unite us—often when we need it most and expect it least.

Paul Sullivan is a composer and pianist who has played and conducted on Broadway, written scores for the Pilobolus Dance Theater, performed with the Paul Winter Consort, and in his own concerts worldwide. He has released several recordings of his music on his own River Music label.

The Gardening Angels

by Marty Hair

The rundown house on Detroit's Belvidere Street was recently abandoned, its windows smashed. Wind and rain blew unhindered across its sills, leaving the house vulnerable to the worst elements. Neighbors were not surprised when drug traffickers moved in to shoot craps and sell crack cocaine. By day and by night, these illegal entrepreneurs flaunted their status up and down the street.

Next door to the crack house, volunteers planting and tending a community garden watched it happening. Some belong to the Gardening Angels, a group of senior citizens who have been around this neighborhood for a long time. Although the gardeners were usually not hassled, there had been shootings in the past and they worried about the potential for future violence.

By spring, the Gardening Angels, and some of the younger people who work the community garden had had enough, so they resorted to chemical warfare. They dumped two truckloads of fresh horse manure from a suburban hunt club on the garden, and added mounds of oozy, fermenting, odiferous grass clippings to start a massive, stinking compost pile.

"That compost got to fermenting real good, with a couple of rains and a few hot days," says Gerald Hairston, who masterminded the plan. The stench wafted through the windowless crack house. "You'd see some of them come up the walk with their hands over their noses," Hairston says. "I told a couple of them, 'You're dead and you just don't know it. That's you starting to stink.'" The drug traffickers got the message and moved out, and the city tore down the crack house in the fall.

It's the latest triumph for the Gardening Angels, an informal band of senior citizens and younger folks who have sunk deep roots in this patch of Detroit, proud of their stake in a city that once boasted the highest rate of single-family home ownership in the nation. While Detroit's population has dropped from the fifth largest city in the nation in 1950 to 10th largest now, Hairston and his friends are among those who have stayed, determined to help knit their city back together with their community gardens. They find space on vacant lots where abandoned houses have been demolished, getting city permission to use the land, or buying it outright. Though the Gardening Angels work in neighborhoods where up to 45 percent of people live below poverty level, they're digging in, and forging some surprising bonds as they plant, tend, and harvest their crops.

Their name came about when Hairston was working in the community garden that once abutted the crack house. A little girl stopped to examine a stepped wooden composting unit that resembled a staircase, Hairston recalls. "[She] asked, 'Why are you building a stair in the middle of the garden?'" By coincidence, he says, he heard the radio playing the Led Zeppelin song, "Stairway to Heaven."

"You believe in the spiritual value of Christianity and you live by the Ten Commandments," he replied, "then you make the transition that you take the stairway to Heaven." Because of the "stairway," neighborhood kids started calling the workers the Gardening Angels. Perhaps they had heard about the Guardian Angels, a citizens' group that made headlines years ago with a vow to take back the streets. For these Angels, however, many of whom are in their 70s, 80s, and even 90s, and faithful churchgoers, the name carries a more important spiritual connotation.

Affiliated with a local 4-H center, the Gardening Angels started reclaiming vacant lots as gardens in the mid-1980s, aiming to raise nutritious food, demonstrate self-sufficiency, and serve as a model for younger people, who were invited to join the project as volunteers. It has now spread, informally, from the near east side of Detroit across the city, with sixteen official Gardening Angel 4-H members and many other similar gardens around the city, according to Hairston, himself a 4-H volunteer.

One person started planting and others stopped by to find out about it. Then they started planting, too. In the process, people were talking with and learning from each other in ways they hadn't before. The garden became a common ground where people met and shared as equals across generational, geographical, and racial differences.

Not that reclaiming vacant city land for gardens is easy. It takes hard work, constant care, and commitment. But organizers say that message, taught through the garden's cycle of death and renewal, are lessons they want young people to learn from the senior gardeners. By taking responsibility even in the face of threats or failures, they can claim a stake in the future of their neighborhoods.

"The issue comes up in the community gardens—are the bad elements going to come around and ruin the garden, or is somebody going to take the produce, or go through and stomp everything down?" says Detroit community organizer and teacher Jim Stone. "Just as in life, there's always a possibility that that can happen, but it very rarely does."

The gardens are quietly changing the way the neighborhood looks. "This is the kind of thing you look at when you drive through a community that is very poverty-stricken," says Sister Jolene Van Handel of the nearby Nativity of Our Lord Church. "People used to come from the outside and dump trash on the vacant lots. They don't dump their trash any more on those gardens."

Some would look at the community surrounding Sister Jolene's Nativity Church, around the community garden on Belvidere, and not see much chance for renewal. But like an experienced gardener assessing a fallow soil's potential, William Mills has seen what urban gardens can do—how they can have a ripple effect in a community that goes beyond any yield of tomatoes and beans and marigolds.

An extension agent for the Michigan State University Extension office in Wayne County, Mills runs the urban gardening program at the 4-H community center, which he says draws visitors from around the country. They are anxious to see how the Detroit center's programs, staff, and volunteers interact with the neighborhood around its boxy, high-set brick building.

About twenty years ago, Mills started the urban gardening program by digging into nearby vacant lots: "A lot of people laughed at us—'You can't grow anything there.'" But 4-H volunteers hauled away old wood and bricks, concrete, and junk. They tilled the hard clay and dug in leaves, compost, and peat. Finally, the soil was rich enough to support new life, and like a chain letter, gardens began to fan out through the neighborhood.

At one time, there were three houses across the street from Gerald Hairston's childhood home on Belvidere, a few blocks from the 4-H center.

One by one, the houses were abandoned and torn down. About fifteen years ago, Hairston, a certified master gardener, started working with a neighbor to garden those lots, and they soon became a 4-H composting demonstration site.

Last year, two new gardeners began working the community garden's soil. A pair of elementary school-aged boys who live next door soon earned the nickname "the cucumber kids" for their successful crop, which they sold on the sidewalk. Hairston says they started asking him, when there was still snow on the ground, how soon they could start planting.

Mills calls Hairston "the key leader" in taking community gardens from a dream to a reality, in making the link between senior gardeners, community resources, and the young people and school children eager to share that heritage. The official Gardening Angel 4-H group began about eight years ago, Mills says, and in addition to their work in the gardens, members take extension workshops and then teach classes at the center on such topics as canning and food preservation. Hairston estimates as many as 600 people— seniors, young volunteers and school children—helped tend about 150 garden sites last year.

Grace Boggs, who co-founded a youth volunteer program called Detroit Summer, says programs like the Gardening Angels reflect a radical approach to rebuilding cities. Rather than an assistance program based on need, groups like the Gardening Angels depend on the strengths its participants have to contribute.

On the three vacant lots next to Lillian Clark's house on David Street, flowers and vegetables grow in unlikely spots: a cast-off toddler wading pool, an old athletic shoe that belongs to Clark's grandson, a rotting tree trunk. Clark's own garden is on the adjacent lot. Next to that is a Detroit Summer garden, tended by youth volunteers who work in Detroit for a month each year. On the corner is a community garden worked by four neighbors.

In the fifty years since she moved to Detroit from Kentucky, where her parents and seven siblings gardened and raised chickens on an acre of land, Clark has kept a few flowers in the front and back. But the house next door was torn down about eight years ago, leaving an eyesore. "I didn't want a lot like that next door to me," she says. "I just started to grow the flowers and the gardens. And then I bought it." She paid the City of Detroit $250 for the property, which is now her garden and a tumble of vegetation—Seventy-five rose bushes, perennials, annuals, and vegetables. She put up seventy-five quarts of beans last summer. Like other Gardening Angels, what Clark doesn't use she shares between friends and local groups, like churches and soup kitchens.

Many days, Lillian Clark is outside working in her garden from just after dawn until twilight begins to veil the rows in shadow. She is out there so much that her granddaughter gave her a portable phone.

At Howe Elementary School, not far from the 4-H Urban Center on McClellan, Maxine Williams teaches students about computers. She also teaches them about gardening. Last year, she and other teachers started a Kwanzaa garden across from the school to improve an abandoned lot and "make it something the community could have pride in and the children could identify with." Kwanzaa, the winter holiday honoring African-American heritage and culture, focuses on principles like self-determination for survival and success.

In the vacant lot, the soil was so poor that Williams decided to make the garden in raised beds edged with old tires. It went over so well that, this year, Howe Elementary students are cultivating the whole lot and have a long-range plan that may involve raising ingredients for making and selling their own barbecue sauce.

Already, students are studying marketing, and learning the math and science they would need to tackle such a project. The students are intrigued, Williams says: "A lot of my kids...think greens come from the grocery store. They have no concept that this came from the soil and that you have to take care of the soil for it to take care of you."

Gardening Angels and 4-H volunteers are helping show how to do that, and other seniors are coming forward, too. One of Williams's students was coming to the garden every day after school. After several weeks, her grandfather, who also lives in the neighborhood, stopped by. That day, the gardening project was composting. "He got to talking about his garden and ended saying, 'I'll show you how to do it,'" Williams says. Since then, he has returned to the garden many times to work and give assistance.

"For us, there is black history here," Williams says. "For us, it's a way of learning about our past. And these seniors are the past. The kids love it. They appreciate each other."

A slender man with a salt-and-pepper beard, Gerald Hairston's articulate voice is so smooth it might be on the radio. In fact, Hairston, forty-nine, once hosted a morning show, reading newspapers aloud for the Detroit

Reading Information Service, a closed-circuit radio broadcast for the blind.

Volunteer activities seem his life fuel, and many of them involve garden-ing. He is currently trying to convince his Detroit Eastern High School alumni group to create a tribute garden and neighborhood focal point on the site of the school, which has been torn down.

Hairston says he has little money, no car, and not much interest in mate-rial goods. He lives with his elderly uncle. Hairston learned about planting rituals and prayers from his grandmother, who was part Native American, and because of her teachings gravitated toward gardening, his skills sharp-ened by a neighbor who was a horticulturist. Hairston says the garden teaches that there is only one race—the human race—and that all people are equally dependent on the earth.

Hairston has had a local landscaping business, worked at a family-owned lounge, been a chauffeur, and a house painter. He has also become so involved in the Gardening Angels and community work that its people are now like his extended family, providing strength through his life's rough times, of which there have been several.

When he suffered an aneurysm a few years ago, Hairston says he woke up in his hospital bed to find it surrounded by Gardening Angels, to whom he is a relatively young man. Queva Anderson, who had had a stroke several months earlier, joked that if he didn't get out of bed soon, "She'd take a walk-ing stick and get me going," he says.

Hairston has also spent time as a patient at the Detroit Psychiatric Institute. He says a doctor called him delusional when he described his wide range of volunteer activities, including his radio show. "I said, 'if you think I'm crazy for doing this, that's your problem.'" And in a way, he had the last word: Before Hairston was discharged, he organized fellow psychiatric patients to start their own garden on the hospital grounds.

Another hard period originated with a 1991 incident, a dispute between Hairston and another man over equipment. Hairston was charged with and convicted of larceny, although he was acquitted of armed robbery and using a gun to commit a felony. Before his sentencing, the Gardening Angels and others who knew Hairston took up his cause, vowing to do what they could to prevent him from serving prison time.

"The whole community group wrote to the judge to say this [was] not a violent criminal who needed to be locked up, but rather someone who deserved to be out there," says Sister Jolene of Nativity Church. The judge gave Hairston two years' probation—"Community service"—Hairston says with a droll smile that acknowledges the situation's irony.

Those who know him say one of Hairston's talents is finding ways to get things accomplished. He knows many people, and he channels donated mowers and tillers and hoes to the right ends. When lawns in the neighborhood needed mowing, he figured out how to set up a program using probationers once a week. Of what drives his near-constant whirl of volunteerism, Hairston says, "I work with these seniors and my batteries get recharged."

Walking into the senior lunch program in the basement of Bethel Baptist Church East, one Wednesday in February, it was easy to see that the Gardening Angels consider Gerald Hairston a battery charger himself. Faces light up when they see him.

The Gardening Angel effort is bringing unity and renewal to this neighborhood. One benefit, notes William Mills, is that seniors and young people feel safer and more at home when they know each other's names. "Gardens also brought people together, people who didn't always necessarily have a reason to go over and talk to each other," he says.

And this spring, there will be some new gardens in the neighborhood. One will be where the Reverend Mack Benton's house stood before it was fire-bombed on Devil's Night in 1994. Reverend Benton, seventy-seven, escaped without injury. Although he now lives elsewhere, he still has strong ties to his home of thirty years. He continues to own the property, along with two adjoining lots. The house has already been leveled, and he says Gerald Hairston has volunteered to help him plow the soil.

Another new garden is planned for a vacant lot across from Hairston's home on Belvidere, and it's a particularly noteworthy site: That's where the smell of composting and the strength of people working together on a garden was powerful enough to run out a crack house.

Marty Hair is the gardens and gardening writer for the Detroit Free Press.

Our Newest Old Friends
by Johanna Garfield

Last winter, after a brief but wrenching hiatus in our lives together, my husband and I spent a snowy weekend in the country with two of our three unmarried adult kids: Meg, thirty-two, and Jim, thirty-one. (The third lives in Colorado.) Just the four of us at the "farm," an isolated house in Massachusetts the kids've been visiting since before they were born. And though God knows we've had our share of *sturm* and *drang* as a family, I enjoyed those two days more than I would a weekend with even our closest and most entertaining friends, people who play bridge, share our preference for Handel over Hootie and the Blowfish, and even more importantly, have negotiated the obstacle course of parenthood with us.

We've gone to the farm with the kids many times before, of course, though almost always with other company—of ours, or theirs, or both. But it wasn't only our being alone together that made the weekend feel different. There was a sense of reunion this time, and the period apart seemed to have heightened my awareness of alterations in them, in us, and in how we were interacting. Had we all undergone a sea change during the hiatus? Or—and this explanation seems more likely—had the changes been happening all along?

I kept thinking of a phrase (later a book title) that's haunted me for years, "Look, We've Come Through." And it occurs to me that while we may not yet have come all the way through as a family, we're getting there. Yet, until we were forced to take a detour, I had been too busy negotiating our particular obstacle course to notice that the road was smoothing out. But what a road it has been! Probably no more filled with pitfalls and hurdles than anyone else's, but it certainly seemed so at the time. To begin with, I had all three kids in less than three years. We married late, and I wasn't sure I could conceive. Ha!

Meg, our oldest, has always been extraordinarily bright, but high-strung and super-sensitive from birth. As a baby, she had an allergy to wheat products that meant monitoring her diet carefully, and when she was only four months old she had to wear shoes with a metal bar connecting them at night to keep her feet from turning in. In those days, that was the approved method for correcting the problem, but to me the contraption resembled an instrument of torture. For some strange reason, though she often cried inexplicably during the day, Meg never seemed to mind the bar at night. But I did. It hurt me every time I put it on and twisted the screws.

Jim had to see a specialist two or three times a week for years to correct an eye problem that brought his early reading and writing to a halt until it was finally resolved. It didn't do much for his social life either, since we spent the afternoons of his childhood driving to various eye specialists while his cohorts were playing with their buddies.

And sibling rivalry takes on a whole new meaning when applied to two brothers just a year apart in age, especially when the younger is slimmer, far more athletic, and better coordinated. Though his brother could ride a two-wheeler by the time he was three, Jim, to his intense mortification, still couldn't at six. The eye problem may have had something to do with it, but that was no consolation for Jim. He and I spent months on a secluded path in the park practicing until he caught on. (And for the first time, I had muscle definition in my arms.)

As I said, I don't doubt for a minute that other parents have the same or worse problems when the kids are small. But these bore our own unique coat of arms, one I see as three lion cubs on a field of red with a fire-breathing dragon on either side.

It was the fights between the boys that brought out the worst in both of us. I am convinced that the adult ear is not designed to tolerate the decibel levels of two or more young children screaming at each other as they roll around on the ground beating each other up. And, to my shame, I have to admit that there were times, when we couldn't get them to stop, that we were reduced to being children ourselves and took a swipe at them. Anything for peace, one foolishly thinks at the time.

"Little children, little problems; big children, big problems." The aphorism must apply more to adolescents than to what comes later. During those teen years, Meg's childhood angst became a maddening alienation and withdrawal. As Joseph Heller's middle-aged protagonist in *Something Happened* said of his teenage daughter, "Her obdurate refusal to be happy drove me crazy." My own running joke to friends: "We have a love-hate relationship. I love her; she hates me."

Jim lost his baby fat by his teens, and could soon rival his brother in sports. However, though seemingly born with a smile on his face, and well-liked, by then he, too, acted out during those years, only more gregariously. A city kid, he preferred nightclubs to homework.

Don't get me wrong. The crises didn't all arise from their side. Having three children in three years is not exactly a recipe for marital bliss, and although my husband, Michael, and I both love our children dearly, we were not great parents together. We disagreed frequently and loudly in front of them on matters of behavior and discipline, though we knew—or at least had read—that a united front was important. Michael thought I was too forgiving and permissive; I was convinced he was too harsh and critical.

In fact, both were true. I couldn't get over feeling guilty towards all three of them, especially Meg, for having had them so close in age. Poor babies, I thought, they never had enough time alone with us. Alone at all, in fact. So I overcompensated by rarely saying "No." I thought—as most such misguided, well-meaning parents do—that giving them their way would make up for the emotional deprivation I was sure my fragmented attention must be causing them. I'd smile bitterly when some of the same people who thought it wonderful that my children would "always have someone to play with" also told me it was "so nice you got it all over with at once," as though having children were some kind of infectious disease, to be endured for as short a time as possible. How I envied those parents the precious hours and years they'd been able to give each well-spaced child, and envied for my own kids the privileged status big sister, older boy, or baby brother bestowed in such families. Most of all, I saw the special attention "only children" received. And so, to compensate, I tried to raise three "only children" myself—an impossible task, I see now.

What they really needed—yearned for, in fact, whether they knew it or not, were reasonable limits. (This was borne out for me a few years back when my youngest said, accusingly, "Mom, how could I ever learn to cope? You always tried to make everything perfect.") Not, however, the unreasonable limits Michael often imposed to balance what he saw as my overindulgence. "Do that one more time and you're not leaving this house for three weeks!" he'd rage at them, for offenses ranging from the serious (playing with matches when they were younger; staying at a friend's house without letting us know when they were older), to the relatively trivial (failure to hang up their clothes when they entered the house; failure to make their beds).

I knew he wouldn't follow through, and so did they. The logistics of school, music lessons, football practice, and my own unwillingness to stand guard, especially when I disagreed with the penalty, made such edicts impossible to carry out even if he—or very rarely, we—had been able to maintain the initial level of outrage. And knowing this would happen, I frequently raised the ante after these outbursts by immediately interjecting, "You know you don't mean that." Which only made Michael angrier. Needless to say, the kids learned early on to turn this dissension to their temporary advantage.

It was after one such quarrel twenty years ago that Michael—who'd had too much to drink, as he often did in those days—stormed out of the summer house we'd rented in Saltaire on Fire Island, New York, threatening divorce. He took the ferry home, only to return, chastened, the next morning. (We all met him at the dock.) More recently, far more unexpectedly, and much more disruptively, I decided I was in love with another man and moved out of our house for six months.

During that period, our family configuration changed. My husband, once the ogre of their growing-up years for his inconsistencies, his drinking, his occasional verbal abuse ("Mom, how can you stay married to him?" they'd ask with disgust—and I often wondered myself) became the major, and favored, parent. All three children, in their late twenties at the time, were protective, and fiercely loyal to their father—the two nearby having lunch or dinner with him several times a week, and all of them calling him often on the phone. They were willing to see me (though far less often than they saw Michael), but never to meet with "him." Though it would have suited my interests mightily for them to have been more flexible, I secretly admired their unbending attitude.

But things had begun to change even before this. Frightened at where the ever-increasing nightly martinis were leading, and the damage they were doing to his relationships with us and others, Michael entered therapy a few years after the Fire Island scene and gave up alcohol cold. He began to think twice before issuing ultimatums and making scathing judgments. He took up cooking and became the chef in the family. And though he'd threatened to leave for good that night at Saltaire so long ago, and on several other occasions, he never did.

I, on the other hand, always the steadfast one until then, was taking flight, a decision that would have made a lot more sense to the children many years before. Not that they didn't understand, on an adult, intellectual level, when I tried to explain what I really didn't entirely understand myself. But the fact is, they were profoundly shocked, both by my frank revelations and what they saw as my desertion. I could see that there were ways in which they were still "kids," in spite of their years and sophistication. "They're grown up now. They have their own lives. What difference does it make?" the other man had assured me, when I'd worried about the effect of their finding out, or breaking up the family. But now I could see it wasn't so, that it *did* make a difference.

As I suppose I should have known, the Great Romance couldn't take the wear and tear of everyday life, or more importantly, the strain of my divided loyalties to Michael and the children, and my undeniable sense of loss. I remember, once, sitting on the porch of the other man's house with his adult children, and his sister and her family, and feeling completely disoriented. "What am I doing here?" I wondered. "These aren't my children. This isn't my family. This isn't my life." And every time he tried to criticize Michael, I'd leap to Michael's defense and infuriate him.

The final straw was learning that, in my absence, the kids were planning a surprise birthday party for their father. I knew that if I'd been around they'd probably have left it up to me, and I felt elated at their seizing of responsibility—and at the same time excluded and useless. But now that the party was in the works, it seemed impossible that I not be there. What, Michael have a birthday without me? After thirty years of marriage? It just couldn't be. There was a quarrel with the other man and an ultimatum. He stalked out of the small apartment I'd rented (we never actually lived together) and I went to the party.

Though I'd obtained the kids' worried consent to be there, to everyone else, especially Michael, I was the biggest surprise of all. He seemed, in fact, to be at least as baffled as he was shocked by my presence. And as for me, it felt a little surreal being the unexpected guest at a party in my own home. But it also felt right. This was my family. This was my life. I knew that if Michael could accept me, I would soon be home to stay.

It seemed he could. Over the next few months, we used the tried-and-true method we'd always used for dealing with our problems in the past, which was the exact opposite of what the psychologists and marriage manuals recommend. We didn't talk it out. As Anne Bernays once wrote in a "Hers" article for *The New York Times* about her long-term marriage, "Somehow, when the crises arose, we just closed our eyes and kept going until we came out the other end," or words to that effect, and essentially, that's what we did. I just hung in there, and gradually, by my coming around night after night, and then beginning to do the things we'd done before, like using our concert subscription tickets, or visiting friends, we began to put our lives together again. Literally. Because four months later I moved back home—though I kept the apartment I'd rented, to use as an office. I'd found that Virginia Woolf had it right about a room of one's own.

Of course, the birthday party marked the real end of the affair. And by that time I was glad. I'd miss the clandestine excitement that fuels any such illicit liaison, and yes, some of the genuine romance, but the price was too high. I was worn out from a relationship that had become more exhausting than satisfying. I'd never realized how much one takes for granted in a marriage; the thousands of accommodations couples make; the things in common—until they weren't there. I'd never realized how much easier it made our lives that Michael and I were equally indifferent to whether the Mets won or lost; how smoothly we went about the ordinary business of clearing the table and putting away food (me); loading and emptying the dishwasher (him). And of course, there was the thing we had most in common; the thing that together we found a source of never-ending interest and conversation: our kids.

Still, however welcome my return, I'm not sure the children will ever completely trust me again. Perhaps not even as much as Michael, whose wary faith in me has grown stronger with every day that our lives resume their familiar—yet now delightfully unfamiliar—routines. But for Meg and Jim, there's been a permanent shift, no doubt about it. Often, they'll call Michael first with news of their jobs, or dates, or even their problems, a habit they developed during the separation. And though I've moved back in with him, Meg often calls our home "Dad's house"—ostensibly to distinguish it from my office and former apartment, but I tend to read more into it than that.

Surprisingly, it wasn't as hard as I thought it would be to yield my position as the reliable parent, or at least to share it. And because their father had changed so much, it was kind of a relief not to have to protect them all the time. Maybe I hadn't realized how tired I'd grown of being a tower of strength; always on red alert. I suddenly saw that I could relax a little.

They've changed, too, though I daresay the changes in them took longer than they might have if I hadn't been so fearful of doing harm, when in fact I was doing harm by doing nothing. Therapy has helped—we've all had some, from time to time—and if indeed I tried to make their lives "too perfect" when they were children, Real Life, in the form of the school of hard knocks, has managed to teach them some lessons as adults that I wasn't able to. As the song says, "I don't remember growing older; when did they?"

As I watched my grown children during those two days at the farm, I wondered, when did they start volunteering to cook or do the dishes? In fact, when did they become cooks at all, who can far outdo their father or me? (Which isn't saying much, in my case.)

In a startling reversal, they fixed our ritual weekend breakfast of Nova and bagels imported from the city for us, and did it right. The coffee was perfect, the bagels toasted, the onions cut fine.

And when did that request to let us know what was left, or needed, find its mark? Meg had provided us with a list of supplies and food she'd left on a weekend a few weeks back. It's still unlikely we'll ever get through the duplicate spices, jams, mustards, and canned goods that crowd the cabinets from the years before she and Jim caught on.

They tolerated "Don Giovanni" on the radio Saturday afternoon, when only a few years ago they'd groan and demand equal listening time on one of "their" stations, or storm out of the room. During the intermission, they laughed with us at the opera quiz contestants, who we agreed sounded uniformly smug and supercilious.

We all read omnivorously (we have no TV at the farm—a joint decision) and went cross-country skiing. Instead of trying to put as much distance between us as possible, my son checked regularly to be sure his aging ma was okay. She was—barely.

And to my amazement, before we all left they emptied the wastebaskets, made their beds without being nagged, and got wood from the basement so the fire would be ready for the next time.

Lest the picture look too rosy, let me paint in some darker tones: Both in the country and the city, they still find things Michael and I do or say annoying, or even infuriating, as only one's children can. But now, our failings have taken on a certain charm for them—identifiable markers of our intense familiarity with each other's strengths and weaknesses. They laugh at Michael's ineptitude with today's technology ("Dad still can't turn on the TV with the remote," I hear them telling their friends in cool, superior tones), at his squeamishness at the sight of blood, at my indecision in restaurants ("Okay, Mom, what's your first order going to be?"). Meg still can't resist taking potshots at me from time to time. ("Mom, you really don't have to explain that it's you on your answering machine. Who else would it be?")

And sometimes the sniping isn't so good-natured. They learned their early lessons in caustic cracks well. But even the hardball family jibes have the strange allure of the very familiar. Not exactly Jung's collective unconscious, perhaps, but something a little like it. Indeed, it's just because of the bittersweet memories of who they were that I found the differences in them that weekend so astonishing, their company so fascinating. For, after all, who else shares the intense intimacy of the thirty-plus years we have known each other? Not our contemporaries, close as we may feel to them. Not the children's future mates, interested as they may be in the old photo albums or the family stories.

Who else shares our memories of Pearly, the capricious cat whose newborn kittens disappeared overnight from their box in the cellar? Our horror at the thought she might have eaten them (a grisly possibility suggested by *Cat Behavior*)? Our relief when Michael found them in the back of a closet in the attic? Who else remembers Meg's long-planned seventh birthday party at a swimming pool that turned out to be closed for repairs that day? Who else would agree to the special rules we've evolved over the years to make our fiercely competitive Scrabble games even more so? (One of them: You can consult the Scrabble dictionary before your turn.)

Occasionally now, when I read articles on appropriate developmental "passages," I wonder if such a close relationship with a single adult child isn't an unhealthy means of prolonging his or her childhood. Apparently the thought has crossed Jim's mind, too. Just back from our cross-country trek, he suddenly said, "Sometimes I think I see too much of you guys."

But compared to what? I mused, as we shared Michael's split-pea-and-ham soup. For centuries, kids lived with or near their parents until they were married; sometimes, even after. Only today is such a relationship regarded with misgivings, as one that "fosters dependence," or is some sort of indication that the young person doesn't have enough friends of his own.

It's not the case with us. Meg and Jim have their own apartments in the city; they have their jobs and their friends. Our weekends with just the two of them are now rare and serendipitous. My adult children (a strangely accurate oxymoron) are not yet involved in the trials—and joys—of establishing their own families. And during this phase, despite all that's gone before, or maybe because of it, they've become our newest old friends, another contradiction in terms that's nonetheless true. It goes beyond the charm of their company which can be, but isn't always, considerable. Their charm for us, in fact, isn't "charm" as in "charming" at all. It lies in observing the thousand ways in which they're like us; and the thousand ways in which they're not. And I find their pleasure at the prospect of spending time in the country with each other and us—and actually doing it—more flattering than a million "I love yous."

"Just when they get interesting, they leave home." I've been hearing that for years. The message is clear. Just when the payoff for the years of changing diapers, wiping noses, and tolerating teenage rebellion should arrive, the kids duck out.

There's still some truth in that. But nowadays, though some do follow the old timetable, many, like mine, are marrying late and having children even later. Out of the house, yes, but by no means out of our lives. And during this period of stasis, made even more precious by my knowledge of how close we came to disaster, I can raise my head, look back at the obstacles we've hurdled and see that yes, after all, we've come through. At least for now.

Johanna Garfield's articles have appeared in The New York Times, Reader's Digest, *and other publications. She is also the author of two books,* The Life of a Real Girl: A True Story, *and* Cousins.

Mamma's Boy
by Peter D. Baird

So many people are coming out of closets, these days, that I suppose it's my turn for a public unburdening. Here it is: now in my mid-fifties, I'm becoming a mamma's boy.

Mind you, I didn't say "mom" or "mother," and I didn't say "son" or "only child," either. No, I said "mamma" and "boy" and I don't care anymore how pantywaisted those two words may sound. Indeed, if Alzheimer's had left my eighty-seven-year-old father with anything more than volcanic rages and a surprisingly dangerous right cross, I would tell him that his taunts from the 1950s have come true, that I'm not a man's man anymore, and, best of all, that I have never felt better in my life.

To put my uncloseted confession into perspective, I'm not a wet-nursed, limp-wristed milquetoast, but a weathered trial lawyer who has fought through uncounted court cases and, in other contexts, has battled for money as a provider, for grades as a student, and for victory as an athlete and coach. At this stage of life, being a mamma's boy means that, for the first time since my mother died more than thirty-seven years ago, I'm finally listening to her, taking seriously what she said, and changing.

If my memory is accurate, I probably stopped paying attention to her advice at about the time I first used the word, "mom," back in 1957. For the previous sixteen years, she had been "mamma"—an organically textured word with a strong, earthy resonance but one which, when enunciated slowly with both syllables flattened out, sounds like the plaintive cry from an unhappy baby. Because of that infantile association, I drew "babycakes" snickers from my teenaged friends and "you're-a-sissy" looks from my oversized father, no matter how adult or clipped my pronunciation of "mamma" was.

Faced with that combination of peer and paternal pressure, I dropped "mamma" and adopted "mom"—a tight-sounding word which, at least back then, lacked the loamy feel of "mamma," and which often carried with it a sense of tidy aloofness and perfect respectability. Quite apart from my friends' noises and my father's frowns, Rick and Dave Nelson didn't call Harriet "mamma" on "Ozzie and Harriet," and Margaret Anderson was always "mom" to Kathy, Bud, and Betty on "Father Knows Best." Besides, my mother baked pies, wore aprons, kept house, and, as was expected in those days, gritted her way through my father's demanding medical practice, episodes of boozy violence, and sporadic indiscretions with a neighbor.

Yet, the momly mold did not fit. She had too many demonstrative, risk-taking characteristics for that designation; too few suburban orthodoxies for the neighbors; no opinionless dittos for her husband; and precious few fawnings for her son. With energy that seemed at times almost radioactive, she was an amateur magician who was not too proud to give rinky-dink magic shows for little kids; a social worker who served outcasts in a Chicago settlement house and an Illinois women's prison; an odds-minded gambler who, after each visit to Las Vegas, lugged away small, cloth flour bags of silver dollars; a dreamer who loved to watch cloud formations, listen to Verdi, and fish for trout; a cancer patient who broke medical conventions of the day by visualizing good cells killing bad ones, and who exceeded medical predictions by living an extra three years; and an inveterate writer who, in long-hand, constantly sent letters to her friends, me, and herself, and who even won a literary prize for a travelogue about Uruguay—a country she had never visited. More than anything else, though, she was a teacher who could have enriched more than three decades of my life had she stayed a mamma, and had I only remembered.

To my embarrassment, I tuned her out for the same reason that I changed her name from "mamma" to "mom"—cowardice. It sounds like a contradiction, but I became a seemingly tough, ferociously competitive man, not out of confidence or out of courage, but out of fear. During my adolescent years, I lived in gutless dread of what my six-foot-two-inch, two-hundred-fifty-pound, combat-veteran father might do with his limitless anger if I crossed him, or if I didn't do what he demanded.

Consequently, while "mom" battled her way through cancer surgeries and radiation therapies, my father bombarded me with edicts that I did not have the strength, Oedipal or otherwise, to resist. Day in and day out, he pounded me with time-tested orders that had been passed down from his father and from his father's father, such as "never need an eraser; do it right the first time;" "don't be a puff;" "win;" "use your head;" "don't cry;" "never quit;" "hit first;" "work like hell;" "never back off;" "fight to the finish;" and the all-purpose, "be a man."

To be fair, those hard-nosed doctrines probably got me through my mother's funeral without shedding a tear, and they may even have goaded me into some academic, athletic, and professional successes that, today, look impressive on my resume. But his tough talk did not help me preserve a twenty-seven-year marriage, reduce high blood pressure, understand children, be patient, find peace, sleep without nightmares, give love, or live without destructive compulsions and crippling inhibitions. And they were no damn good during twenty years of chronic depression, five psychiatrists, and thousands of lithium, Prozac, Paxil, and Zoloft pills.

As if recorded on a tape deck surgically implanted in my brain, my father's fierce commands played on for years, drowning out other voices, blocking out other values, and slowly turning a specific fear of father into a general fear of failure and then into a relentless perfectionism in which enough was never enough, and "the most" was not enough, either. Not until the depression had lifted could I think of my mother as someone real, hear her voice again, and make her in memory what she had once been in life—human, wise, and accessible.

Her insights may not have been original with her, but that doesn't matter. What counts is that, for the first time since 1957, I'm listening, learning, and feeling better.

She'd say, "close your eyes and you'll be invisible." Although I had watched mamma close her eyes and act invisible when my father had chased too many jiggers of bourbon with too many bottles of beer, I usually laughed those words off as the remnant of "the disappearing boy" trick she had taught me when I was three or four years old, and I actually believed that my body vanished if my eyes were shut. What I didn't understand back then was that, when one's eyes are closed, personal essence does disappear from sight and, invisibly, it can go anywhere and do anything, and that those unfettered flights can lead to unseen truths, emotional peace, and even physical health. These days, I close my eyes a lot.

From my father came, "use your head." From mamma came, "think through your skin." Taking my cues from him, I used my head all the time, toiling away on academics, ignoring instinct, treating athletics more as a mind game than as physical fun, and living life as if it were a giant SAT examination. In the long run, though, the only person I outsmarted was myself because, as I've learned the hard way, real wisdom does not march out in formation from above the neck on command; rather, it ferments down deep in the body's juices, it sloshes around without the conscious mind even being engaged, and then it seeps out through the skin at unpredictable rates and times. It's called "feeling," or, more currently, "emotional intelligence."

"Believe in magic," mamma said. Since she was an amateur magician, I misunderstood her and thought what she wanted was for me to do magic tricks. Consequently, I practiced sleight-of-hand moves like "French drops," "Hindu shuffles," "Elmsley counts," "passes," "forces," and sideslips," and gave my own rinky-dink magic shows for kids in the neighborhood. But I didn't get it. For mamma, magic was not just the secret of a theatrical illusion; it was a life-enhancing metaphor that can propel us beyond the conventional and into the transcendent. These days, I am open to almost anything.

When my father barked, "BE A MAN!" she would amend his order with, "Be a man, but stay a boy." At long last, I know what she meant. If necessary, I still slug it out, work around-the-clock, and fight to the finish for clients, principles, and those I love. But today, my battles have limits—beginnings, endings, times, and places. No longer does everything involve winning, getting ahead, proving something, or making money. Besides the man stuff, I now do the boy stuff, like count clouds; raise dogs; skip stones; feed hummingbirds; watch trains; go fishing; give my own rinky-dink magic shows; and close my eyes to be invisible.

Yet, mamma's wisdom didn't just pop back into my head unbidden. Far from it. She had been buried within me for so long as the picture-perfect, 1950's "mom," that I had forgotten what she had *really* been like and what she had tried to teach me. Worse still, I had lost the ability to look inside myself for her or, sadly, for anything else. After decades of following my father's dictates, taking on my clients' causes, adopting my wife's values, and trying to put my children's interests ahead of my own, I had become a man who lived life from the outside in and whose soul was little more than silly putty. No wonder I was depressed.

Finally, in the occluding darkness of my late forties and early fifties, a physician opened my eyes to who I had become, and medication lifted the toxic fog of depression. At the same time, I started to do what mamma herself had done, and began writing, not to recount what was external and remembered, but to explore what was internal and forgotten.

Without using a computer or a typewriter, and without worrying about punctuation, syntax, spelling, grammar, organization, accuracy, or even conscious thinking, I mined my subconscious and wrote whatever came out of my pen and onto the paper. Eventually, after years of scribbling and publishing, my mother came back to me, not as the picture-perfect 1950's "mom" but as the humanly flawed yet insightfully gifted woman she had been. The realities were that she hadn't been ideal; she had been, like me, depressed; she had been in a bad marriage she had helped make that way; she had made mistakes just like my father and everybody else; and she had struggled with life's inflictions and exhilarations.

For more than forty years, I had hidden her memory beneath layers of fiction, idealization, and depression. When once again made real, she could still teach. When once again made whole, I could still learn. And what I've learned is that I may be my father's son, but I'm still my mamma's boy.

Peter Baird has written for various publications, including Newsweek, The New York Times Magazine, The Wall Street Journal, American Heritage, Men's Health, *and* The Chicago Tribune Magazine.

The Strangest Faith
by Edie Clark

On some days it feels as if every time I pick up the paper, there's a story about a woman being beaten or stalked or killed by the man with whom she shares a home. Not long ago, I saw a news report about the capture of Glen Rogers, a rough, bearded drifter with haunted blue eyes and blonde hair long enough to pull into a ponytail. A television news show offered an adjunct interview with a beautifully dressed black-eyed Hungarian woman. With her shiny black hair and sparkling jewelry she could have been advertising cosmetics. Instead, she was weeping at the sight of the arrest of this man who authorities believe had murdered five women on what they called a "cross-country killing spree." This woman claimed she had shared a home with this man for two years. She wept and said she only wanted him back, did not believe that he had done these deeds. Yes, she said, he had been violent with her. Yes, he had served time in jail for supposedly torching the apartment that they shared. But she never believed that he had done that. She didn't believe he was a serial killer. He was so loving, she said.

I watched, silently, as did, I imagine, many other women who have experienced abuse from the person who claims, simultaneously, to love them. Her words sounded absurd. Why wasn't she relieved that he had been captured, that he would be put away, that he would never again hurt her or any other woman? How can someone want such a man back, a man who has injured her? Ridiculous. And yet, as ridiculous as it sounded, as ridiculous as it looked, just seeing these two human beings on the same screen, I knew what she was talking about. It may be the ultimate paradox of human emotion, the twisted impulse to reach out to the one who has harmed you.

It was the winter of 1973, the first full winter that we spent in New Hampshire. Tired of crime, tired of street filth, tired of no place to park the car, Jim (not his real name) and I had moved up from the city the year before. It was impulsive. We were not even married. I was from New Jersey, Jim was from New York, and we had left good jobs and come north to a place we knew nothing about. We thought of it as the great adventure. We had worked, for a few years, in book publishing—good jobs, good futures. We had tasted of it and it repelled us. We had read about the "good life," the simple life of Thoreau and the Nearings, and we were groping our way in that direction. Our families were angry with us for "throwing away our futures." We were young, just a few years out of college, but they had expectations for all the money they had spent on our college degrees.

Jim found work, nothing like his job in the city, but work nonetheless— a desk job at a book manufacturer. I was less fortunate. In the summer I picked asparagus and planted strawberries at a produce farm. And there was a temporary job, proofreading at a printing plant. On the weeks when they called me, I brought home $75 a week. But there were lots of weeks when they didn't call.

We heard about an old farmhouse for rent, cheap. It was on top of a hill and the view went for miles. The only houses within sight were off in the distance, down in the valley. Maple trees lined the road, and a barn with timbers the size of men was set into the bank across from the house. To us, it looked like paradise. The owner was unwilling to rent it to us unless we were married, so we married in a simple ceremony in the middle of a field dotted with Queen Anne's Lace. Our parents came and, skeptically, gave us their blessings. We regarded the whole ritual as a societal encumbrance, not unlike paying taxes or registering a car, something you try to avoid but eventually have to do. We didn't feel that being married to each other affected, in any substantial way, the lives we'd already begun to create.

Like a seductive lover, that house fooled us. The winter air came in through cracks we couldn't believe were there. We tucked blankets under the doorsills and taped plastic to the insides of the windows. We bought two woodstoves and plugged one into the kitchen chimney and the other into the living room, and over the winter, we pushed ten cords of wood through those two stoves. We cut the wood with hand saws. Neither of us had ever lived like this before. We lit the old parlor with kerosene lanterns at night and cooked our meals in cast-iron skillets on the top of the woodstove. Even inside the house, we wore layers of thermal underwear and woolen sweaters, and heavy boots with thick socks. We talked about buying a piece of land and building our own house. The house would be insulated and warm and would use very little electricity. We devised schemes to save money. In our second winter we ate mostly turnips and potatoes we'd grown, and the meat of the chickens we raised. I baked bread and Jim took it to work and sold it from his desk, seventy-five cents a loaf. We saved every penny we could and spent little. We dreamed of being warm.

I am telling you all of this because it was during this time that Jim beat me. I was twenty-four years old. Jim was thirty. I think back on this now and it's like a cut in a beautiful piece of cloth. A slash.

The first time it happened, I was stunned and confused. I can't even remember what precipitated it. I have thought and thought about it but I can only remember his rage, how he grabbed me and threw me against the pumpkin pine paneling of that farmhouse kitchen wall and then took both his hands and closed them around my throat, smashing my head against the wall, over and over again. I don't remember how it ended. I only remember aching for days, and feeling trapped. I had given up a decent job in the city, left my friends, and come north to a little town where the only people we knew were each other. In doing this, I had alienated my parents. And, of course, the first time that Jim beat me was not the last.

This was a time when the issue of domestic violence was rarely in the news. In New England, in the early 1970's there were no such things as women's shelters. I had never heard the terms we use now—abuse, abuser, batterer, victim—in that context. And all the deep psychological insights we carry with us now—that batterers abuse because they were once abused, that abuse victims will do almost anything to protect their abusers, that abuse is all about power and control—none of this wisdom had surfaced, at least not to any surface I knew.

In fact, I had never heard of domestic violence. It wasn't anything I ever saw in my house, growing up. The first time I'd ever encountered it was in an apartment in Philadelphia where I lived briefly, right after college. Early one summer evening, I heard heart-stopping screams, the screams of a very frightened woman, coming from a neighboring apartment. I froze, and listened, my hand on the phone, ready to call the police. I was sure someone was being murdered. There was the sound of a struggle, thuds against the walls, and then the shout of a man, his voice distorted with rage: "I told you I do not like mustard on my ham!" I knew that the police wouldn't come for something like that. I knew that they would consider it a private matter.

I had, on rare occasion, witnessed violence in the city where I lived. It was one of the major reasons I wanted to leave. I lived for three years on the second floor of a three-story brownstone. It was pleasant and sunny and the street was safe. One night, however, I was awakened at three in the morning to the sounds of yelling outside. I could see, below, a car stopped in the middle of the empty street, both doors flung open. The driver was screaming at his passenger, "I'm going to kill you, woman!" He had in his hand a stubby, thick-bladed knife and he began to chase her around the car. I reached for the phone and called the police. I heard the woman run into the vestibule of our building. The man followed her. Under my floor, I thought I could hear him stabbing her. "Ugly woman, ugly, ugly woman!" he cried, as she screamed helplessly, Finally, he took off, leaving a small cloud of burning rubber. I went downstairs to find the woman, but the vestibule was empty. The police came. I told them I didn't know what happened to them and felt somewhat foolish. The police car circled the block for about half an hour. After they had left, I heard the woman again, down on the sidewalk: "Johnny! Johnny! Come back, Johnny!" she cried. "Oh, Johnny, please!" I saw her below my window. She was walking, almost running. Maybe he hadn't stabbed her after all, I thought. The sounds of her anguish disappeared into the night. Within the hour, Johnny was back, stopping his car in the same place he had left it earlier, getting out, brandishing the knife into the still and quiet pre-dawn city. "Where are you, woman! I'm not done yet, woman!" he snarled.

I was probably not in danger from this, which is why the police took it so lightly—a dispute between two consenting adults, no big deal, a danger only to each other—but I was terrified by it, and the middle-of-the-night scene became the single ignition that thrust me out of the city. Jim was my partner in this flight. We weren't necessarily in love. I wasn't sure I believed in love at that point, but neither of us loved the city. We shared an offbeat sense of humor, we liked to camp, and we liked to hike. That seemed enough of a pact.

What I didn't take in about Jim right away was his love of guns. I passed it off. Guns didn't interest me but, well, I reasoned, he was a man; it didn't seem unusual that he liked guns so much. Once we settled into our farmhouse, whenever we went out into the woods to hike or to cut wood, he would pack a pistol on his belt. Along the trail, he'd set his beer can on a stump and pump it full of bullets. Sometimes, he'd wheel around and train it on me. "Just kidding! It's empty," he'd say, laughing and coming over to give me a squeeze. He was kidding, of course. But he was making a point, and the point was about power.

Slowly, he acquired more and more: rifles, shotguns, pistols, big hand-guns. He kept this arsenal under our bed and sometimes, before going to bed, he'd pull one of the weapons out, draw the gleaming barrel from its leather case and set it in his lap. Dressed only in briefs, he would polish the gun, ramming the barrel with a cloth-tipped rod and then smoothing it with one of the chamois-colored soft cloths that he kept sealed in a plastic pouch. I would be lying beside him in our bed, reading, while he performed this ritual. I would fall asleep breathing the faint odor of gunpowder and clean-ing solvents.

I think of it now and I cringe. It seems so bizarre to think of a man in his underwear sitting beside me, polishing a weapon, the air full of the smell of violence. But this is the filament that is so hard to understand about domes-tic abuse. This is about how we shut down and don't notice certain signs. It is also about being young and vulnerable and not understanding the dynam-ics between man and woman. This is the paradox of sleeping with the enemy, not even understanding that he *is* the enemy, that he is the prowler in the night, the Boston Strangler, the Midnight Slasher; that he is the one to be feared above all others because he is the one who is with you so much of the time; the one who knows you. He is the one who wants to control you. He is the one who knows where to find you. Always.

I couldn't acknowledge that Jim was the enemy because to do so would have left me with nothing. That's always the gamble. How bad is it? we ask ourselves, in such deep privacy that we can barely hear our question. Not bad enough to give up our home, whatever money we might have, maybe our children. Not bad enough to expose ourselves to our friends, to let them know Jim and I weren't the model couple. Did anybody really think we were? I doubt it, but that's what I say now. I don't know what I was thinking then. I only know I was shoved deeper and deeper into a pit of shame.

I can remember now being asked by a doctor where the bruises came from, on my stomach and on my breasts. I can remember being confused by his question, not knowing that I was bruised, and trying to think if I had fallen, not even imagining that the bruises might have come from Jim. So deep was my denial, I wasn't even trying to hide what I knew because I honestly didn't think I knew it. When I got home, I stood naked in front of the mirror and saw the dark spots, touched them gingerly and felt, for the first time, the pain of those marks as well as the hot embarrassment from the doctor's question. I thought hard, tracing slowly backward like a finger in the darkness, until I remembered the punches, the jabs, the pokes, some of them done supposedly in fun. But even if in fun, his point was that he meant whatever he said.

A lot of what happened to us was probably exacerbated by our situation. It was a harsher climate than we were used to. We had very little money, and we were caught unaware by a severe winter. Our jobs were unsatisfying and often demeaning. We were, for that brief period in our young lives, the rural poor. I see that now. If someone had said that to me then, I would have laughed. We were striking out on an adventure. We were the young pioneers. That was all.

And yet, surely, we had expectations. I try to get back into the mind that was mine at that time. It is hard. We had ideals, that much I know. We were trying to improve the quality of our lives. I think of that now and the irony shines back at me like a harsh spotlight. In building our lives in the country, we truly felt that our lives were better, healthier, more peaceful. And I am still here and many of these ideals are still part of my life—I love the stillness of the woods and the sharp light of stars in a dark sky. I still heat with wood, I garden organically, and I use a composting toilet. But I do know now that quality of life has not so much to do with lifestyle as it has to do with what goes on in your heart.

We had never seen snow like what came down that winter. It slid off the slate roof into piles across the front and back of the farmhouse, and pretty soon the windows were almost covered. At times it seemed like all we did was shovel and push more wood into those sheet-steel stoves. Jim drove a Ford sedan at that time, the same car he had driven in the city. It had been nice down there, but we used it now to work in the woods, and pieces of trim had fallen off, and the taillight was broken. These details bothered Jim, who normally took immaculate care of his vehicles. The car rarely made it up the hill to our house in the snow. The hill was so steep that sometimes even the grader got stuck, coming up to plow. And, since we were the only house up there, we were the last ones on the town's plowing route. Jim used to drive around with lengths of cordwood in the trunk, to give the car more weight, and better traction.

On one occasion, snow had been falling all day long and the road had not yet been plowed. By the time he tried to make it up that hill, it was dark and the snow was almost a foot deep in the roadway. From the living room window, I watched the car's headlights piercing through the swirling storm. They slowed and then wavered, and then began to recede. He made four attempts, and finally the car swept up the hill and into the barnyard in a shroud of white. He shut off the headlights and came inside. I don't remember an argument. I have thought back on it and come up blank. Maybe there simply wasn't an argument. Maybe it was just blind rage. Maybe he blamed me for the storm, for the cold, for the steepness of the hill. I only remember that he set down his briefcase and came at me, throwing me to the floor and pinning my shoulders with his hands. He straddled me, his knees into my ribs, and he pounded my head against the hardwood floor, over and over and over again. That was the one time when I thought I was going to die. That was the one time I needed medical attention. "Tell them you were tobogganing, tell them you ran into a tree and hit your head," he said, as he drove me to the hospital. We had waited until the next morning because of the snow. My forehead had swollen alarmingly, and a drizzle of deep red curled under my half-closed eye. "They're not going to believe that," I said. "Tell them," he said, his eyes cold.

It's hard to explain to people why you stay in a relationship like that. That's why I never told anyone. I knew I couldn't explain it if I told the truth. Maybe this is why Nicole Brown Simpson had Polaroid photos taken of her bruised face, and locked them away in a safe-deposit box, like some bizarre insurance policy. Maybe she reasoned that if she was ever ready to talk about it, she would have these snapshots as proof to back up her story. Or, as some people have speculated, that if she were killed, there would be some graphic evidence that her husband had violently attacked her.

I never took pictures. The thought never even occurred to me. To take pictures would be to look in the mirror and see what was happening. I stayed underground, almost the whole eight years we were married. I didn't want anyone to know, and part of that conspiracy was that I couldn't know, either.

Of course, I knew. I knew the nights when it happened and the thoughts would storm around in my mind: Where could I go? How could I divorce myself from this man? I had no money. *He* made the money, I made the bread.

My parents would have been horrified, not only about the abuse but about our whole lives. I couldn't face that humiliation. And I felt worthless. When the one person who shares your life beats you, it's hard to imagine anyone loving you, it's hard to imagine that there is any love in the world at all. There's a voice in there that's saying it's going to get better. There's a side of you that listens to him say he's sorry, and that believes him when he tells you he really loves you after all. It's the side that starts to build the wall, even as the bruises are beginning to swell to the surface of the skin, even as they bloom yellow and brown and green and purple, and the plans of escape erode. You go and sit in your favorite chair in the living room and look at all your books on the shelves. This is your home. How could you leave?

A beating is brief. A strike, a blow, takes no longer than a second. Two of them are two seconds. So often it's over before you know what happened. Like a nightmare, the memory of it is hard to sustain. It rises up, a hot glare, and then life intervenes. A phone call, a return to the working day, schedules, needs, dogs, laundry—all of these become willing allies in the need to forget that it happened. Because remembering that it happened means that you have to do something about it. You have to make a change, a seismic change. Somewhere, deep inside, you know this, but the risks are too great, it would take far too much strength to allow yourself to see it, far too much to set yourself free.

I left twice. Once I ran away from his rage, out the door, into the deep summer darkness of the mountain night. I heard him slam the door behind me and turn the lock. "So go," he yelled from behind the door. "You leave, you don't come back." I slept that night curled in the back seat of my car. In the morning, he came out to the car and pounded on the window. "Had enough?" he said, laughing. It was part of the charm that made it all so hard to remember. He'd make me feel foolish, as if I had gone to some extravagant lengths to gain a negligible advantage. Silly me, sleeping in the car just to make a point. He'd always josh me and console me and draw me back in.

The second time, I ran farther. I don't remember the fight. I don't remember any of the fights. I just remember the fear. I ran in the middle of the night and drove forty miles to a motel, the nearest one I could think of. I was afraid he would come looking for me, and think of this place, too. It was probably the only motel near where we lived. I thought that if he were out looking, he would see my car parked in front, so I asked for a room in the back. The man at the desk looked at me suspiciously. I was dressed in jeans and sandals.

Perhaps he thought I was running drugs. But he gave me the key to the room, which was dingy and smelled heavily of cigarette smoke and beer. I didn't sleep. I was afraid Jim would find me and I didn't know where I would go from there. I could barely afford the $40 the room had cost me. I couldn't rent the room for another night and had no further plans. So I went back. Jim laughed when I came home the next night. He laughed, as usual, as if I always made such a big deal out of small matters. "So, Annie got her gun, huh?" he said, mussing my hair. "Come on, I'll take you out to eat."

Wasn't that better than being alone in that ugly motel room?

It's so hard to explain what brings you back. A thousand hopes, a thousand dreams. It is a perverse kind of faith, indeed the strangest faith a woman can muster.

This kind of faith is all about dreams and how we hang onto them, how desperately we want them to come true, how blind we become during the prayers of this faith. If being beaten up is a secret of the night, and if it's the only thing that stands between us and the realization of those dreams, maybe, we reason, maybe it can stay hidden, maybe it will never come forth. The bruises heal, the arguments go long forgotten, but the dream remains, the dream of having a good life, however we interpret those two words. This strange faith is the longing to feel protected, the longing to feel loved, even if not enough, even if not perfectly, even if by someone who might kill you.

I know that I wanted to feel loved, probably more than anything on earth. And I knew that leaving Jim meant being alone, which seemed frightening and uncertain; it would mean that all possibility of love would be extinguished. I had never been alone, and I had no reason to believe I could survive aloneness. I think about Nicole Brown Simpson, whose life as an ordinary high school cheerleader was transformed into one of lavish privilege, with access to money and power and fame, by the simple addition of a powerful man. I wonder if she struggled, knowing that if she allowed the secret all the way out, she might lose it all. I wonder if she felt she was risking her life for her lifestyle. I wonder how much any of us would risk to protect our lifestyle.

I stayed because it was all I had. I stayed because the outside world seemed so much scarier than the one I was already in. I also stayed because Jim was charming enough that I thought no one would believe me if I told them of his dark side. He had so many friends, and I was convinced that none of them had ever seen this part of him. Could I blame them for not suspecting he could do such harm? Sometimes I didn't even believe it myself. His remorse was always plentiful, his sense of humor—a mighty curtain behind which he hid so much—infallible. The abuse in our marriage was not, by any means, a constant battering. Months would pass without incident. What it was, though, was a measured distribution of his power, a numbing of my sense of self, and of those optic nerves that might otherwise have allowed me to see more clearly. All of it left in me a lingering residue of fear.

All the while, though, we were hard at work on our dream. We eventually bought a beautiful piece of land with fields and woods and a view of the valley, and, on successive pages of a yellow legal pad, we drew up plans for our house. It would have everything we believed in for that simple survival of the nuclear age: solar collectors, lots of insulation, woodstoves for heat and for cooking, a root cellar, a composting toilet. We would build it for cash only. We did not want to be slaves to a mortgage.

And so, as we began to build our house, timber by timber, brick by brick, the stakes for my leaving grew even higher. These are certainly aspects difficult to explain at this comfortable distance, some twenty years and a successful marriage hence. I stayed for a thousand seemingly legitimate reasons. I stayed because I hoped, I prayed, it would get better. I stayed because he told me I could never survive on my own. Never. And I believed him. I stayed because he'd told me that if I left, he would find me. And he had all those guns. He would kill me. I was also certain of that. He had made that clear, so many times, in so many different ways. "You're dead, baby," he liked to say.

He didn't kill me. Maybe he never would have. Maybe he just liked to feel powerful. Maybe he just liked to see me look frightened. Maybe he never meant any harm at all, as he always said the next morning. It's just that I love you so much, he would always say. Always. And, truly, the worst of it happened in the first two years we were together, though little assaults, hits and punches, like references to a well-known text, continued until the end. Maybe he mellowed and began to see the futility of his method. It's more likely, though, that his work was done. Like an animal trainer, he'd broken my spirit. The lessons had been learned. I knew the game. I knew the rules—do it his way, don't argue, and don't ever serve anything with gristle in it—and the cost of breaking them.

I also stayed because those fleeting moments of rage were always balanced by hours of good times together. I don't know about other abusive relationships. Are they pure hatred? Ours was not. Jim and I loved to laugh and often did. We found humor in the oddest things, and shared a passion for our own independence and a passion for sex. We had saved up money together with a common goal. We had drawn up plans for our house, laid the foundation, block by block, together, raised the roof rafters, built the chimney, shingled the roof. If all of this sounds too confusing, then maybe you are getting a feeling, just a glimpse, of the confusion that I felt in trying to leave. How could I leave behind all that goodness because of this one flaw? There was a lot about Jim that I loved, and I do look back in fondness for much that went into our relationship. That may sound twisted, I know, but it is true. There are times when I think of us as two children, thrashing our way together toward maturity.

I can tell you that, even to this day, I never felt like a victim. I have felt stupid, I have felt like a co-conspirator, an accomplice to a crime, but I've never felt like a victim. If I resigned myself to that, I would feel I had given up any claim I might have to free will. I won't go that far. Because, in spite of all that I have said here, the fact remains that I could have left. There is no question about that. But I stayed. Way too long.

And I can tell you that I watched that woman on television weep for the love she shared with a suspected serial killer and I understood, some deep part of me understood, but out loud I said, "You idiot!"

We finally parted. It was long and slow, and maybe that's the only way it could have happened, as I gradually realized that I could support myself. I found a good job, as an editor, a job I could have walked right into, directly from the city. It was almost as if my professional life was suspended for eight years, a long sabbatical that, I like to think, brought me more knowledge than any studies might have. We struggled through counseling (though I think of that era as the dark ages of our culture's understanding of relationships: the issue of Jim's abusive behavior came up, but it was more or less dismissed as insignificant). We separated, twice, and reconciled before, finally, we divorced. It wasn't bitter. It was resigned. Both of us remarried. I don't know about Jim, but I know I was happy for the first time in my life. We lived near each other but our paths rarely crossed. Occasionally I would pass him, driving by in his truck.

Some twelve years later, Jim knocked on my door on a Saturday morning. I didn't know what he wanted but I invited him in and offered him coffee. A lot had happened to both of us during these years. He came in and sat in one of my kitchen chairs—and asked for my forgiveness. His voice was quavering and I thought he was struggling to keep from crying. "I'm so sorry for what happened in our marriage," he said. "Can you forgive me?" I have no idea what had brought it on, and I certainly didn't expect it. I'm glad I hadn't waited all those years, anger festering, for such an offering. If I had, I might not have heard what he said. Still, I was surprised. Why now? I wondered. Who knows what kind of timetable these things have? I think of it now as some deep splinter that had slowly worked its way up to the surface, at last. I did forgive him. At that time and from that distance, forgiveness came easily. But it was not insignificant.

Jim's apology freed me from bonds I had forgotten were there. It was one of the greatest gifts he could have given me. Not that I was waiting for it or hoping for it. Not that I had ever even thought about the prospect of an apology. It all seemed like ancient history. But it allowed me new perspective on these stages of our lives. It made me see that we had passed through those times and that we had learned something. I saw that part of my life as a chapter—just a chapter—not the whole book, and that there was more to my life than the fact that I had been abused. Those dark moments in our lives were not forever and they were not unredeemable. They had left me hurting, and if one very special man had not entered my life after that chapter, I don't know how I would have recovered. That new man taught me how to love and be loved. Without that, I wonder if I might have gone on in a cycle of relationships that not only continued the abuse, but compounded it. Certainly this period of my life is not one of which I am proud, and to this day I have rarely spoken of it to anyone, even my closest friends. And yet, of those eight years, taken in totality. I would say that they were perhaps the most instructive years of my life. I learned how to cook almost anything on a woodstove. I learned how to split wood and how to stack it so it will dry. I know how to frame a house and square a foundation. People still call me up when they want advice on composting toilets. I also know how to pace myself through a long snowy winter, how to dress in below-zero weather, and how to keep a house cool in the summer without air conditioning. I can mend almost anything with thread and needle. Ironically, during those eight years, I learned how to survive.

So, while this chapter in my life has closed, and Jim and I have grown and moved on, I know full well that there are other women—and men— living in fear, and terror, and denial. Though it is not easy to dredge up these memories from my past, it seems important to share them, important to recall how terribly easy it is to live that way despite what we know and believe. If I thought that the situation for women had improved, perhaps I would not have dug so deep, but what I hear and read suggests that it's getting worse, even with such "advances" in recent years as women's shelters, the plentiful advice of experts, and a bumper crop of restraining orders.

I have not forgotten the terrible power of that strange faith, and how hard it is to turn from it. But everything about abuse is rooted in fear, and in the illusions it often sustains. My dream now is that men and women will lay aside their arms in this seemingly unending battle for power; that they will seek another route and come together not in sexual combat, armed with misplaced anger and veiled agendas, but as human beings who understand each other's need for compassion and care and help in times of weakness and strength. And who are not only willing to offer this kind of caring, but unafraid to accept it in return.

It is sometimes hard for me to believe that there were times when I thought I had only dreamed that those brief ugly moments of violence had happened to me; that there were times when I didn't remember the bruises at all. Sometimes, when we were still married and I tried to bring it up, Jim would sneer, "You're crazy!" or "What the hell are you talking about?" which always left me angry and confused. But his apology on that morning finally legitimized my experience. The only other person on earth who knew about this had come forward. At last. I was not crazy. It had really happened, and we had survived it. We learned and grew and came to a place where we could finally acknowledge this experience to each other. No ruling in a court of law could have brought me such deep and enduring satisfaction. More importantly, no legal document could have allowed me the opportunity to feel, after so many years, a new respect for Jim. I was so grateful for that Saturday morning visit. It was so sunny that morning. I remember that, especially.

Edie Clark is a New England writer and editor whose features and columns in Yankee *magazine are well known to its readers. She is the author of* The Place He Made, *from which a chapter was excerpted in the premiere issue of* Hope.

Crying for Justice

by Jon Wilson

The call that awakened Thomas Ann Hines in the middle of that February night in 1985 was from the Texas State Medical Examiner's office in Austin. The caller asked if she knew a Paul Hines. Her son, Paul, twenty-one, was a senior at Austin Community College, just a few hours south of her Plano home. The slight, fifty-something woman had once worked in the Dallas Police Department, and she knew what a call from the Medical Examiner meant. "Someone shot him a couple of hours ago," said the caller, and he's dead."

Her heart in her throat, she pleaded into the darkness, "Paul Hines is a common name. My Paul has red hair and blue eyes and a scar across the bridge of his nose and a birthmark on his chest.... Could you just go in there and check? Maybe it isn't him...." Footsteps echoed away, then returned. "Yes," the caller said, "it's him." The police would be in touch, he said, about identifying and picking up the body.

The body. The words hit hard. A single mother with a scarred and haunting past of abuse, Thomas Ann Hines had focused all the love she could muster on her only child. If he was gone, she thought, there wasn't any reason for her to live, either. "Alright," she remembers thinking, a few minutes later, "I can do this. I can go down to Austin. I can bury my son. But when I'm done, I don't want to live."

In Austin, questions seared through her grief. "Why would anyone shoot him?" she asked the homicide detective. "Paul was everybody's friend; he never met a stranger." But the truth was that a stranger had shot her son;

a stranger for whom Paul was doing a favor.

Robert Charles White was a seventeen-year-old drug dealer, and he needed a car. Believing he was about to be arrested for a burglary, he wanted out of Austin fast. He had too many felonies on his record. Near a video arcade, he spotted Paul Hines's Camaro Berlinetta and its lone driver. White asked Hines for a ride to his mother's home, saying she was deathly ill, and Hines quickly agreed. After driving for a while, White directed Hines to an apartment complex—and then ordered him out of the car. What happened next is not exactly clear, but seconds later, Paul Hines lay slumped in the driver's seat, bleeding to death, shot through the lungs and heart. White bolted from the car and the scene, hiding the gun along the way. Police found the gun, and, a few days laters, White.

Thomas Ann Hines endured the investigation and the trial, hoping for the death penalty. White was convicted of murder, but he was too young for Texas's Death Row. His sentence of forty years in prison was converted to thirteen years "flat time," and probation until age forty. She watched as the judge read the sentence, adjourned the court, and left the room. She watched as White was led out in handcuffs. The attorneys left, and the courtroom emptied. Only a news reporter stayed behind. She had never felt so terribly alone.

In our system this is traditional "retributive" justice. At each trial's conclusion, most victims are still left helplessly grasping for closure. There is even a name for their residual pain and anger: It's called "secondary victimization." And it's from this systematized failing of victims that the field of "restorative" justice has emerged, designed to find ways of restoring meaning and purpose to the lives of victims and their families. Remarkably, it has also provided new meaning and purpose to the lives of offenders.

In her aloneness, Hines began thinking about how to end her life. Not only did she feel lost without her son, but she couldn't shake her feelings of guilt. Paul had wanted to come home to Plano—a four-hour drive—the night before he was shot, to check on his mother, who was sick with a cold, but she discouraged him, telling him to stay in Austin. From the moment of the medical examiner's call, she was tortured by the question of why she just hadn't let him come home. "My guilt was overwhelming," she says. I just couldn't live anymore."

Straightening out her personal affairs, she bought a one-way ticket to Jamaica on Labor Day Weekend, 1985, intending to just walk into the water, one calm night. She is not a swimmer, and she is terrified of water. She readied herself, and walked to the water's edge. In desperation, she called out once again to her son.

"If I just knew where you were," she cried, "and that everything was alright, I'd be okay." What she heard, she says, was "...a voice that wasn't a voice, but it was Paul, and he said to me, 'I'm where I was before I was with you, and I am alright.'" It was a profound moment; it released a new promise of peace in her, and she decided to return to Texas. "It wasn't that I didn't cry, anymore, or didn't miss him," she recalls, "but that night was the beginning of my survival."

In fact, years would pass before she began truly to recover. By the next February, she says, "I'd been crying for a year, but it wasn't getting any better. I had to *do* something." At the urging of a friend, she began reading books on the soul and the spirit, and on the criminal mind. The more she read, the more she wanted to know. She regularly wrote letters to the Parole Board to ask if her son's murderer "had died yet," and to remind them that she would fight his release at every opportunity, and that her hope was that Charles White would rot in prison for what he'd done to her son. But the more she read, the more interested she became in who these offenders actually were, and the circumstances many had come from. Struggling to heal, she read voraciously. In 1990, she began working with other parents of murdered children, assisting them through their own ordeals. "It felt great to be able to help others through their pain," she says, "because I didn't have anyone to help me when I was there." Ultimately, however, it would take an encounter with White to ease her inescapable grief and her unrelenting anger.

. . .

The state of Texas is often considered, especially by outsiders, to be a paragon of all that is retributive in criminal justice. Its prison population is high, and its renowned death penalty is the subject of wide debate. Yet, before the mid-1980s, the state's criminal justice system barely addressed the needs of victims. It was only ten years ago that the Parole Board had established an office for victim services, a change due largely to the untiring efforts of Nell Myers, an Austin mother whose twenty-year-old daughter Cydney had been raped and murdered in 1979. Myers knew from hard experience how much help victims need—a number to call, a person to listen, and resources to call upon. She had also struggled alone in the aftermath of Cydney's murder, driven mostly by the ferocity of her anger, but she managed to transform the state's entire approach to victims. The founder of the victim-advocacy group People Against Violent Crime, Myers wrote the first draft of the Texas Crime Victims' Bill of Rights, which was finally amended to the state Constitution in 1989. Texas state representative Terry Keel, the former Travis County prosecutor who finally brought Cydney's murderer to justice after more than nine years—thanks to Myers's tenacity and to DNA analysis—says, "The system today is radically different because of her."

With the new victim awareness, the Parole Board in 1989 appointed a parole and probation officer named Raven Kazen to run the first office of victim services. Kazen, who had a tiny room, a phone, and a part-time assistant, had worked for years with victims seeking monetary restitution in primarily non-violent crimes, and she was now to work with victims whose offenders were about to be paroled. In 1990, Governor Ann Richards took two important steps: she consolidated the Parole Board into a new Texas Department of Criminal Justice (TDCJ), and she appointed Ellen Halbert, a victim of rape and attempted murder, to the Board of Criminal Justice, which oversees the state's massive system. Halbert was the first victim to serve on the Board.

That same year, a young woman named Brenda Phillips had been raped and murdered, and her mother, Cathy, wanted desperately to meet face-to-face with the murderer, Anthony Yanez. There was no victim-offender program in place, then, and no procedure for allowing such a meeting. Undaunted, Phillips pressed all the way to the governor's office, leaving no stone unturned, and no ear unbent. Finally, in late 1991, Kazen was allowed to bring in a mediator from Oklahoma. Kazen believes Ellen Halbert's presence on the Board made it possible. It was Texas's first victim offender mediation in a crime of violence. Preparation was minimal. The night before the meeting, the mediator talked with Phillips and Yanez separately for only an hour, allowing little processing for what was to come. But Phillips got to look Yanez in the eye, to let him know how precious her daughter had been to her, and to express some of her emotions. Yanez showed some remorse. It was only a step, but an important one.

A year later, the Board of Criminal Justice established a full-fledged statewide Victim Services Division—with Kazen as Executive Director—under the auspices of TDCJ. Kazen suddenly found herself dealing with victims from throughout the state, as calls came in at a rate of 1,000 a month. (They now come in at 3,000 a month.) She had already drafted a proposal for a full-time victim offender mediator, and now she pressed more intently forward with her plans.

. . .

The words mediator and mediation are imprecise. These are not disputes in search of resolution. In victim offender mediation/dialog (VOM/D), what is actually being worked toward is "mediated dialog," and the offender must already have owned up to the offense completely. So Kazen needed someone unique for her program: a person not only deeply sensitive to the needs of victims, but one with experience in dealing directly with offenders; someone who understood criminal thinking and behavior. She needed a person capable of enabling honesty, courage, and trust in both the offender and the victim, so that each might express not only what is truly on their minds, but truly in their hearts.

The right person was David Doerfler. Now the Victim Services Division's State Coordinator of Victim Offender Mediation/Dialog, Doerfler, fifty, is a former Lutheran minister, football coach, counselor of sex-offenders and their victims, and father of a daughter who was permanently injured by a drunk driver. Doerfler, who believes the TDCJ program to be the first "in-system" approach in the nation for victims and offenders in violent crimes, has the ability to work effectively on both sides of the table.

Of medium stature and rugged build, Doerfler has a warm gaze and soft-spoken demeanor that belie the power of his mission and tenacity. He has been responsible for mediating twelve violent crime cases and overseeing two others during the six years he has been at TDCJ. Also involved in grant-writing and policy development, he has designed a program for training much-needed new mediators. (There are almost 400 cases now awaiting mediation in Texas, including ten offenders on Death Row. The rate of victim interest in mediation is growing by about sixty per year. Thirty volunteer mediators have now been trained, and more trainings are scheduled.)

Doerfler's strength, says Minnesota counselor and former social worker Marilyn Peterson, who is researching the ways homicide victims' families find meaning after losing loved ones to violence, is that he understands how to help participants go deep within themselves. "He is very gifted and very spiritual," she says, "he can access that yearning that people have for their own healing."

"The thing to remember," says Doerfler, "is that healing is sloppy work; it's *really* sloppy. It depends on facing your feelings, and that means it's not going to be in one-two-three order. People have to be given the opportunity to process."

. . .

Thomas Ann Hines continued to nurse her hatred for Charles White while struggling to keep anger from overpowering her life. She had become an outspoken advocate for victims and their families as Executive Director of Nell Myers's People against Violent Crime from 1992 to 1998. In 1994, Raven Kazen invited her to join a panel of victims of violent crime, to speak at one of the state prisons. The idea was that victims would tell their stories to inmates—not the offenders in their own cases—in an effort to show the human consequences of their crimes. Hines was already convinced that inmates had it too easy, and she thought they ought to be facing "real guilt and pain." If she could make them do that by telling her story at prisons, she was ready. But as she sat there at the front of the room, awaiting her turn to speak to the 200 assembled inmates, she noticed a red-haired young man sitting not far from her who, she says, "...could easily have passed for Paul's brother. I looked at him, and suddenly thought to myself, 'what would his mother want to say to him if she could say something?' I realized that if my son was in this room, I'd want someone to reach out a hand to him." It was a moment, she says, as profound as that on the beach in Jamaica, because she was instantly transformed from an angry lecturer to a compassionate mother. "In that moment," she says, "I realized that, even though victims have every right to their pain, we can also turn it around."

For a moment, she wasn't sure what she was going to say, anymore. When she began her story, she did so not with her usual edge, but with a sense that she could actually touch these men. Instead of merely reminding them of the pain they had caused, she talked about how they could change their lives, and the lives of those they loved; they were not only the terrible things they had done. She talked from her heart about how their lives were redeemable. She also talked about the abuses she had suffered, growing up. When she saw tears in their eyes instead of the blank stares she expected, she knew she was onto something important. By showing them the human in herself, she had unlocked the human in them.

She began speaking to inmates at prisons all over the state, volunteering whatever time she could find for it. Occasionally, she gets up at 2:00 A.M. to drive her Geo to a prison three or more hours hours away so she can talk for an hour or two. The more she did this work, the more she believed in it, and the more she connected with inmates. The effects were as visible among adults as they were among juveniles. She could see that most had grown up in bad family circumstances, and that they'd made bad choices. She wasn't forgiving their crimes, or seeing them as innocent; she was simply seeing new possibilities. But for all her understanding of these inmates, many of whom were in for the most vicious of crimes, she held her ground against Charles White. She was not permitted to speak at the prisons where he was an inmate.

One day in 1996, after one of her prison sessions, an inmate approached her. "You have no idea how important what you said was to me," he said. He told how, at seventeen, he had killed a man in order to steal his car. Hines, suddenly caught between compassion for this man and the knowledge that he could just as well have been the murderer of her son, thought again about White. Maybe she should talk with him, she thought. His release date would be coming up in three years, and once he got out, she'd never have a chance to ask him anything about Paul's death. She'd long struggled with a dreadful image of Paul begging for his life at gunpoint. As one who had known the terror of having a cocked gun held to her head by a threatening drunken husband, this image tore at her. If she could actually sit down with White, he might tell her about Paul's last words.

By this time, Doerfler had conducted several successful sessions with victims and offenders. As a matter of procedure, Victim Services had notified Hines that mediated dialog was available to her, but she had not been interested. Now that she felt more ready, she contacted Kazen's office. Doerfler asked White if he'd be willing to meet, and he said yes. Doerfler then invited Hines to come in and view a videotape of an early mediation session. When she saw the tape, however, it seemed that nowhere near enough was resolved in the session. "I had to get up and leave," she says. "I didn't want to do it."

But by late 1997, Hines again realized that she needed to talk with White. As it happened, a media class at Midwestern State University in nearby Wichita Falls wanted to produce a video documentary on the VOM/D program, and they contacted the office. They wanted to videotape a victim who had managed to turn tragedy to good, somehow, and the office called Hines, who agreed. But then White withdrew.

"This is where the mediator is so important," says Hines. "He took my *pain* to Charles—who just hadn't really thought about it." Soon, White again agreed to mediation, and Doerfler began meeting regularly with each of them.

Doerfler's challenge is to prepare the participants as thoroughly as possible for the meeting. He begins by asking them to examine their deepest feelings—their griefs and fears—not only about the crime itself, but about their lives. These "inventories" help them to identify and connect with their feelings. He asks that the offender take complete responsibility for his offense and be *accountable*—to both himself and the victim. If the offender tends to blame others, or circumstances, for his actions, Doerfler urges him back to an understanding of his own choices. In this way, Doerfler coaxes that yearning to *do right*, which he believes we all have, into the consciousness of the offender. The process involves reading, writing, and talking, and he gives the offender a thick binder full of narrative, questions, and quotations. The offender works through the material believing that his feelings may actually matter.

The victim works with similar material, designed to encourage deeper introspection and insight, and especially to connect with the pain and issues that the trauma of victimhood can swiftly sublimate. Bringing such feelings to the surface allows for greater potential understandings, and the mediator works closely with each to keep them feeling as safe as possible as they explore these realms. The process is deep, and also slow. Doerfler's approach is to bring potential realities to each before they meet. His task of conveying to Hines a sense of the human being inside the killer wasn't that easy. White was considered one of the more violent inmates in the system. During the nearly thirteen years that he'd been in prison, he'd had 148 major disciplinary actions, and was placed in solitary confinement twenty times.

Among the questions Doerfler asks Hines to consider: "What if you find out that Charles White *did* hold Paul at terrified gunpoint while he begged for his life?" Confronted with the question, Thomas Ann realized that she's been living with this image for so long that she *could* handle it. (She will learn that Paul probably never even saw the gun, it happened so fast.) In this way, the participants usually engage in exploration and "dialog" through the mediator for months—and perhaps a year or more—before they ever sit down together. The ideal outcome before meeting, in fact, is one in which they *want* to sit down together, but don't *have* to in order to move on with their lives—because the preparation has already enabled them to begin moving on.

. . .

On the morning of June 9, 1998, in the chapel of the Alfred D. Hughes Correctional Facility in Gatesville, Texas, where White was an inmate, Thomas

Ann Hines finally sat across the table from the murderer of her son. David Doerfler sat at the side. He had prepared them for this moment, and now there was no turning back. They sat in silence for a few minutes, as Hines sought the strength to speak, dabbing at unceasing tears. "This is so hard for me," she said to him at last. "And I know it's hard for you.... The hardest thing, though, was to bury Paul...." White, who had been waiting apprehensively and listening intently, hung his head as tears welled up in his eyes. Hines choked back her sobs. "I appreciate your doing this," she said, "and please know that I will not be unkind to you in any way. That's not why I'm here...." White's head lowered more. "You were the last person to see Paul alive, and it's really important that I know the last things he said and the last things that happened in his life."

It took White a few moments to reply. "I don't know how to start," he said, in barely more than a whisper. "I don't know how to explain. It was just a stupid thing. Just stupid...."

And so commenced a conversation that was to begin to restore two individuals, a violent offender and the mother of his victim, whose lives had become inextricably entwined thirteen years before.

"I don't blame you for how you feel about me," he said. "I didn't know I was going to cause so much pain."

The emotional session lasted eight hours, with a forty-minute break for lunch. "I went in there totally for *me*," admits Hines, "but it changed as he *listened* to me, and I *listened* to him. At one point I remember saying, 'If you knew how much I loved him you wouldn't have shot him, I just know you wouldn't,' and he just folded.... That sad, troubled boy let me see inside his soul. I began to feel such compassion."

White talked about his life, and about growing up on the streets. By the time he was thirteen, his mother told him she could no longer feed and clothe him. She could give him a place to sleep, but that was all. At the time of his arrest for the murder, he was smoking more dope than he was selling, and living with a thirty-something prostitute. He talked about feeling hopeless after he went to court. Knowing he didn't want to spend his life in prison, he considered suicide, but then he thought of the pain he'd cause his mother if he ended his life.

He asked Hines why she wanted to help him. She said, "If the only thing good that comes out of burying Paul is that you turn your life around, then Paul will not have died in vain." Her tears flowed as she continued, "If it had not been Paul, it would have been someone else."

White reached across the table, gently took the tissue she was holding from her hand, and wiped her tears. She'd been telling him almost from the beginning that he could change his life, and she now began to tell him that he was valuable, and important. He started to cry again, overwhelmed. She handed him a tissue and said, "I can't be your mother, but hopefully, I can help you get some direction in your life. There's a good person inside you; don't give up on yourself."

"I just hate it," he said, "that I brought all this pain in your life."

David Doerfler has seen this before, and he knows it's the real thing. "When an offender," he says, "has to look directly into the eyes of the person he hurt the most, or the aftermath of the hurt in the case of a homicide, it's hard to hide; it's hard not to face yourself. This is where the healing happens. And when the tears of the victim intermingle with the tears of the offender, healing takes place for both parties. In the face of a past that cannot be changed—when a victim gets sick and tired of being sick and tired, and the pain is so debilitating—letting go is the only thing we can do to move on."

As the end of the session drew near, Hines was unsure of what to say, or how to say it. In her outreach work, she makes a point of shaking the hand of every inmate she speaks to, but the thought of shaking the hand that held the gun that killed her son seemed a betrayal. Yet, when the moment came, she couldn't help herself, and almost involuntarily, she reached across. As their hands touched, she lowered her head to the table and sobbed. After a few minutes, they stood up. White leaned over and kissed her cheek. Hines left the room so that Doerfler could debrief him on the session before he was returned to his cell. When she was gone, he sat down again in tears, saying, "stupid...stupid...stupid."

Doerfler reminded White how Hines had told him that, while we can't undo anything, this can be a new beginning, and he must try to move forward. When his debriefing was finished, White asked Doerfler if it would be okay to hug Hines. "I may never see her again," he said. Doerfler said it would be alright. She returned to the room, and White got up to leave.

"As he was walking out," she recalls, "I offered my hand to him again, and he took it, but then he reached out and almost picked me up in a hug. I was totally shocked and taken aback—my first thought was that he'd get in trouble with the officers—but then I gave him a hug back. I was crying uncontrollably. He just said, 'I'm sorry, I'm sorry.' It was all so quick; it was over just as fast as it started."

In the year-and-a-half since the meeting, White has changed. "Charles has not only *received* hope, but *given* it," says Doerfler. The inmate who averaged more than ten serious infractions a year before the meeting has had just two minor ones since. He and Hines correspond regularly, and he tells her he wants to get his GED. Some of the rules are crazy, he says, but he's working to follow them. Hines has become a kind of godmother to him, and her letters reflect her compassion, her sorrow, and her mission. No day passes without her thinking of her lost son—"a victim's sense of victimization never really goes away," says Doerfler, "its *intensity* changes—but her work with others, particularly victims and inmates in need, keeps her going. White wants her to visit again, and she intends to, but Victim Services discourages such visits without a mediator, and Doerfler has been swamped. Hines, busy herself but notoriously determined, will probably surprise no one if she takes the matter into her own hands.

. . .

Stories of restoration are happening everywhere, with many different endings; indeed, they are more about beginnings. The pain of loss never leaves these victims; and neither does the shame and guilt of offenders. But how they move on with their lives is very different from before mediation. Cathy Phillips, whose determination helped launch the Texas program, worked with Doerfler and offender Yanez in a second, more productive session, and she hopes for a third meeting, sometime. Ellen Halbert, the rape victim who was left for dead, and then later appointed to the Texas Board of Criminal Justice, thinks it *might* be productive to meet with the rapist, but he refuses. Among the more heartbreaking cases are those in which a victim wants to meet with a willing offender on Death Row, but lack of funds and resources prevents the assigning of a mediator before the offender's execution. On the other hand, Nell Myers, the woman whose untiring efforts indirectly resulted in the creation of the Texas VOM/D program, has never liked the idea of mediation, and doesn't believe in its capacity to heal. "Why would we need to do that?" she asks. "We can work to help other victims. *That's* what we should be doing."

Then there's Paula Kurland, whose daughter Mitzi was murdered in 1986 by Jonathan Nobles, who ended up on Death Row. She met with him and Doerfler just two weeks before his execution in 1998. After carrying her grief and anger for twelve years, she just wanted to get the meeting over with. But what arose in her from seeing the remorse in Nobles was an unexpected compassion. Nobles, well aware of her anger, was overwhelmed by her mercy. The five-hour experience thoroughly transformed Kurland.

"David and Raven absolutely allowed me to take my *life* back," she says of the experience. "After mediation, because Jonathan had taken total responsibility, I walked out a new person. I became a person I didn't know I was capable of being." She now volunteers in two programs where groups of victims find healing by meeting with groups of offenders in prison.

"We can never put a price on a human life," says Doerfler, "but in a strange twist of logic, we ask for nothing of real substance when we just incarcarate offenders, even for the rest of their lives. Yet, in this restorative process, where offenders face their victims, themselves, and their shame, it *is* possible to give something back: hope. When we stop reacting only out of our anger, and instead ask 'what is the most *healing* thing we can do?' we'll find an answer in victims screaming to have their grief acknowledged, and in offenders screaming to be accountable. If we're really looking for healing and accountability, we'll find it where it can truly happen—between victims and offenders in dialog together."

Jon Wilson is Publisher & Editor-in-Chief of Hope.

Sowing Seeds of Hope
by Bill Mayher

Like roadside ice cream stands or country churches, summer camps in Maine have a reassuring orthodoxy all their own. Visit one and you'll probably find a line of cabins strung out along a lake. There will be a main lodge and a jumble of lesser structures, each with its own blend of rumpled out-of-plumbness speaking of light construction and heavy winter snows. On your visit, you're almost certain to hear the shriek of whistles from the swimming dock, the sound of distant shouting as a well-hit ball arcs deep to left, dusty footfalls clumping closer and then suddenly tripping on a well-worn root by the dining lodge, as a thousand teenage feet have tripped a thousand times before. At summer camps, what you'll mostly hear is laughter, and in the spaces between the laughter, the plaintive song of a white-throated sparrow from the woody margins, the uncertain plunk of tennis balls, and the snap of a wet towel with its answering yelp of pain. In the long inhale and exhale of summer days by a sandy-bottom lake, what you'll surely find among the grassy spaces and dappled shade of camps is a special mix of away-from-home safety and risk that helps kids grow right.

Not surprisingly then, when it came time to find a place for the children of Arabs and Jews—bitter enemies who have been killing each other for generations—to attempt the painful and uncertain work of making peace among themselves, a summer camp in Maine seemed like a natural place to locate. To make peace, these kids need distance from their homelands. They need neutral ground. The cultural, political, and personal walls that separate them are incomprehensibly high. There is, in the words of contemporary historian Mohamed Haikal, such "fury and revulsion" between them, that most of the teenagers chosen by their countries to attend a camp called Seeds of Peace in Otisfield, Maine, have never met a single one of their opposite number. For this reason alone, they need time to talk together; they need time to listen. Most of the 162 campers at Seeds of Peace have traveled from Egypt, Israel, Palestine, Jordan, Morocco, Tunisia, and even Qatar to eat American camp chow and sleep in open cabins with people they have been taught their whole lives to hate. For taking these risks, they deserve a chance at reconciliation and friendship. At Seeds of Peace, they'll get it.

On a dazzling July morning, Seeds of Peace founder John Wallach opens this year's session with a challenge to the teenagers gathered around him on the grass. "Today this is the only place in the world where Israelis and Arabs can come together on neutral ground and try to be friends," he says. "Because of this, I would ask one thing of each of you. No matter what else you do in your time here, make one friend from the other side."

In laying down his challenge— regardless of how idyllic the setting, or how eager the kids—Wallach is saying that building friendships between enemies is, after all, no easy thing.

John Wallach left a high-powered journalism career to launch the Seeds of Peace International Camp in 1993. Wallach had been a White House correspondent for thirty years. He had broken the story of the CIA mining Nicaraguan harbors, and he had covered the Middle East. He won the National Press Club Award and the Overseas Press Club Award for uncovering the "arms for hostages" story that led to the Iran-Contra scandal. When few people had thought such a thing was possible, he had written, with his wife Janet Wallach, a biography of the elusive Yasser Arafat.

But Wallach didn't feel satisfied being, in his words, a "fly on the wall of history." Perhaps he felt a sense of personal destiny because his parents had escaped the Holocaust. Perhaps he has always had an instinct for seeing beyond superficial differences because Catholic priests had guided his parents through the Pyrenees to safety. Whatever the reasons, in 1985, when the Cold War thaw was merely a trickle, Wallach initiated a program in what he called "citizen diplomacy" at the Chautauqua Institute in upstate New York to bring ordinary Russians and Americans together to search for common ground. For this work Wallach received in 1991 the Medal of Friendship—the former Soviet Union's highest civilian award—from then president Mikhail Gorbachev.

At news of the World Trade Center bombing in New York City in February 1993, Wallach again heard the call to action. A month later, an idea came to him: Because the adults of the world had so clearly failed at peacemaking in the Middle East, he would skip the present generation of leaders and go straight to the next. He would bring together young people who had been born amid the violence and searing hatreds of the region, and allow them to explore their mutual humanity.

"I spent my whole life with the powerful," Wallach recalled in an interview with Susan Rayfield in the *Maine Sunday Telegram*. "I can't tell you how many times I've been on Air Force One, or with the White House pool, or world leaders. I had a lot of power as a journalist. I've learned that the answer to life is not the poohbahs, it's the basics. The coming home to Maine; to what is human in all of us, that ties us together as human beings."

Wallach needed staff, kids, and a facility to realize his vision. He found his first staffer, Executive Director Barbara "Bobbie" Gottschalk, in Washington, D.C. Gottschalk's book group had invited Wallach and his wife to discuss their book on Arafat and afterwards, he shared his vision for Seeds of Peace. Gottschalk was so intrigued, she left a secure job as a clinical social worker to join him.

To find kids for his camp, Wallach approached the Middle East's major players, each of whom he personally knew: Yasser Arafat, the Chairman of the Palestine Liberation Organization; Yitzhak Rabin, the Prime Minister of Israel; and Hosni Mubarak, the President of Egypt. "Trust me with your children," Wallach asked each of the beleaguered men. "Give me the next generation. Give them a chance to escape the poison." His years of journalistic engagement and fairness were to have an unforeseen payoff: all three leaders answered Wallach's plea, an acquiescence little short of miraculous. Serendipity intervened when Wallach found that a Camp Powhatan in Otisfield, Maine, would let him use its facility after the camp's regular session ended. Touring the camp, Wallach met Tim Wilson, Powhatan's co-director, whom he immediately recognized as a Maine-camp classic with his own dazzling bag of tricks for keeping things lively and yet under control at the same time. An inner-city teacher and football coach around the steel mills of Pittsburgh, Wilson is as good at the up-in-front-of-everybody bluster that keeps things cooking as he is at the quiet arm-around-the-shoulder buck-up that helps an exhausted and melancholy adolescent get through another day. So in the summer of 1993 with a camp facility and a core staff in place, Wallach had assembled the basics of what would become Seeds of Peace.

In four short years, the camp has won awards including a 1997 Peace Prize from the United Nations Educational, Science, and Cultural Organization (UNESCO), and drawn accolades from world leaders. Kofi Annan, Secretary General of the United Nations, wrote in a letter to Seeds of Peace this year, "There is no more important initiative than bringing together young people who have seen the ravages of war to learn the art of peace." In her speeches, Secretary of State Madeleine Albright has mentioned Seeds of Peace as a bright spot on an otherwise dark Middle East horizon. Yasser Arafat has said, "Seeds of Peace represents the hope and the aim which we are working to realize, namely, just peace in the land of peace." Before he was assassinated, Israeli Prime Minister Yitzhak Rabin noted after meeting with campers, "Witnessing young Arabs and Israelis together gives me great hope that soon all Arabs and Israelis can live normal lives side-by-side."

The new arrivals, all between ages thirteen and eighteen, plunge into the usual sports and games, ready to fulfill the camp's mission to make peace among themselves. That is, until the hard work begins. Staff assign campers to Co-Existence Groups, where the most intense, and arguably the most important, work of the camp occurs. Here, campers learn to listen to the histories and feelings of age-old enemies and begin to move toward accommodation and, ultimately, empathy. Led by pairs of trained facilitators, these groups of about fourteen campers meet daily in a cycle of three sessions, and then move on together to a new pair of facilitators who, using a variety of techniques including oral history, role playing and role reversal, art, and drama, teach effective listening and negotiating skills. The group work is at first designed to create a safe space between participants. The facilitators then direct the group toward more difficult issues.

In one group, facilitators Linda Carol Pierce and Janis Astor deValle delve into intense racial tensions in Brooklyn, New York. Their role-play, in which a black camper from Bedford Stuyvesant runs into a white camper from Bensonhurst, starts out as friendly banter. Suddenly, it veers into a dramatic shouting match recapitulating incidents of muggings and mob murder that continue to divide their neighborhoods to this day. As the actors shout at each other, "You people," this, and "You people," that, campers see graphically that bone-deep prejudice is not confined to the Middle East.

Following the role-play, Pierce and deValle ask individuals in the group to share with a partner a personal story of prejudice each has suffered, and then have that partner report the story to the entire group—a well-known technique that builds listening skills among the youngsters and, as they tell each other's stories, helps put them into each other's shoes. An Arab girl tells of being snubbed on the Internet by members of her chat group when they discovered she was from Jordan. She relates how one of them shot back, "Isn't that where people with bombs come from?" and refused to acknowledge her further, letting her twist in cyberspace—a new style victim of a very old disease.

In another group, campers who already have represented the opposition's side in a mock Middle East negotiating session are now allowed to present their own points of view in debating who should have control over Jerusalem. But before the teenagers begin, the facilitators ask them to assemble pictures from colored toothpicks in a tabletop exercise that serves as a metaphor for issues of personal and collective space. The kids' individual designs—stick figures of people, houses, stars, and suns—soon expand to cover the entire table. The facilitators then start with the questions. "Were there borders there for you?" one facilitator asks. "There were borders on the table. Whoever was stronger took more space," a camper replies. "The quick and the strong get it all," adds another. "Let's relate this to Jerusalem," the facilitator then suggests, giving the kids fresh angles of approach to discuss this contentious and emotional issue. The debate that ensues is spirited, often heated, but it is also respectful because both sides have established the need to honor each other's "space."

Through the process of working with different facilitators—each with different strategies—campers cannot avoid getting down to the most stubborn problems that divide them. There is too much bad blood, too much history to let campers play at peace like they play at tennis. This camp, by Wallach's own design, is no feel-good paradise; rather it is a camp that compels them to look their enemy in the eye and in doing so, begin to know their enemy's heart. When the kids get down to it in the groups, Wallach says, "It doesn't take them very long to realize that they don't like each other very much."

As they hash out their deep-seated differences, the kids at Seeds of Peace also spend plenty of time on the playing field—a few individual events, but mostly team sports that put individuals from opposing political factions on the same team: baseball, tennis, lacrosse, soccer, swimming, volleyball, relay races, basketball. The theory is that, in the heat of competition, young people will become teammates and forget the elemental differences that brought them here.

Nowhere is this more apparent than in the Color Games, a competitive crescendo in the final days of the camp. Guided by the skilled (and wily) hand of Tim Wilson, the camp is divided into two teams: Greens and Blues. Tee shirts are donned, separate cheers invented. The teams are then turned loose to relentlessly compete against each other across the entire spectrum of camp sports and activities. Every camper has to contribute, the efforts of each essential to the whole. It is raucous, loud, dusty, and hilarious: transcendent partisanship forging white-hot loyalties—if only for the moment.

As the Color Games rush toward the final events, in the age-old tradition of a summer camp, it becomes increasingly impossible for the participants to assess with any precision what it might actually take to win. The totals for each team remain maddeningly close until, in the final event, one team surges to capture the crown only to discover that, in fact, there is no actual prize for the hard fought victory except the opportunity to give an enthusiastic cheer for the losing team and to jump in the lake first.

At this moment, the Color Games become a metaphor for sharing the victory equally between "winners" and "losers." After days of running their guts out and shouting over the treetops, the campers begin to understand that most elusive of truths: People on each side of a conflict must be truly satisfied if there is to be peace; victory can and must be a shared thing.

Perhaps Egyptian camper Silvana Naguib said it best in a film made at the camp several years ago: "The first step we have to make right now is not only to want for your own people.... You have to really, really want, really desire for the others. If you are an Israeli, you have to want for all the Palestinians to feel happy and feel safe and feel comfortable. If you're a Palestinian, you want the same thing [for the Israelis]. All the people in the country have to really want everyone else to be happy."

On July 30, 1997, a double suicide bombing by radical Palestinians tears through a Jerusalem marketplace called Mahane Yehuda, killing fourteen Israelis and wounding more than 150 others. The horror of the attack is captured by Serge Schmemann writing in *The New York Times*: "Witness after witness recited the same litany of flame, flesh, and horror. They described bodies covered with fruits and shoes; a man sitting on his motorbike dead; limbs flying."

Reports of the bombing rip through Seeds of Peace as well. When the news breaks, John Wallach addresses the whole camp. Special groups are formed with facilitators to help campers ride out the emotional storm. In the first hours, a deep sense of mourning and sympathy pervades the camp. In the next few days, as the initial shock wears off, the work in Co-Existence Groups takes on a harder edge; it becomes more difficult to maintain safe space and good listening. At this point, says facilitator Cindy Cohen, "It's almost impossible for kids to [acknowledge] the suffering of the other side without feeling it as an attack."

In the groups, tension is palpable and harsh phrases fly: "Palestine does not exist!" "Israel has no culture!" "You people always bring up the Holocaust to justify everything you have done to us." Historical interpretations are shot like missiles; it is raining verbal SCUDS. Of this phase Wallach says, "You could leave a Co-Existence Group and feel pretty discouraged by the depths of anger you see there. But it's all part of the process of peacemaking. It is the beginning of wisdom."

At first it's hard to see much in the way of either peacemaking or wisdom happening. It just looks like bickering. But then, through the sluiceways of talk, one suddenly glimpses—washing along amid the hard, gray slag of ancient enmities—bright nuggets of reconciliation: "I can understand your fears." "Everyone has the same sort of pain.... We share that." "We hear history repeats itself, and that's really scary." "If we can't compromise here, how can we expect two whole countries to compromise?" Finally, in one combative session, a particularly hard-line Israeli boy turns and looks into the eyes of the Palestinian youth next to him—a boy who was jailed at the age of eight during the Intifada, and who saw his uncle killed by Israeli soldiers. The Israeli boy says, "I can't guarantee that my government won't kill your people, but I can guarantee that I won't."

In the days ahead, the kids will be allowed to exhaust themselves in passionate arguments—no matter how futile. Eventually they will reach the point when they look across the abyss that divides them and finally see other human beings. It is the tradition of this camp that, amid the games and cheering and fireside songs, amid the long, hot days of talk, trust will be built on the simple idea that if each side listens attentively enough to the other, each will at long last realize there is no alternative to peace.

Wallach's charge to make one friend from the other side seemed like a modest goal in the first, euphoric days of camp. In the darker days following the bombing, it seems nearly unreachable. This is the point when a paradox embedded in the way Seeds of Peace works becomes clear: The pain of the journey is the very thing that insures both its validity and its durability. Without hardening-off at camp, the tender shoots of reconciliation nourished there won't be hardy enough to survive transplanting to the rocky, unyielding soil of their homelands.

Role-playing and other group work gives the campers a sense of how to cope with the re-entry process. But when the teens return home, they will still face formidable obstacles to keeping in touch with new friends from the other side—especially since the suicide bombing has led Israel to impose even stricter control over border checkpoints. A Palestinian camper explains that he had to stand in line for four hours to apply for a pass into Jerusalem. He then had to wait about a month for the pass to be processed. After his request was approved, he had to stand in line for another four or five hours to cross into Jerusalem to visit his friend who lived only twelve kilometers away. And that was before the bombings.

Luckily, there is e-mail to keep kids communicating with camp friends, and Wallach and executive director Gottschalk—who maintains contact with all of the kids—have developed other techniques for helping them stay in touch. A full-time coordinator in the Middle East works at establishing events for alumni, who also write feature articles for the organization's quarterly newspaper, *The Olive Branch*. Two years ago, King Hussein of Jordan welcomed 200 campers to a Seeds of Peace reunion in Jordan and symbolically donned a Seeds of Peace necktie.

Towards the end of camp, evidence of friendship is everywhere—in arms casually twined around another, in easy banter and teasing. Hazem Zaanon from Gaza and Noa Epstein from just outside Jerusalem are hoarse from cheering and flushed with excitement about the Color Games. Hazem says that he got to know Noa at their lunch table when they "just began to talk, first about Palestine and Israel, but then about everything. We became friends because everyone listened to the other's part," explains Hazem. "We became easy in this. We listened and respected each other without yelling and screaming." Noa agrees: "Camp is wonderful for me. I wouldn't have made a Palestinian friend back home." She then speaks of the "easy" luxury of time with her friend, "not in Co-Existence Groups, but eating lunch and playing ball games. Things that require friendship." Of course each of them knows it will be hard to keep in touch when "they face reality back home." But, Noa adds, "I think we have taken a step toward a new reality."

Whether this new reality is to be born in the region may end up being a matter of sheer numbers. When this year's campers return home, there will be 800 Seeds of Peace graduates in the region; next year, close to 1,000. The Arab-Israeli conflict has been fought out in a tiny theater of operations. For the most part this geographic compression has intensified the struggle, allowing enemies to throw rocks at each other, shoot into each other's homes, launch inter-neighborhood rocket attacks, cross the street to blow each other up.

If every problem contains its own solution, the solution in this case is to unleash what Wallace—now a Senior Fellow at the U.S. Institute of Peace—calls a "small army" of peacemakers. Kids who can speak clearly and listen carefully. Kids who have learned to negotiate patiently and who know that to achieve peace, each side must leave the table feeling safe. Kids who, by any accounting, are among the best their countries have to offer. Kids who, as Wallach predicts to the camp, will surely return to Seeds of Peace as the presidents or prime ministers of their countries. Kids like Noa and Hazem, who have had the courage and suppleness of mind to make a friend from the other side, who have combined to make a double-play together, dished-off for a winning basket, collaborated on a sculpture. Kids who together have watched the moon rise over a lake, and in its soft light seen that their enemy has a human face and known, in that moment, something of their enemy's heart.

Bill Mayher, a former teacher and college counselor, is the author of The College Admissions Mystique.

An Outward Bound Epiphany
by Garfield

I wanted to tell you about two of the guys on my Outward Bound course. One was named Dave. He was a real macho athlete type. He was a football star at his high school and could do everything better than most of the rest of us could. He could run faster and farther than any of us and he wasn't afraid. He was first on the ropes course and the first one to climb the cliff and rappel down. He made everything look easy.

The other guy was William. He was kind of the opposite of Dave. William was overweight and uncoordinated. He really enjoyed camping and hiking, but he had a hard time doing some things. But I'll say this: he never gave up, and he kept a sense of humor about it. Everybody liked William. He was good at planning and organizing our expeditions and he really understood how to read a compass. After a week together we started depending on him to make sure we were going in the right direction.

Most days, after we had finished our activities, we did a three-mile run. They told us we were competing with ourselves instead of each other. That was a laugh because none of us could compete with Dave. I was pretty fast, and Susan and Leslie were both faster than me, but Dave always finished first. He was always trying to beat his own time. We all thought being first was the most important thing to Dave, and we made jokes about it behind his back, but it was only jealousy.

On our next-to-last day we did our run, as usual. When I got to camp, Dave had already been there, probably five minutes. He wasn't even breathing hard. Susan and Leslie were already there, and the rest of our group straggled in pretty close together, but William took even longer than usual. It was almost dark, and we were going to go back to look for him when he finally showed up. He kept to himself and didn't say anything. I think he had been crying. He was soaking wet and breathing really hard, and he just sat down on a log and sort of hung his head down. I saw Dave looking at him and I thought how much he must look down on somebody like William.

The next day was our end-of-course run, our last personal challenge. It was sunny and cool and I really felt like I could beat my best time. I had gone about a mile and a half and was starting to get winded. Susan and Leslie were in front of me about fifty yards. We came around a curve in the dirt road and saw Dave up ahead. He had stopped and was just standing there with his hands on his hips and his head down, like he was thinking. He looked up as we got closer, and then he started running toward us.

I heard him say "Come on," to Susan and Leslie, and he kept on running in the opposite direction. They turned around and followed him. I stopped in the road to catch my breath. "Come on," he said to me as they went by. I knew he couldn't have already finished the run, and now that I had stopped, I knew I couldn't beat my time. I wanted to know where they were going, so after I got my breath I started running after them.

After a while I caught up to them. Three of the other guys and girls in my team were already running with them. A couple of minutes later we passed two more of our team, and Dave said the same thing to them: "Come with us." And they did. After a while we had the whole team running back toward the starting line. That's when we saw William.

He was struggling like he always did, but you could tell he was determined to finish. He was shocked when he saw us running toward him. That's when I understood what Dave was doing. We all ran up and gathered around William in a group and started running with him. Dave was right next to him, talking to him while they ran together, telling him he could do it and that we were with him. Then we all started talking to him.

It took a while, but we finished the run as a group, and Dave and William crossed the finish line together. It was William's best time ever, and of course Dave's worst.

I learned two things that day. One was how easy it is to misjudge people. Of all of us, I would have thought Dave was the last one who would give up his lead to help someone like William.

The second thing I learned was how it feels to put your own goals aside and help someone else achieve theirs. Of all the things I remember about Outward Bound, crossing that finish line together as a team was the best moment of the whole course.

I hope I never forget that feeling.

Garfield, who grew up in New York City, experienced his epiphany at the North Carolina Outward Bound School. The experience was powerful enough to inspire his continuing commitment to outdoor education.

Beneath the Skin
by Colin Chisholm

W hen I was growing up, my mother often said to me that the world would be a better place if it was run by women. She didn't say this with anger or spite, but with a sigh or a shake of her head as she turned away from yet another television news report about another massacre in another war in just another country half a world away. I didn't really understand what she meant, but I knew from watching the news that it was men who ruled the world, and that I was one of them.

Although my mother was no June Cleaver, she and my father lived well within the ironclad gender roles so dominant in their generation. My father was the main breadwinner, a man wed to his work even in his dreams. He traveled as much as half the year, leaving my mother, who had given up her nursing career, to care for the five of us children. She had seemingly boundless energy, always giving of herself in ways that I learned to take for granted. Late at night, exhausted after a long day, she'd let us nest in her bed while she read us stories or massaged our scalps with her long, willowy fingers. Sometimes I'd have the treat of having her to myself, and I'd rest my head on her stomach and burrow into her. She'd hold her book in one hand and with the other firmly run her nails over my scalp before gathering a handful of my hair and pulling on it just enough so that it was wonderfully close to pain but never close enough to really hurt. Over and over she pulled me back and forth between near-pain and ecstacy, until I'd drop into a place where nothing existed save the two of us held together by longing fulfilled and immeasurable trust. With one ear I could hear her stomach gurgling, with the other the cadence of her breath. Nothing in the world, then or now, could make me feel so loved, so safe in her breathing belly of home.

My father was modeled on Hemingway: strong, silent, unemotional. He had even gone hunting in Africa, had been attacked by a lion, and had four large fang holes in his left thigh to prove it. He was a good man, generous in all ways but one: he heeled in his emotions like well-trained dogs. He cried rarely, with great restraint and silence. I learned from a young age how to push my tears aside like anything else that got in my way. My mother hugged; my father shook hands. Even today, at seventy-five and my mother long since gone, my father turns wooden in embrace.

But there were exceptions: Alcohol made shape-shifters of my parents. My mother could be cruel; my father could be tender. My mother sometimes drank too much, and I remember the confusion and fear this wrought in me as a child. Red wine revealed a side of her few people outside our family circle knew, raising her hidden sorrows to the surface where, exposed to light, they lashed out in a barbed and crimson tongue. Sometimes I'd find myself curled on my bed, weeping uncontrollably because I didn't understand who this woman was, nor what I'd done wrong. Through my tears I'd pray for my father to return. I'd call his name again and again, because I knew he'd understand.

If he did come home I'd hear him, first his car in the driveway, perhaps a few sharp words between he and my mother, then his heavy creaking on the stairs. He'd open the door gently, in case I was asleep, then sit on the bed and rub my shoulders with his big hands. Unlike my mother's perfectly tuned caress, his hands were rough and clunky, heavy on my back. But he was trying, and in those seemingly desperate moments his touch felt to me like that of an angel. "It's okay," he'd say. "Everything will be okay." If I hadn't eaten he'd bring me food—toast or a hot-dog—the few things he knew how to prepare. He'd stroke my head and I'd fall asleep under the spell of his simple words.

In those moments I glimpsed aspects of my father I barely knew. In my child's imagination I came to believe that there were two of him, one the distant stranger, the other a fearless lion hunter come to carry me away. I wanted him always to be my rescuer, not just in the ugly moments of my mother's illness. But he was usually so far away, physically and emotionally, that I learned how to feel emotion from my mother. Despite the bouts of drinking, it was she who showed me the relief of tears and the pain of awareness, she who revealed touch—skin to skin—as a small act of love and forgiveness.

I didn't escape the hard blue gaze of my father's masculinity, but neither did I settle like hardening wax into the mold of him. Thanks to the shaping of my mother and three older sisters, I'm more comfortable in a room full of women than men, more at ease with their language of emotion and touch. I'm an outsider to be sure, still thick-skinned and crippled, at thirty-two, by stillborn tears. My closest friends are men, but even with them, emotions lie dormant, like water behind a papier mache dam. Their fathers resemble mine, a generation of hand-shaking, rough-hewn men. As children, my male friends and I bonded through games and sports, honing our egos and tools of war on the Darwinian field of play.

My mother lived by her intuition, which is to say, her heart. With no religion, per se, she read prolifically about alternative ways of seeing the world and matters of the spirit and soul. I can see her still, reclined in the library guest bed, squinting through narrow grandmother eyeglasses propped half-way down her nose. While my father was grounded in the black and white figures of an engineer's mind, my mother wandered from meditation to the moon. She felt things, perhaps, too deeply, and I wonder if her mourning for the victims of this world helped lead her to wine. When she found me pulling the wings off a fly she reacted not with anger but deep sorrow. Years later, when I went weeping to her about pictures I had seen of coyote pups burned to death in their dens by ranchers, she held me close and cried with me. When my tears dried she helped me pen my first letter to our congress-man. I was seven years old. In these small moments she taught me that it was okay to feel things deeply, that in fact it was wrong not to.

Her crying allowed me to cry. I didn't know it, but she was teaching me to live and speak through my heart, even when it hurt to do so. It is this language of tears, of heart, of open emotion that I yearn to know better, and that I wish for other men, including my father. In his generosity he invited strangers home, but it was my mother who fed them and, after my father went to bed, listened to their sad stories late into the night. She took care of them. Taking care. This, more than anything, defined my mother and count-less other women I've known. What would the world be like if the other half of us learned to care as well? Or learned to feel as deeply? A man will sacrifice his life for his nation, but withhold from his children the contents of his heart.

Ironically, it took my mother's death to unveil the father I'd seen in the shadow of her drinking so many years before. More painful than seeing my mother waste away to cancer was watching my father watch her. Controlled for so long, his tears stung him. He writhed under them, as ashamed as he was devastated. Even at her funeral, when I held him and cried onto his shoulder, I felt the shield of the man, his shoulders and back rigid as steel, his jaw clamped and quivering. Despite all of his children surrounding him, he was profoundly, undeniably alone. The most difficult moment of his life, and he couldn't let us in.

In the ten years following her death, the lion hunter has returned, slowly, to his children. Forced into the role of caregiver, he sees us through my mother's eyes. He has softened in old age, slowed down enough to listen. For years after her death he couldn't bear to speak of her; now tears pool in his eyes as he recalls the years with her. He calls me on the telephone to tell me about the squirrels living in his woodpile. They remind him of our family, he says, now that we are gone. When I go to visit him, my father lets me hold him, if only for a moment. I feel her there, my mother, just beneath his skin.

Colin Chisholm is a writer whose work has also appeared in the magazines Audubon, Climbing, *and* The Sun. *He lives in Prescott, Arizona.*

Giving Thanks for Grief

by Jennifer Armstrong

....

I am standing in the circle of friends surrounding Melanie by the tiny, newly-dug grave. I have wept with her as she and her husband looked their last on their baby, Magnolia, lying in the small homemade coffin. Dead at three days old, she looks like a perfect porcelain doll. A tiny, stuffed bear is beside her and yellow, spring flowers, placed by many loving hands. I could hardly breathe as the bereaved parents cradled the coffin in their arms and gazed on the still face. At last they closed the coffin and lowered it reluctantly.

Now Melanie is gripping a shovel in her trembling hands, readying her-self to throw the first shovelful of dirt over the coffin. She can't bring herself to do it and no one comes forward out of the circle to help her. We all hold our places and will her to be strong. My own knuckles are white as I watch her clinging to the shovel, weeping. Her legs are buckling and her body presses against the shovel as though it were the one thing keeping her from falling into the abyss of grief. We are a circle of love and grief around her, holding her. My mouth is full of silence. We wait. I feel the moment she is ready. I feel her deep shaking breath through the soles of my own feet as she straight-ens, digs the shovel into the loose earth and sends the first clods of dirt over the coffin. A clump of earth strikes the wooden lid and we all hear the final, hollow tone and are caught once more in the passage of time. One by one we come forward then and throw handfuls of earth into the grave. One by one we struggle to let go of the need to understand.

Walking back toward the house and the community meal, my ten-year-old daughter, Georgia Rose, turns and asks, "How old were you, Mommy, when you lost your baby?"

"Nineteen," I tell her. Nineteen years old, six months pregnant and three weeks married I awoke one morning to terrible pains and a gush of blood from between my legs. As if in a slow-motion dream, we went to the hospital, then home to sew a shroud and build a coffin and then to the cemetery. Twelve years ago I was standing in a graveyard on a May afternoon like this, throwing handfuls of dirt over my infant son born three months too soon.

I am called back to the present by my daughter's voice asking, "Mommy, who was with you when you buried him?"

"Your father and I were alone," I say.

"Oh," she says, "Oh, Mommy, that must have been so hard."

The compassion in her voice wraps around me like loving arms and I sink down into my own grief to feel myself standing where Melanie was standing only moments before. Where I thought I was alone, I find the whole world encircling me whispering, "This is the bread of life. This is the cup of faith." Is this what Melanie just experienced when she took that deep breath? Is this what happens when we contract down to the smallest point of ourselves? When we are drawn into our deepest darkness, the world suddenly opens up and there is light pushing its way through the darkness like grass breaking through pavement? In our darkest hour, the barren ground comes alive with new green. I want to hold both my girls. I open my arms to Georgia Rose and...where is Suzannah? Turning, I re-trace my steps and find her placing green sods over the raw, black earth of the grave, tears streaming down her cheeks. Her nine-year-old face looks both painfully young and old as her hands smooth over the grave like one smoothes the covers on a bed of a child being tucked in to sleep. "I wanted to make it beautiful," she says. "I couldn't leave the ground looking so ugly."

I wait in silence as she fits the broken pieces of sod over the wounded earth and tucks them into place. When she is finished, we walk together, all three of us toward the house and the meal. Our wounds are beautiful, I want to tell them. Fierce testimonies to joy, for it is where we are broken that the light can shine through. Would they understand that? Do I? I say nothing. It is enough to walk with their hands in mine under the arching trees above us and then out into the warm afternoon sunshine of a Spring day.

Jennifer Armstrong has spent her life writing and singing and making music.

Widow Making

by Helen Joyce Harris

In the words of D.H. Lawrence, I have something to expiate. It haunts me still. About six months into my widowhood, when I was still a veritable black hole of grief and most of my friends and family were avoiding me, I was finding solace in a sort of compulsive walking. So when a friend of my dead husband Joe's—we'll call the man Al—lost his wife of forty-plus years, I attended the memorial service with a kind of sick, familiar relish. At least now, I congratulated myself, I knew what other bereaved needed: a copy of *A Grief Observed* by C. S. Lewis, and a stiff hike. I loaned Al my book on the spot; a month later, I called to invite him on an upcoming Sierra Singles walk to Muir Beach.

"Do you know," he said over the phone, "that she saved her every pair of glasses?"

Ah. I was at home. For months I'd been where Al now was: sifting through Joe's belongings and making for them arbitrary final resting places, decisions which felt like little mini-murders: driving to the Goodwill with shirts and shorts; offering to squeamish friends his art supplies, his better clothes; boxing up his books and other treasures. Throwing away or giving away his life. Not a single piece of this was easy. Not one pair of dime-store glasses. Much of the time, I expected him to show back up and be really, really upset about his things. Now Al was having to snuff out the remains of a life. The day of the hike, I met him at his house, and he drove us across the Golden Gate Bridge into Marin County. We talked ashes. I had yet to lift off the top from the urn and face into mine.

"They're not ashes, really," he warned me. "They're more the consistency of Kitty Litter."

I brought up my problem with Joe's wallet, from which I had guiltily taken and spent thirty-two dollars. Al covered me: "Her purse is still where she left it in the kitchen."

At the trail head we met a dozen other singles, strangers to us. I could already smell the tart ocean on the soft June air. The light would hold for hours. I studied the other hikers with a kind of awe: focused on their water bottles and the lacing of their boots, they did not, like me, appear to feel aberrant because they were uncoupled.

The trouble began when, just before we headed out, I decided to take off my cardigan. Had he been other than who he was, would I have invited Al out walking? Accomplished, tall, broad-shouldered, urbane; if he'd been only those, I'd not have called, because the invitation would have seemed too much like a date. But he was Joe's friend; that made him my brother. More importantly, he was sixty-eight. If I felt sexless at fifty-one, I figured (insofar as I figured at all) that he, seventeen years my senior and barely back from the mortician's, was definitely sexless.

Except, of course, deep in my heart I must have hoped I wasn't sexless. So, after I slipped my camera off over my head, Al helped me out of my white zippered cardigan. His big hands were tender on my sweater there, and then he offered to put it in his day pack. He put my sweater in his day pack. In an instant the whole late-afternoon scene buckled and swirled: the other hikers; the sandy trail; the nearby brush; and this tall, kind, suddenly dangerous man. I wanted those hands on me. I grew giddy, dramatic, grew flirty and girlish and witty and wry.

How, as I recount all this, can I be fair to myself? I didn't know what to do about anything at the time. It was taking all my courage and my Walkman on loud to propel me into the supermarket once a week, where I'd grab seven identical frozen dinners and more ice cream and beer. I didn't feel entitled to eat. I didn't know how to make sleep happen. I was taking stabs at things to fill up the endless void of my days. This was one of the stabs I took.

The beach didn't help. That ocean's pounding invites in me disclosure, so when at the water's edge some geese flew overhead, I told Al a secret of mine: that I'd always thought geese very brave, laboring up there, borne along by only God knows what. He smiled. I had no business telling that man my secrets. I still don't know what I had any business doing at all.

Then, the moon. As we drove back across the Golden Gate there it was, as big and orange as a pumpkin, low on the horizon, its light reflecting off the Bay. "Reminds me of what you more commonly see in the fall, a harvest moon," he said quietly. I didn't know much about harvests at that time; I'd have called it a Senior Prom moon, and me a full thirty-four years past my last one. Mean old moon—didn't it know people had died around here?

But I am responsible. I asserted myself into the gape of that man's vast and terrible loss. And though later that night when he kissed me my panic was real, it was not as real as the way, there in his living room, imaginary violins swelled and the world lurched to a momentary stop. Not as real as what beckoned beyond that fumbled kiss—two place settings, maybe, someone to say my name, a lap to put my head in, someone to lie down with.

I wanted to break from the kiss, cut the swelling string section in my mind, up the lights, and blurt loud to God, that consummate rip-off artist: "You mean, *I* didn't die?" I felt as choked and dizzy as I had at fifteen when my hand first got held. I felt—maybe for the first time since Joe's terrifying heart surgery eleven years before—thrumming, pulsating, entirely alive.

I thought of nothing else for many weeks, during which time Al and I executed a few entirely chaste walks. Even Joe, ten years my senior, had been too old for me; in falling for Joe I had been ultimately shortsighted. I now wanted a man who saw the doctor only for an occasional tetanus shot, a guy maybe thirty. A man certain *not* to die. Fair's fair: I wanted someone to die *on*.

In time, I had to tell Al this. It was brutal. I was brutal. He'd spent his last several years tending to a wife devoured by cancer, and I, callow and needy, first encouraged him romantically, and then kicked him while he was still down. My whole doomed, bittersweet "relationship" with this man consisted technically of about six kisses. But in "leading Al on," I tarnished all four of us. Al? I clearly further jeopardized Al. His wife? I stole for a time from a heroic dead woman the attention of her ravaged husband. Myself? I pried the cover off some nasty secrets about my own sexual gluttony. And Joe? I revealed to his good friend the ultimately bad taste in women of my defenseless, shining Joe.

My widowhood from then on expressed itself in this turgid, relentless lust—the kind I assume appropriate in adolescent males—and in other bewilderments: the need to change everything about me, restlessness and discomfort around old friends, heedlessness around new ones.

I couldn't have what I thought I wanted, which was either Joe back or unleashed wall-to-wall sex without consequences. But I was a stranger to myself, erratic; I felt toxic to men. I felt I should probably register myself as a lethal weapon, like fighters who register their fists.

I resorted instead to a new kind of sexual act: abandonment into near-ecstasy through wracking, full-bodied sobs. In my womb was a pulsing, vacant sensation, a deep ache that would find expression on demand. Maybe the crying felt so much like sex because it allowed me momentarily to turn off my furtive, panicked mind. This physical grief paralleled my experiences with labor: My body was taking instruction from sources far more compelling than my head.

My crying was most satisfying when done in isolation in the deep red-woods a few miles from my house. I'd sink to my knees, drape myself over a rock or a stump, and the sobs would heave out in great rhythmic chords. The tears seemed to come from a new part of my eyes, drooling from the center of my lower lids, flowing out clear and ample. I see now that this is how I made a widow of myself. This is how I threw the new pot which is me.

When it wasn't crying, my body wanted action. At least twice a day, I hiked. In the dark night I'd watch through my curtain for the first tint of dawn, and then I'd be into my boots and out the door almost before the toilet finished flushing. I'd turn the Walkman music up loud. I had privacy, a route, a purpose. Out flowed the new day's tears. Sometimes I'd moan; I'd call Joe's name. Over time, after the tears, strangely, strangely, I might even begin to sing. After many months, unbelievably enough, there were mornings when I ended my hike at a skip.

During the lunch hour I walked the beach near the high school where I taught. I'd sit on a piece of driftwood, eating my sandwich, draining the new tears, watching the gulls. Once, after many months of this, I invited the rest of the English department to eat there during an extended-lunch day. We bought sandwiches and pop nearby, then trudged through the sand to my log, where we sat looking out at the gray-blue bay and San Francisco's sky-line in the distance.

I felt deeply happy, that I'd had the courage to suggest this spot, to attempt this connection. I ventured to explain: "This is where I come to cry at noon," and, of course, I started again.

The Chair said, horrified, "Helen, we could have gone somewhere else. We still can. People? Shall we move?"

It was another stab run amok. Asking others to witness one's grief, I learned the hard way, is like asking them to undress with you in public. But one colleague, Warren, made a place for me there on the log, and loaned me his shoulder, and did not flinch. For that moment on the log he, I, and the others, whether they wanted to or not, had Joe back.

Oh, Joe was a happening dude. Life was an art form to him, and he was its artist. My sons called him "the poor man's Christo." When our neighbor, Marc, worried about termites, Joe stenciled onto our street dozens of giant, black, anatomically correct wood-chewers storming toward Marc's house. He also baked tuna can lids into our flapjacks, short-sheeted our beds, and squirt-gunned the neighborhood kids.

At the middle school where we both taught, he animated the whole place with his pranks. He'd walk the halls with an arrow stuck through his head. For the faculty pot luck, he once chocolate-frosted tiers of round Styrofoam. The higher the regard he had for a colleague, the more subject that person was to assault. He once elongated the painted lines on either side of one faculty parking space in the lot, labeling it for Virginia Pratt, a sixth grade teacher who was a full six feet tall.

He was irreverent, and yet entirely reverent. He carried our household's spiders out into the yard. His patience felt like the ocean's. He wrought miracles with leftover students. I remember one undersized, none-too-clean seventh-grader whose forearms bore scars from self-inflicted cigarette burns—a boy who gave the rest of the faculty the creeps. Joe and he worked after school for maybe forty hours, building and painting in bright abstractions a kayak of plywood and canvas. I hope the kid sailed into safety in it; I have my doubts.

How I loved him. I never tired of looking at Joe. I was always photographing him: the squint of his eyes, his long straight nose, his salt-and-pepper beard. Joe on the tennis court. Joe in the classroom. Joe bent over a painting. I could not believe that in a world as huge as this, we had been lucky enough even to meet. I dressed the way he liked, biked with him, watched his tennis, learned to tell the works of Diebenkorn from those of Thiebaud. When, seven years into our marriage, he had his first heart attack, I, too, gave up salt, cooked low-fat, watched his rest. I held the termite stencil, I made the frosting for the faux cake. But when I try to talk about this love, I feel as if I'm trying to justify myself; as if even now, almost six years later, I'm compensating for being, finally, unfaithful to him after he died.

He loved me back, that's for sure. While I'd begun admiring him from my first day on the job—and envying those whom Joe cared about enough to tease—the first I knew that he'd noticed me as well was one spring in the early seventies. The students began complaining of a bad smell in my classroom. I paid little mind initially, because they always ragged on each other about B.O. And it was true: they often did stink, especially after P.E. So, afraid of embarrassing some kid, I went perhaps a week not deigning to acknowledge the heavy stench near the front of the room. But after school one day, I opened the lower drawer of my desk, and the smell almost knocked me down. There lay a large, flat, oily, dead fish, which I knew instantly as an invitation to play from Mr. Joe Dawkins. It was easily the most romantic overture I'd ever had.

Since all four of our parents were dead when Joe and I married, both for the second time, we were each other's family. Together we painted our house; built a huge deck, two fences, and a retaining wall; drove our four sons to Vancouver; drove ourselves across the U.S.; flew to Quebec, to England, to Mexico. With me on piano and Joe on guitar, we joined in music.

We also had in common our jobs, which kept us together virtually twenty-four hours a day for most of seventeen years. We did some grand things. Once we squired nearly two-hundred junior high kids to the Renaissance Faire, and, since admission was free for those in costume, we created for most of them period wear. With the girls we braided dried flowers into garlands. For the boys we made tabards—tunic-like garments—out of old sheets, me at the ironing board and sewing machine, Joe staining the finished products with coffee, and stamping each with a black fleur-de-lis.

So when he died, I was a husk. I didn't know who was left when his light was extinguished. Finding out had its ruthlessness. In time, feeling like a traitor, I stripped the many abstract expressionist paintings he'd made from the walls of our house. No. My house. I had the walls repainted, and left them bare and white for most of a year. When friends would drop by, I'd say, "This is me. Tabula rasa." They'd blurt out shocked disavowals: how could a mother—a teacher, even—be completely undefined?

Eventually, some time after our family had at last cast Joe's ashes into the ocean, I put back up some pictures: one of myself as a child; some black and white photographs I'd taken, developed, enlarged, and framed; and some paintings by women artist friends of mine. I got my graying hair permed, my first in thirty-three years. Worse, I dyed it a ghoulish black that reflected back Morticia Addams whenever I checked the mirror.

I bought clothes as gaudy as my hair: bright pink, maybe, or something to show my legs. I am someone younger, my new image screamed, someone aggressively not sad, someone no longer near a death. I am not an absence.

And, unleashed by Al's kiss, I now felt that all males over the age of about fourteen were displaying themselves shamelessly to me: their heart-catching leather belts, their helpless T-shirted shoulders, their busy, capable hands. I knew Joe through them, and them through him. I'd feed myself on all of them together, and they'd compile into a presence that would cover up the hole where he used to be.

My predations after men now make me shudder. At a local dancing place not long after my First Kiss, a woman told me, "Sometimes I ask the men to dance, usually the ones I feel sorry for." So I did that too. But only the ones I didn't feel sorry for. What's the worst that could happen? I asked myself. The men obliged or didn't; it made no difference. Later that night, soon after I'd delivered to Al my "too old" speech, I sidled up to a man and said the following: "May I stand near you? You look like my husband, Joe Dawkins, who died." That's how I got my Second Kiss.

I was out of control. Caring for Joe, especially once his health began to fail, had seemed to have a sanctity to it, a wholesomeness. With that veneer off me, who was left seemed sometimes like a harlot. And the worst of it was that I felt my actions still reflected on him, even though he was now pebbles of bone washing around in the Pacific. He still had me, I guess.

My friend Kathy called my cravings "the life force." Though my brazenness still embarrasses me, I do believe that she was at least partly right. Carnal knowledge—and, maybe even more importantly, the blithe touch it then permits—is such direct access to the fullness of life, at least for me. I was vibrating with appreciation of all males, with the starved appetite of someone who'd been shipwrecked and was now facing a replete buffet. Talk football, I must have communicated just by standing near one. Let me watch you chew. My God, you are entirely alive. Do you have any idea what that means?

In time, I achieved a certain personal integration. I gained some decorum; I pursued some passions not man-related, like biking and whitewater rafting; like writing. I took a leave of absence from my job and sought a graduate degree in Montana. There I hung out with the twenty-year-olds, read a lot of books, got good grades, listened to my music, made myself thick soups, found a church, and gradually began to sleep through the night.

After I got established in Missoula, I began to follow the singles' ads. I had a lot of coffee dates. I did this because my body required it of me: Don't abandon me, it seemed to say. Get me some company. Connect me back in.

In my dating life, I eventually learned how to blunder through "no" a bit earlier, before any real blood was flowing. I accumulated some ignominious purple hearts of my own, I the sadder-but-wiser rejectee. But getting rejected is such a small sting. Compared to, say, poor health. Such a triviality. This is the deep lesson I have learned: As paper covers rock, death covers pride. In this long, slow process of achieving peace about my widowhood, which in my case lasted about four years, I grew a new self.

And then, two years ago, I reconnected with "Bobby" Freeman, a former southern California neighbor whom I hadn't seen in thirty-seven years. I'd grown up across the street from Bob. Our families had been friends; his father my doctor, his mother my best Girl Scout cookie client. He was a couple of years ahead of me in school, and we'd always been shy around each other.

When we met at the airport on the way to our high school reunion, one of the first things he spoke of remembering was that I'd taken fourth place in the Eighth Grade Oratorical Contest. Why, after all this time, would that fact stick? Because he'd taken fourth place two years earlier.

"You cried, I believe," he said.

"Of course I cried," I said. "There in the auditorium, in front of probably four hundred kids. I always cry."

Each of us, it turned out, had studied literature, had three children, been divorced, taught English, and written books. Both had turned rather forcefully away from those Homet Road years. Over the reunion weekend, as we got reacquainted, we realized that we shared a whole fabric of childhood assumptions and experiences: a childhood I—because of the relatively early loss of both my parents—had almost completely repressed. Being with him helped me recover the person I'd been before I became a wife and mother.

Of course, it seemed sudden to my sons when I called them a week later and said I'd be moving from Montana to Colorado to be near a man named Bob Freeman, a man I almost certainly would marry. "Who is this guy, Mom?" my Dylan demanded, aghast, from California. "What's he do?" Good question. Good son. Initially, Bob could not seem more different from Joe. Joe owned only two neckties, and dressed in tennis shorts, even while teaching. Bob is clean-shaven, gets regular haircuts, and routinely wears ties, pressed slacks, and shiny wingtip shoes. Their orientations also seem opposite.

Maybe it was Joe's sky-blue eyes that directed his attention so often heavenwards. He loved the World War II British Spitfire and wore its insignia. He read astronomy. He built and flew countless gliders and kites. By contrast, he knew the names of virtually no plants except daffodils and roses, regarding such green things as mainly raw material for his play: he'd hang plastic oranges in our camellias and wait for folks to notice. Bob, on the other hand, has deep brown eyes and is of the earth. He can still enumerate the plants that grew in our childhood neighbors' yards, even the weeds, though in fact he sees not even crabgrass as a weed. He lives most fully in the intricate and mysterious interactions between soil, seeds, water, and sunlight. He values manure, and he absolutely loves dirt.

These differences aside, however, their kinship is unmistakable: both gentle, both kind, both rebellious, both with keen, questioning minds. And had I not known and loved Joe as I did, I could not now love Bob as I do. It feels as if Joe gave me universal access—a kind of code—a sense of deep familiarity, of meeting and honoring Bob where he was and is. Joe never argued; Bob does. I must have tried Joe mightily, but he held his tongue. Bob doesn't. "You hurt the boy in me," he told me once, "and the man fights back." With Bob, I've learned to argue and to fight. The process of grieving has incorporated Joe into myself, and the newly recombinant me loves Bob. Once in a while I still dream, though, that Joe's not dead, and that now I have to choose. After these dreams, I waken to feel relief that Joe's gone, but then, of course, I feel like a murderer.

Where is Al, the first casualty of my widow-making, in all this? For me, Al was a gift, an indispensable bridge back to life, not just from Joe to Bob, but from feeling dead to realizing that there was life yet in me. I owe Al a great deal. I think of him often. I love him, in a way. I admire him for his dignity and courage. But when I've called a few times over the intervening years to say hello, and to attempt to forge a friendship, he's said bitterly, "Why would I want to talk to you?"

Why, indeed? Why chat with Hannibal Lecter?

I wish, though, that I could achieve peace about him—pay some kind of reparation. I can only hope that I initiated a reciprocal process in his life, one that has since led to one or more of my sisters holding him and rocking him and loving him as he deserves to be loved. I can only hope that the new mysteries of his life have unfolded in ways as surprising and powerful as have mine. And I can keep reminding myself, in Al's name, that one is never too old to be dangerous, to be capable of causing injury and pain.

It makes sense, somehow, that this should be so: that the fine-motor skills of loving require a level of perfect attention from which there will necessarily be lapses. During these lapses I feel as if I'm peering deep into a cold, dark, pitiless crevasse. I hate those times. But it still makes sense to me that, in loving another person, I can't feel the soaring and the connection without the risk of that free fall of loss.

Out my window in our back garden is Bob's handiwork. On beds mounded with straw live the potatoes, spinach, and lettuce. In cavities he's scooped out of the cover crop with his post-hole digger are the artichokes, asparagus, corn, kale, and Anaheim peppers, among others. In thick rows are beets and parsnips. In hills are the squashes; in water walls are melons and tomatoes; in a raised bed, the carrots and herbs. We brought most of these seeds—nearly a thousand of them—to life in trays indoors while there was still snow on the ground. I recall one of our Anaheim peppers from last year's garden, one whose stem got folded over when it was perhaps only three inches tall. I'd have tossed it in the compost pile, but it was Bob who found it, and he fashioned a splint from three wooden toothpicks, which he positioned around the little plant. He then wrapped a strip of cloth around the toothpicks, inserting a sort of poultice of peat moss between the bandage and the injured stem. The pepper healed and bore.

Across the room from where I now write, Bob himself is in the bed. I hear him breathing: in, then out; in, then out. I can turn my head and see how—even as tall and strong as he is—the covers hardly mound; how easily that might be just a few pillows and blanket folds under the quilt, making the shape of a back, a straight leg, a bent one. But his head is on the pillow there—that dear head of shining white hair—and I can hear him breathing. I cannot contain my joy, and so I weep.

Helen Joyce Harris is a novelist and teacher of writing.

Fossil Brothers

Peter H. Spectre

....

George said—and you'll have to trust me here, because George is no longer with us and therefore can neither confirm nor deny any of this—"Pete, don't kid yourself. You don't find fossils. Fossils find you."

Which at the moment sounded like the biggest pile of hogwash I'd heard since one of our associates had suggested that the way to a higher level of consciousness was to build an orgone box and get inside it.

George also said that once the ice had been broken, once the first fossil had found me, fossils would be coming on like gangbusters ever afterward. That's because I would have tapped into the basic hum of the ancient universe.

Which is interesting, because George, who to my mind was wrong more often than right when it came to touchy-feely matters, turned out to be right on both counts. In short order I found a fossil, or, perhaps, a fossil found me, and more fossils came on like gangbusters ever afterwards.

As evidence of the latter I offer a subsequent experience one winter in England. I was staying overnight in Lyme Regis, a tiny town on the sea between Dorset and Devon, on the South Coast. After supper I strolled up the street to The Volunteer for a pint or two of bitter ale. The publican, in response to my query about whether his town had a claim to fame and what that might be if it did, said, "Fossils."

"Really?" I said.

"Really," he said. "Tomorrow morning, if you have time, walk up yonder hill to the second lane on the left and take it down to a path that leads to the shore. Follow the shore to the base of a cliff. The fossils are there."

So, the next morning after breakfast, before I pulled out of town, I took the lane, the path, the shore, the cliff. There were seagulls and salt grass and crashing surf. There were driftwood, flotsam, and jetsam at the high-tide line. There were million-year-old fossils sticking out of the face of the cliff like nuggets in Eldorado. I picked up enough to set off the "Overweight" light at the airport on my return flight, including a piece of ancient shell so big and so heavy that I now use it for a doorstop.

George, on seeing the haul when I got home, said, "See what I mean?—Gangbusters."

My first fossil came some time in the early 1970s. My guess is that it was in the late spring, because I recall the weather was cool, yet we were slapping the occasional mosquito as we walked. I had taken the ferryboat from Rockland, Maine, on the western side of Penobscot Bay, to the island of Vinalhaven, in the middle of the bay, to visit George. He was living with the fishermen while trying to make a go of it as a freelance writer. I used to travel out there every few weeks or so, and we would take long walks around the island and tell each other long, shaggy-dog tales about things we had seen, or heard, or thought we knew. Mostly it was ranting and raving.

George might ask what I had been doing for fun in the last few weeks, and I might say I had been organizing my workshop to build a rowboat, but I was having trouble finding the right tools, and he would take it from there.

"You can't get decent tools, you know," he'd say. "You can go into a hardware store and they throw blister-packed trash at you. If there's any steel at all in them it isn't tempered steel. And most of the time there's only one size of each tool—medium and useless. Who ever heard of medium for crying out loud? Everything is either small or large. Look at a proper tool kit and the medium-size tools are the least worn. And of course the bloody good tools that used to be available are all hanging on restaurant and bar room walls. Oh sure, you can send off to these fine-tool catalog outfits and get English and German planes at $30 apiece, $500 workbenches, monogrammed screw extractors, and full-size drawings for a seventeenth-century mandolin, but try to get a boat slick or a lipped adze; show me a ship auger—and I'll quit smoking. Lead me to a boat-builder's bevel, backing iron, or spud, and I'll take esoteric vows. And materials to work with, Great Hornytoads, you can't get the wood, and no copper rivets and roves—it's a conspiracy, some heinous troll is sitting atop a mountain of our tools, our wood, and we gotta find the bastards to liberate what is ours, to find peace and freedom and the knowledge that we can do it ourselves once again, to know joy again in the beatitude of one's very own shop where personal expression once again blossoms across the land, oh Lordy...."

I'd take a hit off my can of beer and ask what he meant by "joy."

Generally, we had an informal division of labor when it came to rants. George took care of technology, science, what he called "psycho-emotional matters," and manly stuff—guns, fishing, dogs, thickness planers—with a strong emphasis on geology, coastal ecology, and the management of wood-lots. I was in charge of personal history, interrelationships, the meaning of things, nostalgia, politics, and gender studies, which in those days came under the heading, "Women." We tended to share literature, rock 'n' roll criticism, and the analysis of stupidity.

The way it worked was this: I'd come in on the early-morning ferry. George would meet me at the landing, usually in an old rusting pickup truck with his high-strung dog, Sylvia, a long, lean Borzoi, pacing around in the back. We'd drive into town for fried eggs and home fries at a little greasy spoon, and we'd always have lots of coffee. Lots and lots of coffee. Enough so that afterwards it seemed as if our eyeballs were rolling around on sticks.

"What'll it be today, Pete?" George would say, out in the street, wired.

"What've you got?" I'd say.

"Let's see," he'd say. "I've got summer beach, winter beach, woods and fields, bushwhacker's paradise, historical quarries, heights with an overlook, lighthouses and headlands, or freeform. Take your pick."

On the day in question, I took winter beach; so we got in the truck, drove over to the East Side, and parked on the side of a dirt road that led down to an old saltwater farm. Sylvia took off like a rocket into the puckerbrush.

We walked down the dirt road for a while and then took a shortcut through the woods. George went off on a monologue about the deleterious effects of blow-downs on stands of mature spruce. We came out into an open field. I countered with an analysis of why exposing Richard Nixon as a pathological liar was right and good for justice but bad for the future of ratio-nal political discourse. While we crossed the field, we both agreed that if we had it to do all over again, we'd learn lead guitar, strike a pose, and join a rock 'n' roll band. ("Stratocaster," George said. "Pink with powder-blue appliques.")

At the far edge of the field was a berm of loose stones, broken lobster traps and crates, bits and pieces of frayed pot warp, rusted oil cans, and plastic detergent bottles brittle from exposure to salt water and ultraviolet light. This marked the limit of the most extreme high tides—the highest high tides—the most awe-inspiring ones, at once pulled by the moon and driven by the furies of winter. (The existence of such a berm was what identified this as a winter beach.)

We climbed over the top and—bango!—there we were, face to face with one of the most spectacular sights on the coast of Maine. Ocean and ledges and islands and half-tide rocks to the horizon. Wreck Ledge, Bunker Ledge, Old Horse Ledge; Sheep Island, Hay Island, Brimstone Island; Shag, Yellow, and Diamond Rocks. The lighthouse on Saddleback Ledge to our left, the one on Heron Neck to our right.

In the far distance the ocean rose and fell in long, undulating swells, as if it were breathing. In the middle distance it surged through passages between the ledges and rocks. Immediately offshore, it gathered itself together, drew itself up to full height, rolled forward like a freight train without brakes on the steepest of grades, and threw itself on the beach. The effect was like 500 strongmen hitting the same stump at the same time with ten-pound sledge-hammers. The sea thundered. The ground shook.

The beach consisted of huge boulders as big as a man's head, rounded and ovaled by centuries of rolling in the surf. The rocks rolled forward as the waves surged up the beach, they rolled backward as the waves receded; they ground against each other; they bounced along like giant marbles. The rote—the sound of the ocean working the shore—was horrific.

So there we were, walking along our winter beach, George and I, Sylvia off in the distance spooking the sea birds. George, inspired by the beach stones, was declaiming on geology. I was lost in my own thoughts, following a line that branched off the main into...where?... I'm not sure I can say. Something about the setting—the violence of the sea on the land, the slant of the light, the barrenness of the ledges—had turned me inward. I could register a discrete word here and there from George, but I didn't have the foggiest notion what he was saying.

"Strata"... "Devonian"... "Glaciated"... "Schist".... "Fracture zone"... "Sedimentary".... "Fossil"....

"Fossil?" I said, wallowing up from the depths. "Did you say something about a fossil?"

"Three or four years ago," George said, "Right here on this spot."

Now, I don't know much about geology, but I do know that fossils are generally found in soft, sedimentary formations, and that pieces of rock from such formations wouldn't last fifteen minutes on a beach such as this. All those rolling granite boulders would grind them up in no time at all.

"Impossible," I said.

"But true," George said.

"Well then," I said, "I've always wanted to find a fossil. If you found one here, so can I."

And that's when George said, "Pete, don't kid yourself. You don't find fossils. Fossils find you."

And that's when I reached down and picked up a long, thin piece of stone. It was of the sedimentary type. It had broken away from another stone, and the flattish seam of the break was studded with scores of tiny shell fossils, somewhat like miniature scallops.

I can't begin to describe the feeling of triumph, of power, of blessedness that that first fossil gave me. If I could have done a standing backflip, I would have. I showed the prize to George.

George turned the rock over and over in his hands, feeling it, studying it. He seemed perplexed.

"What's the matter?" I said.

"I've seen this stone before," he said quietly.

"What?"

"This is the fossil I found a few years ago."

"You mean you found it and then left it behind?"

"No, I found it and took it home."

"Then how did it get back here?"

"Maybe it's in both places."

We called for Sylvia and ran back along the way we came. The beach, the berm, the field, the woods, the dirt road, the truck, George's place, the front door, the hall, the living room, the windowsill. There on the windowsill was George's fossil. It was a long, thin piece of stone. It was of the sedimentary type. It had broken away from another stone, and the flattish seam of the break was studded with scores of tiny shell fossils, somewhat like miniature scallops.

I aligned my fossil, face down, with George's, face up. They fit together exactly. A sedimentary stone had survived for centuries on a beach that was anathema to it. It had broken in half along a seam. One person had found half. Three or four years later, another person, a best friend in the presence of the first, had found the other half. I won't bore you with an accounting of the odds.

. . .

I am sitting in a room in a house on the coast of Maine, about fifteen miles as the crow flies from our winter beach on Vinalhaven. In the distance I can see a similar beach, and islands, and rocks, and ledges, and the ocean surging among them. On the table in front of me are our fossil-bearing stones, George's and mine.

As I said, George is no longer with us. Before he left we were talking about old times, about some of the wondrous things we had seen over the years.

"Do you still have the fossil?" I said.

"Of course," he said.

"Good," I said, but I wanted to say more. I wanted to ask him if I could have his fossil. I didn't want to see it simply disappear because those left behind might not know what it really meant. But I couldn't ask, and, I suspect, he couldn't offer. To do so would be to admit that our island-walking days were about to be over.

George died of cancer a few days later. At his funeral, on a wild, stormy day on the island, I asked his wife if she had seen the fossil. No, she hadn't. I asked his daughter. No, she hadn't. His son. No....

One day, a couple of years later, there was a knock on my door. It was George's wife. She came in and sat down, and we drank coffee and talked for awhile.

"I was going through George's things," she said, "and I found something you might be interested in."

She pulled the fossil from her bag. "Show me how they fit together."

So I did. Like a glove.

"Keep them together," she said. "They belong that way."

I have been studying the stones off and on for a couple of days now. One side of mine is the outside of the original stone before it broke and is therefore smooth. The other side, the seam side, is jagged with fossilized shells. One side of George's, the matching side with mine, is jagged with fossils. What I have never noticed before—or what I have noticed and have never registered—is that the other side of George's stone is also jagged with fossils. My stone had split off from George's, and George's had split off from another.

Somewhere on our winter beach, or somewhere on someone's windowsill or someone's mantelpiece or someone's kitchen table, lies a piece of stone that fits together with ours as cleanly as the elements of the most expensive Swiss watch.

I won't bore you with an accounting of the odds. But I will suggest that, given everything that has come to pass already, the odds that this is true, as great as they may be, are with us.

Peter H. Spectre is a writer, editor, and author of several maritime books and innumerable magazine articles on a variety of subjects, mostly having to do with boats and the water.

Cultivating the Magpie Eye
by Clinton W. Trowbridge

I look at the sign in disbelief. NO DUMP PICKING! Next to it are exhibited various items for sale, all neatly categorized: lamps, couches, overstuffed chairs, tables, and straight-backed chairs, TVs, radios, cartons of books. The dump flea market. End of the freebies road at last. I think of the Paulsons, of golden moments in our own past, of Hugo, our French artist friend—of our society and what it has come to. Definitely the close of an era.

Our friends the Paulsons moved to Plainfield, Connecticut, mainly because of the Plainfield dump. It contained so many goodies that even then, in the early 1960s, it was kept under lock and key. Every day at 6 AM, the gates swung open, and every day Don and Rosie Paulson were first in line—until their house was furnished, in about a month. Beds, tables, everything—including the kitchen sink—was there for the taking, much of it in matching sets. Twin beds, solid brass, for the boys' room. A round oak table for the dining room—with six sturdy chairs. Even a device to take the top off a boiled egg. They were rightfully pleased with themselves and delighted in telling guests where it all came from.

Today, if you want to get things for nothing, you have to get to them before they get to where they're going. Spring-cleaning day in Chappaqua, New York, where my sister lives. Whole kitchens are out by the curb; three dozen still-packaged alarm clocks; a brand new rake, thrown away for want of a nail. It would pay us to hire a U-Haul. Pickup day in Boston. My eye is caught by a crystal bowl. Also in the pile are three new-looking futons; a portrait of a prosperous-looking man in a powdered wig; six cartons of books; two standing lamps; four boxes of kitchenware; no partridge in a pear tree, but some rugs and lesser things. The man carrying them up from the cellar, the building's custodian, mumbles something about fire laws—and about the moving van being filled up. Our son, who lives in Boston, speaks glowingly about the Harvard dumpsters at graduation time. His own apartment is richly furnished with castoffs—from down comforters to drinking mugs—but there is a new double-lined T-shirt for me, a ski parka for his mother, the promise of more.

It is Hugo, however, who is most attuned to these things. At a restaurant, his hands will automatically make birds, kites, tiny hats out of napkins. The lead foil from a bottle of wine becomes a knight's profile with helmet, the cork (on toothpicks) the body of a horse. But these are not just nervous tics that help him pass the time between slurps or bites. A sculptor, he has long made use of pieces of wood thrown away by the cabinetmakers. Among his creations are massive iron structures made from the rusted hulks of earthmovers. Recently, when he needed fifty or so bicycle wheels, he pondered for a while and then settled on an island community near his home. One ferry a day. Few cars. There must be a dump. There would be bicycles there. Sure enough, there was a mountain of wheels, his for the taking. Glad to be rid of them, said the man in charge. On his own seaside property, Hugo sets up rocks in interesting poses—a limestone/coral sculpture garden. Which rocks he sells—at a good price.

On a bicycle himself, his eye lights on the rusted head of an ancient Peugeot. He gathers it up and puts it away. A month later, from beneath the weeds surrounding a large fig tree, he spies the rest of the engine. Not the same engine, but the parts match. He makes the gasket and waits for the transmission, the wheels, and the rest of the car to show up. Which of course it will (and eventually does). One cannot really compete with Hugo.

When we lived in Long Island, our firewood was free. Probably we could have gotten paid to remove the blow-downs. In Maine, where we now reside, people are more aware of value. Even hubcaps are collected and sold. Now that the town dumps are closed, the best places for treasure hunting are the beaches of the outer islands. The ten-foot beam that serves as our door stoop has an adventure story behind it, and the lignum vitae deadeye that graces our mantelpiece, found on the same beach, is a treasure that is also a part of history—recalling, as it does, the days of the coasting schooner.

Driftwood itself, of course, has value. On some of the islands, whole houses are made from it. Wharf pilings are converted to sills and beams and rafters. A lifeboat blows ashore and becomes a roof. Framing a porthole on the view side of one house is the perfect sea gift: a toilet seat. Fine paneling? All you need is a love of patchwork, a delight in wormy wood, a preference for silver sheen. There's plenty of that out there.

When our children were very young, their favorite toys were cardboard boxes. They served as hiding place, bed, house, and room of house. Table. Chair. Boat. Car. Thoreau, who claimed that a large, wooden packing box made the ideal dwelling, would have approved, as would his hero Diogenes, who made do with a barrel.

People have made fancy houses out of old tires, even cans. Everything from adobe brick to bales of hay. Why settle for familiar materials, ordinary plans? "Be a person on whom nothing is lost," was Henry James's advice to aspiring writers. Instead of spending precious time scouring the shelves of the wholesale emporiums for (unneeded?) bargains, or beating out the early birds in the "everything goes," (mostly clothing) sales, why not consider how much there is of value all around us—and cultivate our magpie eye?

Clinton W. Trowbridge is an author, essayist, and retired English professor. His books include Crow Island Journal, *an account of his life on a Maine island. His essays appear in the* Christian Science Monitor *and other publications.*

Selling the Camp
by Kimberly Ridley

None of us took the For Sale signs seriously at first—not me, not my husband, Tom, not his three sisters. His parents had talked about selling their small, knotty pine-paneled camp on a lake in Maine for years. So we ignored the signs the realtors planted on the beach. They faded into the scenery as we lounged in webbed lawn chairs, swam, had cookouts, ate raspberry pie. We forgot about them. After all, this camp on the lake was the place where nothing bad happened, the place we dreamed about all winter, the place I reminded Tom to imagine, with eyes closed, when he had trouble falling asleep. The lake had claimed us, soothed us, washed away our worries for years. We thought we'd always return. We thought it would always be there.

And why not? The place never seemed to change. Same brown deco sofa, musty from years of holding family and friends in wet bathing suits. Same sunset view of pine-crowned islands like giant bonsai gardens. Same mattresses sagging in the middle from years of the kind of lovemaking that only happens at summer places. Same rituals, the first breath-stealing swim in June; picking blueberries from the canoe in August; closing up in October: thumb-tacking old white sheets over the picture windows, scattering mothballs under wool blankets, capping the chimney.

My in-laws bought the place twenty-five years ago from the couple who built it in the fifties. For Tom and his sisters, the camp is layered in memories like last year's leaves; it's a place where everything is all right, where stubs of birthday candles roll around in the silverware drawer, where everything is beloved and familiar: the feel of warm wood under bare feet, the curve of the cove's long dark arms, the call of loons out on the water.

Despite the illusions of constancy, this silver stretch of water and pine-rimmed shore has changed, even in the twelve years I've been coming here. It has begun to attract hordes of people who can't have fun without at least one loud motor. If they're not tearing across the lake in their jet skis and cigarette boats, they're blowing leaves or mowing lawns or riding three-wheelers back on shore. By seven on a Sunday morning in summer, there's almost always someone who can't abide quiet, who can't resist racing across the lake's calm surface with the throttle wide open.

The consequences go beyond noise. Algae slicks the rocks and clouds the water. Developers are carving up the last wild stretch of shoreline, where the loons have nested for years. I know the lake's decline saddens Tom's father, even as he tells us, in a level voice, that all the noise and pollution will inevitably drag down the camp's value.

But can we tally in dollars the things that are priceless? Despite the smell and whine of motors, I've swum so much in this lake and floated on my back so long that I imagined my boundaries dissolving and turning to silver, reaching toward every shore at once. Back in my own skin, I've witnessed things here that have made me stop. On one of my long swims, a loon flashed past me underwater. Once, while I was daydreaming on the dock, something swift and dark in the shallows caught the corner of my eye: a pair of horned pout herding their roiling mass of inky fry over the yellow sand. Small things: Meteor showers. Coon babies wrestling a chicken carcass up a tree. Pale olive vireos feeding their hatchlings in a papery pouch of a nest smaller than a tea cup. The patch of shinleaf by the back steps that doesn't seem like much until you kneel in the pine needles to smell the tiny white blossoms. The names of the things themselves are divine—sweet fern, shinleaf, pitch pine. Wood thrush, vireo, whip-poor-will, horned pout, pumpkinseed, perch—they fall from my lips like an incantation.

For me, this place is steeped in human events that transcend nostalgia. It's where I've seen all of my blessings before me, and where I've witnessed things now engraved on my heart. This is the place where my husband taught my mother—in her late fifties and terrified of water—how to swim. It's the place where I've watched the three men dearest to me get to know each other over the clang of horseshoes. It's the place where we last saw our friend Rob, happy and playful, the week before a drug overdose ended his life.

When the camp first went on the market, Tom and I blamed ourselves. "If only we had kids," we said. His sisters sometimes regretted living so far away. The truth is, the camp often sat empty. Tom and his sisters talked in twos or threes about buying it together, but deep down, we all knew it wouldn't work. Four sets of summer schedules to juggle, plus friends; we knew it would get crazy.

The phone call came on a raw day last February. This time it was for real. If there was anything we wanted from the camp, Tom's mother said, we needed to pick it up before the closing in April. Tom and I made the three-and-a-half hour drive south in March. He dropped me off at my parents' place and drove the final half hour to the camp alone. He wanted it that way, and he let me off easy.

The New People wanted the big stuff: the funky sofa, the canoe, the funny lamps. Still, a couple of hours later, Tom returned with the horseshoe set, an old wool blanket bordered with pines and cottages silhouetted against an orange strip of sunset, a good garden shovel, and a crude, hand-carved rudder an elderly antiques dealer gave him when he was twelve. But back home in Down East Maine, these things seem strangely out of context. What Tom and I really wanted were the things that we couldn't cart off: the smell of sun-warmed pine needles, the fluting of wood thrushes at dusk, cove-long swims.

After the closing, I asked Tom's father point-blank what made him ultimately decide to sell the camp. "People come to the lake to do what they can't get away with in the city," he said.

It's probably true. There are no speed limits on the lake. No rule enforcers. No signs that say "quiet please." Not that there should be. And not that it would help. It's the tragedy of the commons, played out under the pines. The lake is as much "theirs" as it is "ours," but something has gone terribly wrong: The lake has become a place to use, not a place to share. And what's happening there is happening everywhere.

Although we've relinquished our place on that particular commons, it's hard to let go. What saddens me most is the possibility that the New People may fail to notice the camp's true treasures. When we stop noticing, things have a way of disappearing. That's why I hope they hold handfuls of sweet fern to their noses and breathe deep. On hot summer nights, I hope they skinny-dip and haul mattresses out to the bunkhouse porch and listen to the night sounds. I hope they swim with goggles on so they can see all the life still left in the lake: pumpkinseeds circling nests like small golden craters, painted turtles scuttling along the bottom. I hope they don't mistake the shinleaf for weeds. Honestly, I hope the place gets into their blood the way I carry it in mine.

Kimberly Ridley is Editor of Hope.

My Father, My Son

by Melissa Kent

He was there. Hunched in a wheelchair on the far side of the cafeteria. Older and smaller than when I'd seen him last, my father was barely recognizable. The wall between the cafeteria and the hall was glass, and when I spotted him, I stopped and gasped. Travis, my eleven-year-old son, took another couple of steps and then turned.

"Mom, what's wrong?"

It took me a moment to recover. "Honey, Grandpa Duane is here. Let's go on in." But Travis was slumped against the window, searching for someone familiar inside.

"I don't know who he is, Mom. Do I have to go?" His voice quivered. Old people scared him, he said.

I walked in alone and a silence fell as I made my way through the tables, across the cafeteria. As I neared him, he looked up. Our eyes met and I stopped. The floor seemed to be moving. I put my hand on a table to steady myself. My God, he really doesn't know me. And then, as if he knew how frightened his little girl was, he smiled, threw his good arm above his head, and waved.

Almost instantly, his smile gave way to tears. I gathered courage and moved to him, put my arms around his frail body, and kissed him.

My father was an extraordinary man. He had been a track champion in school; written a dozen books and more than 500 articles and short stories for numerous magazines; drew cartoon characters like a professional; could cook better than anyone I've ever known.

As Executive Director of the local association of Home Builders, he took on City Hall, fighting for strict building codes when certain builders might have wished for more lenient ones, and won the case. He ran a one-man advertising agency, doing everything from finding clients to writing copy. He won trophies for golf, he bowled, shot pool, jogged. He could argue any point and usually had the last word. I was fortunate to be his daughter. But life with him wasn't always an easy ride. He was a perfectionist. He expected 110 percent from everyone. And 200 percent from himself. He hit the ground running every morning, couldn't sit still for long, and was always planning three steps ahead.

When he reached his mid-seventies, it was hard to recognize and acknowledge the early indications of Alzheimer's. We thought the forgetfulness was part of his ability to talk about one thing while thinking of a hundred others. But the absent-mindedness gradually became more pronounced. A temper surfaced; his fears developed: Suddenly he was scared of thunderstorms; nervous about driving his car; terrified by the thought of air travel. After three years of such changes, he took to his room and spent his days working crossword puzzles and watching CNN. Old friends made him uncomfortable. Then it happened. In March, 1992, he suffered a massive stroke that left one arm and one leg paralyzed. My father was a big man; it took two people just to get him in and out of bed. He didn't understand that he could no longer walk, and every day he would try to get up out of the wheelchair. Finally, after many falls, he broke his hip. And as the Alzheimer's took hold, he became increasingly angry and agitated. I was living halfway across the country, and my stepmother was struggling to cope. Finally, we accepted the inevitable, and placed him in a nursing home.

Within six months, his mind was gone. Although he lost his short-term memory, he could still recall his youth, and friends from long ago. He remembered everything up to his marriage to my mother, but there the memories stopped, just short of the birth of my brother and myself. And he could no longer control his emotions. This man I never saw cry or show weakness was reduced to tears when I visited. He knew he should know me—but he didn't.

When he had been in the home for three years, I decided the time had come for me to move closer to him. I had left when Travis was just one year old, and his few memories of his grandfather had come from our occasional return visits. Suddenly, at this late stage, it became important for me to be near my father, and for my now-eleven-year-old son to know him.

That first time we visited the nursing home, when Travis was so hesitant, I told him he could watch me through the window. I'm not sure how long I sat and talked to my father. Maybe ten minutes, maybe thirty seconds. Time was distorted. I was scared. All he could do was rock back and forth in his wheelchair and cry. I didn't know how to handle it. I wanted to scream, "Stop it, Dad. Please." I was lost. This was my father. I was confused, hurt, angry, frightened, and I wanted him to make it all better; to fix it, like dads are supposed to do. I remembered Travis out in the hall. Torn between my father who didn't know me and my son who needed me, I glanced up. But he was already coming toward us. As he passed each table he looked at the group gathered there and said, "Hi." By the time he reached us, every resident was grinning. In that instant my fear left me: My father could no longer help me, but my son could. Travis smiled, and I touched my father's arm.

"Dad," I said, "Would you like to meet your grandson?" When the tears stopped, he said, "Yes." Travis came up to him, "Hi, Grandpa Duane." I had warned Travis that dad might cry and move away from him, and my father's first reaction was just that. But my son sat down quietly next to his grandfather, and through his tears, Dad smiled. Within a couple of weeks, Travis had it figured out, as only a child can. When we went to visit, he would talk to anyone on the way to his grandfather's room. If a resident asked a question, or said something nonsensical, Travis would merely respond, and smile. He didn't try to make sense of any of it. He simply entered whatever conversation came his way. He got smiles. He got tears. He was amazing. He and Dad formed their own relationship. Dad would look at things occasionally and see something that wasn't there: a pitcher of water became a telephone, a pillow on a chair became a puppy. Travis would join him; the puppy was cute, and at least the telephone wasn't ringing anymore! Dad had someone to talk to.

If my father was in his wheelchair, he could get around. He would put up the foot rest and pull himself up and down the halls with his good foot. There were times when we'd visit and find his room empty. Travis would say, "I'll find him," and away he'd go. A few minutes later, there they'd be. My father and his grandson. Travis loved to push him in the wheelchair. He knew Dad had been through the halls thousands of times, but he also knew that, for my father, each time was new.

As Dad moved through his final days, my son understood the increasing silence, and while I had a tough time dealing with the loss of the man I'd known, Travis just loved him as he was.

On the morning of Friday, March 29, we made plans to go for a visit after school; we hadn't been for a couple of weeks. The call came at 10:30. I thought

I was prepared, but the words hit me like a giant fist to the stomach. "Your father just died."

To this day, I don't remember going to pick up Travis at school. I don't remember how I got to town. All I remember is my son's reaction. He didn't have one—not visibly, anyway. Later in the day, he told me, "It's not that I don't care, Mom. I guess I just look at it differently. I can't cry. I feel this is a good thing for him." And he was right. It was a blessing.

The rest of that day moves through my memory in a blur. I remember going to the funeral home to sign papers. Dad had arranged everything years ago. There was nothing to decide; just papers to sign. Then on to the nursing home. I can still see the rain on the windshield as we pulled the car into the Loading/Unloading zone. This time, we were allowed to park there. As we walked inside, I turned and looked through the windows into the cafeteria. A fragile memory: "Dad, would you like to meet your grandson?"

We were stopped before we reached his room. A sympathetic, if somewhat nervous, head nurse told us the room was already occupied. They were going to bring Dad's things up from downstairs. I stood against the wall looking at my son leaning on the opposite wall. He was smiling. I didn't intrude. My stepmother was deep in conversation with the head nurse when the elevator door opened and a young man emerged pulling a cart. On it were two cardboard boxes and a TV. Thoughts tore through my head. How, in God's name, could my father's entire life be condensed and placed on one cart—in two boxes?

A staff person stepped off the elevator, pushing Dad's empty wheelchair. Travis crossed the hall and tapped my arm, "Mom?" I turned. "Can I push the wheelchair?" He looked at me with tears in his eyes, then toward the wheelchair. "Just one last time?" All I could do was nod as he moved toward the waiting woman.

"Ma'am, I'll take this," Travis said as he moved her over. Then he lowered his head, took one last look around, and pushed the empty wheelchair toward the door. The young man with the cart followed. I walked behind, stepped through the double doors for the last time, and left the building. The rain had stopped momentarily and I took a deep breath as I walked slowly toward the car where Travis was loading the boxes into the back seat. My first steps into the rest of my life. The part without my father.

Thank God for my son.

Melissa Kent, a former Financial Analyst, teaches computer software classes.

My Mother at the End of Her Life
by John Daniel

Zilla Daniel was a treasured friend and co-worker at WoodenBoat magazine during the 1980s. She had been everywhere and done everything, it seemed, and although she was by far the oldest among us, her energy and spirit were indomitable, and she was an inspiration to all. As her health grew more fragile, she left Maine to live with her son, John, and his wife, Marilyn, in Oregon, and though she suffered some effects of dementia in her last years, she lived in the comfort of familiar surroundings. This chapter is excerpted from the book John has written about caring for Zilla during those years.   —JW

In my mother's last years she ate her breakfast and lunch at a small oak table in our kitchen, by a window that looks out on the limbs and leaves of a dogwood tree. With ferns below it, the tree makes a small, dapple-lighted garden of that side of the house, screening us from the neighbor's place next door. The pink blossoms gave my mother pleasure in the spring—though, like me, she preferred dogwoods that bloom white—and she also enjoyed the sparrows and finches and chickadees that came to the bird feeder with a mossy roof that hung from the dogwood's central limbs. My mother took a long time with her meals. She looked out the window as she ate, and some-times the food on her plate seemed to surprise her when she looked down and saw it. She usually sat at the table long after I had finished my meal and gone out back again to write or run off in the car on errands. My mother spent many hours with that dogwood tree.

I can see her clearly as I write this, and I can smell her, too. It's a fresh and musty smell of sandalwood and damp sweat, of skin cream and urine, and it's as vivid in my memory as her stooped back and curling white hair, as clear as her slow, flat-footed shuffle in bare feet or slippers, her hands flying out sporadically to a wall or table edge to steady her on her way. That smell of her old age is as sure in my mind as her quick scowl and sharp remarks, her laughter and childlike smile, her frowning concentration as she tried to listen with her bad ears, the look of her reddened eyes behind her glasses as she doggedly tracked lines of print across page after page of the books and papers and magazines she kept piled beside her on her bed.

Her eyesight, unlike her hearing, stayed sharp until the end. As we drove in the car she would sometimes speak out loud the names she read on street signs and billboards, as if to fix our location in memory—or maybe simply for the exercise, for the pleasure of forming words, for the happiness of being out of the house and in motion through the streets of Portland. Her eyes saw clearly the birds that came to the kitchen feeder, but she often asked their names. Sometimes she asked about the same bird at breakfast and again at lunch, sometimes at the same meal.

"What is that one," she would say, intently, "with the bright red...?" She gestured at her throat with her long, purpled fingers.

"That's the finch," I'd tell her.

"Finch," she'd say. "That's what I thought."

A black tomcat, not ours, once in a while would rocket from the ferns and almost capture a finch or sparrow, upsetting the feeder in a spray of millet and sunflower seed. My usual response was to charge out the back door and throw a stick of firewood at the fleeing cat. My mother would watch through the window, looking at me and the wobbling feeder as if the scene had never occurred before and was as delightful as anything that had ever happened in the history of the world. And sometimes a particular image would come to her, a known shape of words, a recurrent visitation from the mists and shadows of the past.

"Do you remember," she would ask, in that way she had of giving each syllable its full enunciation, "when the cat brought a poor bird to the door, and I scolded it? And you were there, all of six"—she'd be smiling now—"and you said, 'Mother, it's a cat's nature to hunt birds.'"

"I remember," I'd tell her, though in truth I didn't remember saying it so much as I remembered hearing her tell the story about me. I remembered being remembered. But I cherished those moments, brief and infrequent as they were, when the two of us could pause together in the shared light of each other's recall. In those moments we were all at home—me, my mother, the family, and friends we spoke of. I felt myself resting then, relaxing from some continuous effort I hadn't known I'd been engaged in and would shortly resume.

Sometimes when she brought up a glimpse of the past, I would try to draw her out, try to enlarge the landscape of her recall. But memory for my mother was a thing of moments, as mutable as the lightplay in the dogwood tree. What I searched for with my questions usually wasn't there. She knew the names I spoke—my father's, my brother's, the places we had lived—but much of the time the names had come loose from their moorings, like boats adrift on the sea. If I told a family story she would recognize it with pleasure, but my mother herself had few stories left.

In the hot summer months the dogwood leaves curled on the tree, and then as fall arrived and the light turned pale, the leaves took on a tinge of red—a subtle red, nothing vivid—and began to drop and gather on the ground. The gray Northwestern season that starts in mid-October and lasts through late spring was hard on my mother's spirits. In the spring she could watch the dogwood twigs hopefully for evidence of buds. In the fall she could only watch the tree unleaving itself. By late November of her last autumn the branches shook in the wind with only a smattering of leaves still clinging, and there came a morning when only one was left, on a lower branch near the window at my mother's end of the breakfast table. She pointed it out to me, and again the next few mornings. "Still there," she said, smiling as if with a secret we shared.

One morning, as I heard her feet begin to shuffle from her bedroom, I glanced at the window and saw that the leaf had fallen. I pointed as I poured her coffee. "It's gone," I said.

She gazed blankly out the window.

"The leaf is gone," I told her. "The last leaf."

"Oh," she answered vaguely. "The leaf."

Because it was absent from her present sight she had only the faintest memory of it. The leaf was profoundly gone for her, and soon would be absolutely gone, but in my own mind it still hangs on. I can see it now. I can't stop seeing it: a dark curled form infused with red, a beautiful ghost that by chance or willfulness still holds to its place in the world. In memory I circle and circle that leaf. I watch it much more carefully than I watched it before. I want to know what makes it hold on in the cold wind, how it somehow emerged out of sap and fiber, and grew in the sun, and remains now only by habit, by a spell of nature, by nothing at all. It's only memory that holds it now, and memory, at last, that lets it go.

My mother kept a clock on her nightstand, a battery-powered portable that had accompanied her on many of her travels. She paid attention to it—when it stopped she asked me to replace the battery—but I don't know for sure that she could read the time on the clock, or if she could read it, I don't know if it meant to her what it meant to me. If I told her that she needed to be ready to leave the house at 11 A.M., for a doctor appointment or whatever, I'd be likely to find her sitting on the side of her bed, fully dressed with her purse strapped across her shoulder and cane at the ready, by 10:30. Maybe she knew how long it took her to dress and prepare herself, and she was over-compensating. Or maybe memory could give her no guidance on how long her preparations would take, and so she began right away to be safe. Maybe she didn't trust the clock to tell her, or herself to understand, when "11 A.M." would arrive. On a few occasions she wasn't ready when the departure time came and had to finish hurriedly as I stood holding her coat like an impatient husband.

Aside from her infrequent appointments, of which I always reminded her several times, clock time had little bearing on my mother's life. We had meals at no set hour; when the food was ready I came by her room, or else clanged the brass yacht bell she had ordered from a nautical catalogue and I had mounted on the dining room wall. She didn't watch TV or listen to the radio, so she had no need to check program times. She didn't divide her day into various activities with budgeted time for each. She had, for the most part, drifted out of time's main channel and was turning slowly in the eddies.

She lived in an older kind of time. She saw the light changing in the shrubs and trees of the backyard, their shadows shifting, reconfiguring. I'm sure she saw the dawn of many mornings. She saw blocks of sunlight move across her room as the day progressed, she saw color in the western sky at sundown. She watched the beginning of rain and the end of rain, the gray sky brightening and darkening. She watched wind stir the birches and pines. She saw leaves drop away in the fall and watched closely, intently, for their reappearance in the spring. "We'll see the leaves soon, won't we?" I remember her asking as early as January with two to three months of leaflessness still ahead. "You can tell by the twigs," she observed one late March morning, studying the dogwood tree at breakfast. "They're getting fatter. Don't you think they are?"

As the days and seasons turned around her, my mother gazed and drifted. She had no need to know what time it was. Her personal river of more than eighty years had borne her close to its mouth, to that great mingling of waters where the current slows, where the channel widens and deepens, where time itself is drowned in timelessness. One afternoon when I stopped by her room, she had just wakened from a nap, and she said "I hope it's the same season. I feel as though I've lived a whole life." There was a tone of wonder in her voice.

"Since when?" I asked.

"Since I fell asleep."

Physicists from Einstein on have insisted that our sense of time as separable into past, present, and future is an illusion. A peculiarly tenacious illusion, but illusory all the same. Time does not happen incrementally second by second. Like space, with which it came into being and from which it is inseparable, time is all here all the time. Past, present, and future are one. No one knows why we don't perceive them as one, but writer-physicists Paul Davies and John Gribbin have speculated that it may be something in the working of human memory that creates our certain sense of immersion in a moving present flowing out of the past into the future. We think of memory as a function of time. It may be truer to say that time, or our illusory sense of time, is a function of memory.

And if that is the case, it may well be that when memory fails, as it did in my mother, a physically more accurate sense of time may come to awareness. Who was experiencing the greater illusion? I as I worked at my desk with one eye on my digital clock, or my mother as she drifted, unmoored to the clock by her bed? It was as though eternity was opening to her, showing glimpses of itself as the ocean sometimes will, appearing and disappearing in fog. In medical and psychological terms, my mother was a cognitively impaired octogenarian suffering the confusions of senile dementia. But in terms of her own sense of being, in spiritual terms, I believe she lived a good part of her last years in the presence of the eternal and in the eternal present.

I also believe she saw differently than I and most people do. At times, at least, I think she experienced a visionary kind of seeing, a seeing perhaps like the psychedelic awareness that many of us sought in the 1960s, a see-ing-into-things that reveals a deeper level of identity than name or category. A seeing in which all things glow with the fullness of their being. Like me on LSD, my mother didn't always know who she was in a personal sense and couldn't always name the city she was in or the day of the week, but in her visionary moments she always knew where she was—deep in the world's unspeakable being.

On one of our walks in the rainy season she couldn't stop looking at the brilliant green moss that lined each crack in the sidewalk and lay in velvety waves here and there along its borders. "So green, so green," she said. She seemed transported, ravished, as if the beauty of it hurt her eyes. She reached a hand down, wanting to touch the moss, to feel its greenness with her fingers, but even with me to steady her she couldn't stoop that far. At the corner of the block, the sidewalk makers had stamped into concrete the date—1911, I think—and the name of their company: a partnership, Miller & Bauer. The lettering was filled with emerald moss. "If only they knew," my mother said. "Their names magnified in moss."

Then there was the morning I set a large nectarine on a saucer at her place at the breakfast table. It was an especially colorful fruit, its rich yellow shading into orange and a large splotch of deep purple. My mother shuffled in, got herself dropped into her chair and her cane hung on its hook, and when I scooted her chair into place she saw the nectarine. She stared disbelievingly, her mouth agape. She seemed aghast, horrified.

"Is it...corrupt?" she said.

"It's just a nectarine, Mom," I said in my let's-get-through-breakfast voice.

She ate her soft-boiled egg and toast, but wouldn't touch the fruit. She stared at it, silently, for long intervals. It was not "just a nectarine" to her. I don't know what it was—vision fruit, ember of the other world, portent of her own consummation and decay—but it was no mere docile object. My mother may have been seeing, in that moment, as Van Gogh or William Blake must have seen. She was not looking at a thing. She was in a presence.

Very little was "just a nectarine" to my mother, and in a way this was the triumph of her late life. The diminishment that her dementia brought, though a very real impairment, allowed at the same time an enlargement of her spirit. It may have allowed, in a way she didn't foresee and perhaps would-n't have chosen, a culmination of her spiritual quest. Her forgetfulness had an aspect of remembering—a spiritual remembering, a cleansing of the doors

of perception. The conventional certainties we carry in common in our
ordinary lives are themselves a forgetting of the primary world, the world
we knew best as children and are in danger of never knowing again. The
world, in the words of painter Harlan Hubbard, whose "radiant beauty should
be an unending source of wonder and joy, yet most people live and die without noticing it." What could be more fitting, as one draws near death, than
to slough off by one means or another the tired definitions we have imposed
on the world and remember it in its unfathomable mystery? "The invariable
mark of wisdom," wrote Emerson, "is to see the miraculous in the common."
By that standard, my mother at the end of her life was a very wise woman
indeed.

One evening in the fall of 1990, when my mother had just read an essay
of mine about the limits of our visual perception of nature, she and I were
having a drink in the living room. I argue in the essay that nature's chief
beauty and value lie not in what we see of it but in what remains hidden and
mysterious. It ends with an image of a desert canyon opening itself to a hiker
but always withholding its further reaches in mystery.

My mother rarely commented on my work, but this time she had been
moved. We had a conversation I think of often, a conversation I'm grateful
for. She asked if I knew ahead of time where I was going in my writing, if I
had a destination.

"Not usually," I told her. "Or if I do, I only see it in a nearsighted way"

"It's like the canyon?"

"It's like the canyon."

She seemed happy to hear that, and she seemed to have taken some kind
of important inner step on her own journey. There was exaltation in her voice.
"I think we know too much now. And if we don't know everything, we think
we do. We need more mysteries."

I asked her if she was afraid of dying. "Not so much," she answered. "Not
so much. I worry more about things I haven't done."

"But you've done so many things...."

"Oh, I think of what it would have been like to explore unknown
terrain. I think of the explorers."

"I think of them too," I told her.

I wish I had told her that she was an explorer. I wish I had told her that
I was proud of her. I hope she knew it.

We were silent for a time. We looked out the window at our neighbor's house across the street, glowing softly yellow in the failing October light. A man walked by, limping. Crows were flying among the tall trees of the park. After a while my mother raised her glass of whiskey.

"Here's to the Unknown!" she said.

John Daniel is an author, poet, and teacher who writes regularly on the natural world. His books include The Trail Home *and two collections of poetry,* Common Ground, *and* All Things Touched by Wind.

Invitation to Rapture
by Candice Stover

One

Sometimes it calls to me unsuspecting, pulling me up from tides of sleep, and leads me to a window overlooking someplace I love.

This time, it happens to be a city in spring. And though I know some version of what I'm witnessing occurs daily all over the globe, this time something leads me to draw a stool to the window and watch, as if rapture herself had invited me to take a seat and read the tinted script emerging from that envelope of possibility we name dawn.

Here the sun is climbing its own ladder of light up the glittery geometry of skyscrapers; here an old silver wing of cloud lifts away. When I crack the window, the low roar of traffic sounds as if the city itself is about to lift off, like some jumbo jet full of rain-washed rooftops, chunks of chimneys, and plum trees in foamy bloom. A siren loops its wail through the streets. A helicopter chugs through the sea of sky—an odd dark bee strung with its own chuff and whir of intention—then disappears over the pale blue fence of horizon.

The birds know what time it is and wake up singing every song they know. Here it is finches, swallows, crows. A gull flaps past, breast flashing white.

Flashes of white, too, when I look directly west, where mountains are rising from cerulean gauze, their architecture of cleft and snow still holding their place on the planet. The mountains remind me this is a planet, and each of us one blink of its ancient eye.

A bumper sticker might proclaim such available glory: I Brake for Sunrise. My feet are cold and it's time for coffee.

I have been looking out the window of rapture a long time.

Two

Barely an hour after watching this sunrise, I find myself in a seedier section of the same city, at a bus stop opposite the Union Gospel Mission and across from a tiny Cuban restaurant with elaborate pink molding and a gallant palm tree.

I ride a bus to the outskirts of the city, past signs advertising used tires and new air conditioners and live naked girls; I get off at a stop where three men sit on the curb watching traffic. When I double-check for directions to the school, one of the men points the way and asks for spare change. I give him what's in my pocket and follow a side street to a courtyard, where a radiant fifteen-year-old dwarf from India introduces herself and offers to take me to the English-as-a-Second-Language classroom.

Mooshi's heavy braid shines against her short sturdy spine in the sun; she tilts her head up at me and smiles. "A lot of stairs," she says, "and then— here we are."

How we all got to this place we call here is, of course, another question. Something about timing. Something about chance. Something about a whole lot of other sunrises in the dark. Something about rapture, too.

The teacher of these students had indicated some of the shadows behind the faces around this table, where two Latino girls are painting their finger-nails frosted green from a bottle they pass back and forth, and a tall solemn black boy looks directly into my eyes, and another girl folds and unfolds one edge of a sheet of paper containing a poem she's written and may or may not show me.

I know that the regal-looking girl from Somalia spent weeks hiding in her tent in a refugee camp in Kenya, terrified of rape, and that she has already survived a clitorectomy. I know that one of the Somali boys in the same camp entered this country under an assumed name and that neither of them may see their parents and siblings again. I know that one of the boys from India stayed as long as he could with an uncle who received repeated death threats and that the girl from El Salvador discovered her uncle's name on one more list of the dead.

I know none of them may know the word, "rapture"—perhaps have never used it, even in their own languages—whatever their skin and tongues and bones have memorized of it, wherever they have seen the sunrise. I haven't really come here to talk with them about rapture, as word or concept. Instead, I want to know what I always want to know, with students and writing groups, with the men on the sidewalk, and the beautiful young dwarf who brought me to this room: "What do you remember?"

What we remember, I'm convinced, is one of the roads to rapture, and I trust that what these students, flung together from war and ache and running, carry as memories in and out of these worlds will be valuable.

"Sitting in the garden on hot afternoons," offers one of the boys from India.

"Everybody says hello," Jessica from El Salvador muses. "Even if they don't know you, people say hello."

"Eating mangoes," says the girl from the Philippines. "Sometimes, all day long, we would just eat mangoes and play."

All around the table, again and again, specific memories tumble and land in a sleeve of light. Sometimes, recollections from the dark slit the edge.

"I saw a woman on the street fall over from starving," a boy from China says.

"There was a bus accident," says Berta from Spain. "There were arms and legs torn off, thrown around, all over."

"My mother hid behind a tree and waved goodbye to me," says another. "I know she was crying inside."

Gifts are not happiness only.

It is an odd and unexpected quotation to return to me here at this table of young survivors (the oldest is eighteen) with their remarkable faces full of stories. When our hour together ends, most of them head for classes where, one tells me, they often feel less open and understood than in their sudden international community. Many go after school to part-time jobs at Taco Bell or Burger King or a local chowder house. The Indian boy who loved sitting in the garden lingers to talk with me and his teacher about hunger: his hunger simply to walk down a street filled with the music and history of his own language. "Just to hear Punjabi in my ears and speak it with everyone," he says. "That would make me so happy."

Three
　　Gifts are not happiness only

　　I had read this on an airplane somewhere over the Pacific Ocean on my way to teach in Shanghai in 1984. Liv Ullmann wrote it in her 1976 autobiography, *Changing*, and though I knew before I landed that Shanghai was a gift, I did not—could not—know the shapes and tones, the textures and resonance this gift would take.

　　As the plane descended toward the gray and fecund expanse of concrete and humanity—twelve to fourteen million people living in that city then—how could I know I would wake morning after morning to the grace and poetry of Tai Chi outside my window, that the shadows of rats would cast themselves against the wall behind my bookcase, that I would plunge head-first into an icy pool at the top of a sacred mountain, and that the flower-seller with the missing tooth would one day give me the warmest smile and thrust her weather-chapped hand into mine—her hand that had cut and arranged blooms for weddings and funerals and the small celebrations of everyday for a lifetime—and that her hand would feel like a claw?

　　How could I know I was descending into rapture?

　　That was a decade before a friend mailed me a card with this quotation from Virginia Woolf, sending me on rapture's trail.

　　"....I mean," Woolf wrote, "life has to be sloughed; has to be faced: to be rejected; then accepted on new terms with rapture. And so on; until you are forty; when the only problem is how to grasp it tighter and tighter to you, so quick it seems to slip, and so infinitely desirable it is...."

　　Sloughed and faced. Rejected and accepted. New terms. Rapture.

　　Sometimes, the process starts when we are young, wrenching us away from roots to strangers, and even the tongues in our own mouths must grope around another language to name new terms.

　　Sometimes, the blow of rapture stuns us, and we stand dumbstruck on some balcony or ledge, overlooking another piece of the world that takes itself for granted—a flock of herring gulls pulling up fog, a finger of desert stone pointing at sky, an avenue flowing with a river of human beings—and we see it, however many times we have seen it, for the first time.

What is sunrise but a chance to meet the day on new terms?

Four

That first sunrise in China struck such a blow. Barely ten hours after the plane touched down, rapture arrested me and brought me to an instant of absolute attention. The twentieth-century French philosopher and mystic Simone Weil equated such an instant not with rapture, but with prayer. I wonder about the difference.

"Absolute attention is prayer," Weil wrote.

What gives us a moment of such attention?

That dawn, the murmur of Shanghai had floated up to my windows; the sunlight had begun weaving its own skeins of song. I heard that song and rose; actually began running down the stairs to discover what I could of this universe unfolding on the other side of the world. Halfway down, I ducked onto a second-floor balcony and stopped.

Was stopped. Seized. The word, "rapture," meant just that in its Latin and Middle English roots: carried away; to seize. Standing on that balcony in Shanghai, I was seized—motionless, rapt—as a steady flow of humanity passed, carrying baskets of vegetables, riding bicycles, strolling in clean white shirts and smart dresses and simple trousers. A group of old women swung their legs up on telephone poles and touched their foreheads to their knees. One man carried a fish in his bare hands. Everywhere, much jabbering and nodding and smiling, a bustle of purpose and direction.

Five a.m. on Mao-ming Lu: I have never seen so many people on the brink of day in my life.

Five

Pull a stool up to one window to witness one kind of dawning; stand stock-still and pray in a new language on the balcony of another. Either way, rapture compels us to attention, brings us to an instant that dissolves the boundaries of time and charges the space before us with insight, washing every particle in a vision so luminous that how we got there—how many stairs we climbed or oceans or deserts we crossed—falls, for that instant, away.

That simple. That pure.

It's the instant where a child lives: the little girl I passed a few weeks ago hanging upside down on a jungle gym, calling out to the upside-down world and sneakers of her mother: "It's-ab-so-lute-ly-splen-did!"

She was in rapture, all right, and who knows where her touched-down feet might take her?

Maybe into the counterpart of a classroom a woman in one of my writing groups remembers: "I was reading something—I don't know what—but whatever it was, I was gone, deep, way down into it. I didn't hear a thing. Then, when I looked up, everyone—I mean everyone—in the class was staring at me. It was fourth or fifth grade. Some of the kids were snickering. A red-haired boy I thought I liked was yawning and rolling his eyes. The clock looked like a giant moon, and the hands pointed to five past three. I can still see it. Everyone—everyone—was waiting for me to wake up and put that book away so we could all go home. I felt my face turn bright red. 'Moon Maiden,' said the teacher 'Where are you? Daydreaming? Again?'"

Another possible bumper sticker on that counter promoting rapture: Have you hugged a daydreamer today?

Six

Virginia Woolf knew something about the care and feeding of daydreamers. In her essay, "Professions for Women," based on a speech she gave to the London National Society for Women's Service on 21 January 1931, she urged the women in her audience to recognize daydreaming as an act of creativity, from the taproot to the nectar of the imagination, where the daydreamer sips and is restored—not to the world of clocks and corridors, but to the privacy and sheen in the spiraled chambers of rapture.

Woolf writes:

"... I must tell you about a very strange experience that befell me as a novelist.

And to understand it you must try first to imagine a novelist's state of mind... a novelist's chief desire is to be as unconscious as possible... so that nothing may break the illusion... so that nothing may disturb or disquiet the mysterious nosings about, feelings round, darts, dashes, and sudden discoveries of that very shy and illusive spirit, the imagination. I suspect that this state is the same both for men and women. Be that as it may, I want you to imagine me writing a novel in a state of trance. I want you to figure to yourselves a girl sitting with a pen in her hand, which for minutes, and indeed for hours, she never dips into the ink-pot. The image that comes to my mind when I think of this girl is the image of a fisherman lying sunk in dreams on the verge of a deep lake with a rod held out over the water. She was letting her imagination sweep unchecked round every rock and cranny of the world that lies submerged in the depths of our unconscious being."

About the act of daydreaming, Woolf also wrote, "It is in our idleness, in our dreams, that the submerged truth sometimes comes to the top."

Feed the daydreamer, Woolf knew, encourage her to suspend that line over the water, and you sit her on the banks of rapture. Encourage the day-dreamer, and the fish she emerges with may be a creation so shimmering— a creation made of words, wood, paper, color, clay—that it offers her and random souls who encounter it, if not a gift of happiness, then at least the possibility of new terms for accepting life.

Seven

My Moon Maiden friend was not among the designers of a survey last year for The Wall Street Journal and NBC News—though her teacher may have been. According to *The Wall Street Journal's* report, the survey questioned 2001 Americans about how they are managing time and money as we approach the 21st century. One section of the survey asked participants to identify some of the ways they waste time. The survey deliberately excluded television as a choice, according to *The Journal's* report, "because typically it dwarfs all other responses."

Here are choices the survey did include: Riding in the car. Talking on the phone. Reading junky books. Playing on the computer. Shopping. Oversleeping. Other. Not sure.

Two other options appeared on this list of time-wasters.

In this group of North Americans, nineteen percent—380 individuals— claimed they waste no time at all. "None," they checked. Nineteen percent!

But another 140 souls—seven percent—'fessed up and checked off one other option. Yes—in a culture where the word, "rapture," rarely occurs and opportunities to cultivate it are increasingly scheduled out of the day they do it.

They daydream.

They dip their feet in the pool of rapture, recognize its tingle, and con-tinue, on new terms, with life's mud, stones, and shallows. They watch the sky wash its face in the water; they see their own faces rearrange into reflec-tions of trees, mountains, clouds.

They speak, in one language or another, with a Chinese scholar and painter whose work I saw years after that sunrise in Shanghai. Chen Jiru lived from 1558 to 1639, and he knew the way to rapture.

His list of "fond interests" reads like one long daydream:

"Studio. Clean table for painting. Cool breeze and beautiful moon. Vase of flowers. Tea, bamboo shoots, oranges and tangerines, all in season.

"Amid mountains and rivers. The host not being formal. Stretching under the sun. Famous incense as offering. Research. Peace in the world. Talking to high monks in the snow.

"Having strange rocks and bronzes by my side. Getting up from sleep. Recovering from sickness. Freely displaying objects but slowly putting them away."

Eight

I don't doubt Chen Jiru's spirit stops in now and then to sip tea with another Moon Maiden I know who's homesteading on an abandoned strawberry farm in the Pacific Northwest. She raises chickens and told me she spent a good part of one summer marveling at the copper iridescence of a Rhode Island Red rooster named "Tank" stalk from spindles of gooseberry bushes to the first crazy hen house she built. Between chores, she sometimes bicycled to an old grove of madrona trees and listened to the ruddy-barked trees talking in the wind. She said she sometimes sat there for an hour; the creaks and chirpings reminded her of the clicking lyrics of dolphins.

I like to think Chen Jiru also walks with a friend I met in another writing group.

"What do you remember?" I asked, as always.

My friend wrote about seeing a spot of blood on one of her husband's teeth when he was dying of cancer. She had just entered her forties—that decade Woolf says is the one we begin to want to grasp life "tighter and tighter... so quick it seems to slip, and so infinitely desirable it is...."

That spot of blood commanded my friend's attention and turned into a prayer; it seized her and cracked open the chalice of love to contain every holy detail.

After he died, she began climbing mountains. Her husband had asked her to do this: to find one where she could scatter his ashes. Day after day she climbed a certain western slope. She followed switchbacks and came to know a swamp where she watched the wild iris bloom. She met the steepness indicated only as tightening circles on a topographic map.

"A lot of stairs," Mooshi said, "and then—here we are."

The more steeply she climbed, my friend said, the more deeply she breathed. And in climbing and breathing, she discovered a gift: "The breathing let me cry."

"I was Sisyphus," she told me, "and grief was my stone. Every day I pushed it, and I only knew it was important that I push, even though I knew the stone would roll right back down again. In the months immediately after his death, I don't remember a thing about taking care of my children. I know I must have, but I don't remember it. Time broke down."

At the peak, she stopped. The spot of blood had transformed again: this time, into a fold of ocean cleaning the shore every day; this time, into a lip of sunrise kissing day awake once more.

What does she remember?

In that time without time, the wild iris bloomed.

She watched. And she cried.

Then, she continued down the northern slope of the mountain.

Nine

One more sunrise.

I am on a mountain in the Adirondacks, being ravished by a pear.

For a week now, every one of my senses has been seized. I've brushed the pear's cool skin against my cheek, inhaled its perfume, pressed my thumbs against the give and nub of its contours, traced the shapes of light slipping it in burnished silks.

I've nosed the shelves of the second-floor library and downstairs common room, searching for anything I can find on *Pyrus communis*, this pear of unexpected rapture. Along the way I discover *Four Hedges*, Clare Leighton's gorgeous 1935 collection of wood engravings and chronicle of cultivating a garden on a slope of chalk in England's Chiltern Hills.

In this book, Leighton translates her moments of absolute attention to chisel and boxwood, training a steady eye and hand on the lineaments of rapture. Meeting her in a room overlooking a lake, with the gift of time to write, I fall asleep with Leighton's engraving of pears beside me and wake to one in three dimensions—plump, pocked, fragrant—on the sill before me.

Once, before dawn, I hear someone, or something, calling from the lake.

Maybe it's the spirit of Chen Jiru, "getting up from sleep," moving towards "peace in the world."

Maybe it's the echo and syntax of one of Woolf's sentences, spilling her translucence into ripples across the surface of water.

Maybe it's the abbreviated shadow of Mooshi, taking me by the hand in the bluegrained, unwinding dark. "A lot of stairs," she says, "and then—here we are."

I am standing on the edge of the lake in a flannel bathrobe. It is mid-October in the Adirondack Mountains; the water will be freezing. I drape my robe on a tree, wade in, and dive. The shock of the cold strips me breathless.

I could cry out, "It's-ab-so-lute-ly-splendid!" But rapture is often mute, and when I emerge a few seconds later with the sun in my eyes, I see the gift of why.

Five deer are grazing in the first streaks of light; they lift their heads but hold their ground as I pull my robe around me and pass.

Once again, rapture is standing before me.

Candice Stover leads writing workshops and teaches at College of the Atlantic in Bar Harbor, Maine. Her collection of poems, Holding Patterns, *won the 1994 Maine Chapbook Award.*

Without Wings
by Claudia Schmidt

She moves across the parquet dance floor in a solo sashay, balancing a drink on her head. Black Russian on a beehive. Hands on hips, triple-E powder-blue pumps planting themselves one chunky step at a time, pulling her forward with head held rigid, the rest of her body swinging gently and relentlessly. She is so perfectly bell-shaped as she swings. "MY LIFE IS FULL!"she announces with her whole being, bursting at the seams in every possible way.

It is late afternoon at a hotel lounge jazz jam. At one point the drummer, at the mention of Hoagy Carmichael's "Skylark,"leaps over his drums and hastens to feed a strangely mutant skylark to a sour-toned, snaggle-toothed piano. But my belle of the ball doesn't miss a beat. Tapping out her chunky rhythm, rivulets of mascara cascading down both sides of the nose shining like a beacon in the well-cocktailed, scorching August Charleston afternoon. Nothing coy or seductive in this performance, just a forthright, exuberant statement: MY LIFE IS FULL! She comes right toward me. It happened years ago, but she rises up again and again, clear as the bell she so resembled on that afternoon. She rings true.

Did she change my life? Just maybe. Sometime back I heard myself telling a friend, "My life is so full!"and she said, "What about the loneliness? Don't you get lonely all by yourself out there on the road?"I responded without even thinking, "Well, then it's full of loneliness!"And poof, there was that woman, smiling and swinging in the air between us.

Can we ever know the impact we may have had on another's life, or how something in our own is triggered by someone bumbling through like a Mr. Magoo?

Once, as a guest on a national radio show, I sang a parody of "Forty Miles from Albany."The new lyrics concerned the misery of traveling in a van with cats yowling and puking. A few years later, when two friends were moving in a van from Milwaukee to San Francisco, the owner of the van asked the passenger if she would please leave her cat behind. This she did with no apparent regret until about halfway across North Dakota. In the sweltering absence of air conditioning, with nothing coming through on the radio but static or Jesus lounge music for hundreds of miles, she realized suddenly that the biggest mistake of her life was leaving that cat behind. A terrible fight exploded, eventually settling into a thick silence with no resolution in sight. After a while, the driver jerked the radio knob across the band one more desperate time, and darned if he didn't land on a replay of that very radio show, with me smack in the middle of singing about cats trembling and puking in a van. That was the end of the fight. They laughed about it for days. I only know this because they know me and were able to pass it on. But what about the little visitations from strangers who save the moment, if not your life?

What I'm saying is, I believe in angels. Angels minus the diaphanous wrappings and dazzling, otherworldly light. I see angelhood as a particular state of grace into which any of us can step. You can do it in your sleep, on the radio, certainly in your street clothes. If you're hanging out right in the middle of your own life (that's the trick) with all the edges sharp and clear, you're a candidate for angelhood. That's when you will be noticed by someone who needs a visit from an angel at a precipitous moment. They might sail right on by and knock the drink off your head to boot, but if the light is just right and everyone's at least half awake, the foray into angelhood may be successful.

When it works, a tiny moment may stay with you for keeps. Like the morning I was up early after a troubled, wakeful night during a period of life as memorable as a mildewed dishrag. I was heading for the park by the lake to brood at the sunrise and there, all by himself, was the garbage man singing, "On the Street Where You Live!"at the top of his lungs with perfect passion... all the while picking up everyone's crap on the street where I lived. It had the instant effect of eight hour's sleep, and hope crept home again.

You see, that's just how it works. Recently I had this revelation that my life is like stretch pants: The fuller it gets, the more it gives. Now, I don't see just any stretch pants here. What I see are some Kelly-green numbers packed to the brim, like the ones on the waitress at the burger joint in Duluth who was telling the cook while she waited for my order to come up, "I'd rather regret all the things I did than all the things I didn't do!" I realized that packed in there were the bell-shaped woman ringing and the garbage man singing, right along with the old guy clog-dancing at a festival spilling his philosophy in the middle of a nimble hop: "Live and learn, die and forget it all!" Who knows how many angels it takes to fill up a pair of Kelly-green cosmic stretch pants, big as life? I aim to find out.

Claudia Schmidt is a well-known singer, writer, recording artist, and concert performer.